HOLY HIMALAYA

Owing to the antiquity and rarity of this book, certain pages are regrettably absent, and readability is compromised due to the blurring of the original text. If you possess any insights regarding the availability of these missing sections, kindly inform us. Your assistance is crucial in ensuring the completion of this significant work for the benefit of future generations.

HOLY HIMALAYA:

THE RELIGION TRADITIONS AND SCENERY OF HIMALAYAN PROVINCE (KUMAON AND GARWHAL)

E. SHERMAN OAKLEY

GYAN

Published by

Gyan Publishing House
5, Ansari Road
Daryaganj, New Delhi-110002
Phone: 011-47034999, 9811692060
E-mail: books@gyanbooks.com

Distribution Network
gyanbooks.com
India, USA, Canada, UK, Australia

ISBN:**978-93-6920-359-8**(PB)

First Published, 1905

2nd Impression 2025

Printed at: Gyan Press, Delhi.

HOLY HIMALAYA
Author: E. SHERMAN OAKLEY

NATIVE PICTURE OF THE GOD SIVA AND HIS WIFE PARVATI

HOLY HIMALAYA

The Religion, Traditions, and Scenery of a Himalayan Province (Kumaon and Garhwâl)

BY

E. SHERMAN OAKLEY, M.A.
Of the London Missionary Society

EDINBURGH AND LONDON
OLIPHANT ANDERSON & FERRIER
1905

TO

MY DEAR BROTHER

HENRY HISLOP OAKLEY

I DEDICATE THESE PAGES

WITH MUCH AFFECTION

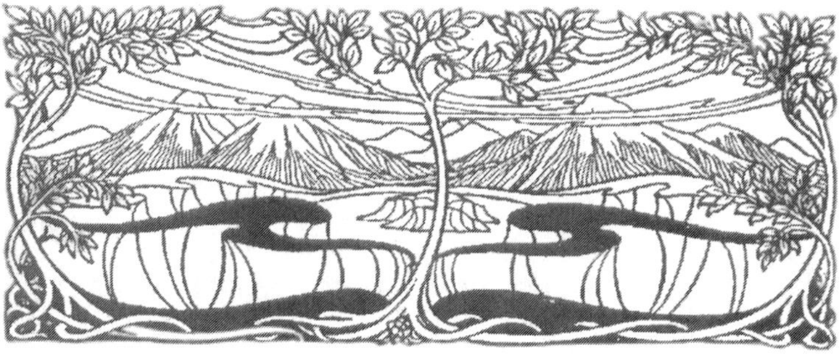

CONTENTS

CHAP.		PAGE
	Introductory	9
I.	The Journey to Almora	17
II.	Almora	36
III.	Highland Fairs	56
IV.	Byways in Kumaon	62
V.	A Chequered History	82
VI.	An Indian Holy Land	128
VII.	Kedar and Badari	141
VIII.	The Greater Gods	162
IX.	Ghosts and Godlings	201
X.	A Chapter on Customs	233
XI.	The Village Wiseacre	255
XII.	The Roots of Hinduism	281
XIII.	Conclusion	297
	Index	313

LIST OF ILLUSTRATIONS

PAGE

1. Native Picture of the God Siva and his Wife, Parvati . . . . . . *Frontispiece*
2. View of Naini Tal 10
3. A Dak Bungalow (Dhaulchina) . . . 31
4. The Panch Chule Peaks 31
5. View of Almora 50
6. Corner of a Village Fair in Kumaon . . 59
7. The Pass into Tibet beyond Milam . . . 81
8. A Village on the Way to Bageswar . . . 81
9. An Almora Temple 102
10. A Bazaar in Kumaon 113
11. A Brahman Official of Almora 125
12. Badrinath and Kedarnath Peaks . . . 142
13. Kumaon Yogis 161
14. Ascetics returning from the Great Pilgrimage . 192
15. A Brook by the Way 225
16. A Baniya or Shopkeeper in Kumaon . . . 259
17. Bhotiyas at Bageswar 275
18. The Gori-Ganga River, with Mission Camp . . 295

The Author's best thanks are given, for permission to use photographs by Miss Meachen, Rev. W. R. Le Quesne, Mr. E. G. Hill, and Lalla Gangi Sah of Naini Tal.

HOLY HIMALAYA

INTRODUCTORY

INDIA is Britain's great romantic asset, and one of her chief claims to historical distinction. The nation that dominates the Indian peninsula is, from the standpoint of human interest and culture, the most enviable nation of the world. "The glory that was Greece and the grandeur that was Rome" have passed away, and their sites only are left as relics of the past. India, on the contrary, has the more vivid charm of a treasure yet unexplored, a storehouse of existing marvels, a vast and complex field for research of every kind. Many secrets of bygone races and eras are yet to be wrung from its buried monuments and unpublished manuscripts. Here the ancient world yet lives on in the daily lives of men. Customs, cults, and ideas that have perished from the memory of the rest of the human race are here in full force. India is the land that above all has power to stir the imagination.

It has nowadays become a trite remark to say that India is not a single country, but rather a continent—an aggregate of many regions, tribes and tongues differing widely from one another. This fact must be borne in mind in reading any book on India. The value of works purporting to give a general view of Indian life and religious custom is often seriously lessened by the writer's ignoring of such diversities, and when they have been borne in mind, the attempt to weave a description that should apply to all the peoples of India has sometimes resulted in vagueness and sketchiness—and what is vague is always uninteresting. The way to understand India is to take a part of it, gain a clear idea of its history and life, and work outwards from that centre of observation. The history of Kumaon is one of these coigns of vantage from which the wide field of North Indian antiquities and religions can be viewed, and the reader will find that it presents many fresh vistas of interest.

The present volume will, it is hoped, have some value as an attempt to show the romance and reality of a corner of India remote from railways and the usual tourist lines, and little known to Europeans in general, though famous in the annals of Hinduism, and a region of great sanctity and popular resort for the people of the country. A residence of fifteen years in the province gives the writer some claim to speak with adequate knowledge, and he has endeavoured to consult the best authorities in bringing out the story of the past and apportioning its interest to the present. The writing of these pages has been the recreation of leisure hours in a busy life under Indian skies. If they express, however faintly, the charm of Himalayan days, to those who have not known them; if, moreover, they bring back to old friends, dwellers now or formerly in beautiful Kumaon, the memory of mossy oak and

View of Naini Tal

rhododendron woods, the sough of the breeze in deodar and pine, the glittering snows, the verdure of the "rains," the rich brown and emerald of the mountain-sides in drier seasons, the bright sunshine over all, or the poetry of winter evenings by the glowing oak-log on the open hearth—above all, if they awaken in the mind of any who may chance to read them an abiding interest in our great Indian Empire, its people and their deeper needs—his pleasant task will be amply rewarded.

The purpose of the work is far from being wholly a controversial one, yet I shall be very glad if it helps to prove that India needs a better faith. I have tried, in describing the forms of religion current in this part of India, to keep well within the bounds of sober truth, and to state nothing that does not admit of the fullest verification. It is easy to paint lurid pictures of the lower types of idol worship and demonism, but every religion may justly claim to be judged by its best, or at any rate its average, level. Those who have lived among the Hindus on familiar terms and studied their literature in a sympathetic spirit would be the last to deny that there is much that is amiable and worthy of respect in the life and character of the people; but I think most will confess that such better features are little due to the prevailing types of their religion. Moral precepts abound, and religious books like the popular Ramayan of Tulsi Das are full of the spirit of faith and devotion; but when one comes to examine the actual forms of religious belief and worship, the wonder grows that the people are half so estimable as they are. As regards India, at any rate, the conviction appears to be forced on one's mind that the outward symbols of religious belief have less influence on the daily life of individuals than the social standards that exist independently of the strange and often very unedifying religious cults professed by the people. Yet what a sad confession it is, that the very influence which should be most elevating and inspiring falls here below the common level of moral feeling, and has to be ingeniously explained and interpreted before it can be made to accord with ordinary notions of right! It is this, more than anything else, that keeps back the Hindus from attaining the place in the world that their intelligence and ability fit them to occupy. They need a high and inspiring ideal, a hopeful and energising faith that will lift them out of the slough of fatalism which their religious creed, under all its manifold forms, has inculcated. A consciousness of this need has made itself felt of late years, giving rise to a desperate and forlorn attempt to revive the belief in Hinduism, with all its ancient practices, among the educated classes. While acknowledging the zeal and self-denial which have led modern workers like Mrs. Besant to aim at the regeneration of the Hindus by a revival of their old religion, one cannot but regard such efforts as a very questionable service to young India. As a non-Christian Hindu, writing lately in the *Kayasth Samáchár* (an ably conducted magazine published under Hindu auspices in North India), says: "The recent Hindu revival is a backward movement, inasmuch as it tries to reintroduce into our creed those doctrines of a bygone age which we threw away long ago. To attempt to assert the divinity of the Puranas, to find innumerable beauties and lessons, from the spiritual standpoint, in the obscene farces of Krishna related in the Bhagavat Purana, to defend idolatry with plausible, long-exploded arguments, is to lead us back to the stage from which we started, and to undo the labour of years in the cause of religious reform. I believe the Theosophical School is a great favourite because it panders to the vanity of the young patriots and enthusiasts who want to defend even the Puranic customs, so absurd in themselves. It is the fashion in these days to discover hidden truths in the most trivial, ridiculous practices of Hinduism, to apply all the force of ingenious sophistry and misguided zeal for the purpose of extolling everything ancient. This arises from a mistaken notion of patriotism, which makes our young students forget the wise maxim of the late Sir T. Madhava Rao, 'What is not true is not patriotic.'"

It is probable, however, that the belated effort to revive belief in Hinduism among the educated will not have much permanence, and it may serve a useful purpose in showing the uselessness of all such endeavours, and in leading to a truer appreciation of spiritual needs. It will be seen that Hinduism, from its very nature, is incapable of supplying the energy for moral and social reformation. A brief illustration of this incapacity may be given in passing. The common explanation of the cessation of the worship of Brahma, the Supreme God and Creator of the universe, is that he was deposed from his eminence for telling a lie (in reality the legends assign a far more atrocious cause). The impassable gulf between pagan and Christian thought is revealed here. To Christians, God is the moral ideal, all-holy, incapable of wrong, towards whom the soul aspires as the only good. To the Hindu, the

Supreme is a sinner. God may be Satan, Satan may be God, if by His austerities or ritual performances He can win the power. The divine is only divine because it is powerful, not because it is good, and religious faith is thus only a desire for material aid. The root-ideas of religion and spirituality are thus totally diverse in the two creeds. The fatalism of the Hindu system, again, is its most hopeless feature. There is no hope in the future. The Hindu is taught to believe that all that is heroic and good lies in the past, and that the present age, or Kali Yuga, is steadily deteriorating from the imaginary ideal state of the golden age, and will go from bad to worse. He is thus made sceptical about the possibility of any real reform. The gloom of Fate overshadows all man's hopes. Hinduism regards with a contemptuous smile the plans and aspirations of philanthropy. If he is true to his faith, the Hindu cannot believe in progress, which for him is a pure fallacy, the fad or pretence of foreigners. The Hindu religion, in short, is not the friend of man. The religion which could produce, and which sanctions and supports, *caste*, is an inhuman religion. It has no "enthusiasm of humanity," and its revival can do no one any good, except the Brahmans, in whose interest it was framed from the beginning.

Along with the return to the old Puranic ritual, there has gone in recent years a marked revival of Vedantist philosophy, especially under the leadership of the late Swami Vivekananda, who was the means of introducing it to the English-speaking public at the Chicago Parliament of Religious. The Swami, with whom I had some acquaintance, was a man of remarkable ability, and full of ideas, which he expounded in various published lectures. It stands to reason, however, that an abstract and difficult speculative system, like the Adwaita or non-dual Vedantism, can never be made the basis of a popular religion, and must always remain the creed of a select few who are capable of appreciating it, even if we overlook the character of the system itself—a theory that does away with earnest effort for the general weal, and concentrates the faculties on a vague system of self-refinement which has no real aim beyond the self, even when it professes to regard others. It will be seen in the end that there is only one religion in the world that spells Improvement, and leads men and nations to their highest capability. The nationalist feeling in India, so natural and comprehensible in a people suddenly roused to self-consciousness by the new Western enlightenment, is in its present form crude and mistaken. India cannot close its gates against the new influences that are pouring into it. It is hardly reasonable for the widely differing castes and tribes and creeds of India, which owe their only semblance of national unity to their combination under the British Government, to bid progress cease in the attempt to revive a national union that never existed, except in the dreams of some of her recluse writers. In reality the British is hardly more of an alien element than any of the others that go to make up the complex of Indian society, and there is every reason why India should not cut herself adrift, in spiritual and intellectual sympathy, from the Western Aryans who are co-operating with her for her true advancement.

A clear understanding of the origin of Hindu religion, and some knowledge of the mundane sources of its creeds, will probably do more than anything else to lead intelligent Hindus to see that truth must be sought where the vanguard of the human race has found it, in those spiritual ideals that win the heart and convince the intellect of men of every nationality who regard them in sincerity and in truth.

The writer does not claim any originality for the historical part of the work. Especially in the chapter on the History of Kumaon, I am largely indebted to the voluminous *Himalayan Districts*, compiled by the late Mr. E. T. Atkinson, and published by the Indian Government. As this work, with its three portly tomes and aggregate of some 2500 closely printed pages, is practically out of the reach of the great majority of readers, I make no apology for giving a brief outline of the full and admirable treatment of the subject there presented. It is indeed the one authority on the history of this part of India. Many other books have been consulted, as well as articles in the *Asiatic Researches* and *Calcutta Review*. But I would especially mention Pandit Ganga Datt Uprety's *Folklore of Kumaon and Garhwál*, which has proved a valuable mine of information. I have also had the advantage of the same writer's MS. notes and collections on the history, antiquities, and customs of the province, and of much information gained in conversation with him and other Indian friends in Almora, without whose help some of the chapters could not have been written.

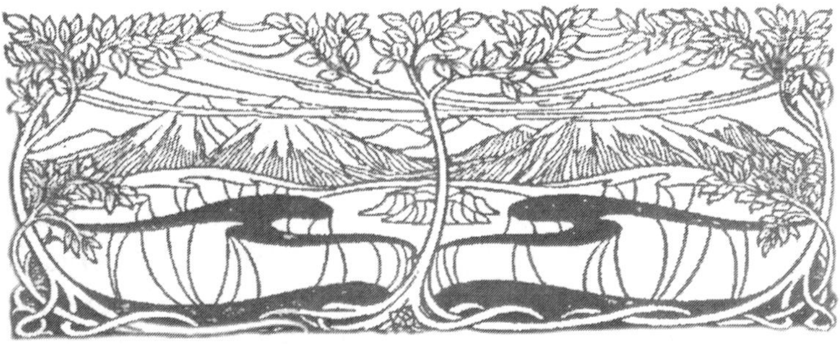

CHAPTER I

THE JOURNEY TO ALMORA

THE traveller whose destination is the mountain province of Kumaon must first of all make his way to the large city of Bareilly, the capital of Rohilkund, about sixty miles from the foot of the Himalayas. There he will transfer himself to a single line of railway which runs up to Kathgodam. For many miles the train passes through a flourishing agricultural country not differing in any respect from the usual scenery of the Indian plains, with their wide stretches of unfenced fields and level wastes diversified here and there with clumps of trees. The name Rohilkund perpetuates the memory of a race of fierce Afghan invaders, the Rohillas, who on the fall of the Mogul Empire seized the lands between Delhi and the Himalayas. The British came into collision with these warriors in 1774, when Warren Hastings sent a force to help the Oude Vizier to drive them off his frontier, and the Rohilla leader, Hafiz Khan, was slain on the field. Before leaving Bareilly we see the little fortress standing a short distance from the railway station, and are reminded of the wild events of the Mutiny year. When the news of the outbreak among the native troops at

Meerut and Delhi reached Bareilly, the three native regiments stationed there were thrown into great excitement. The commandant, Brigadier Sibbald, a veteran, sixty-eight years old, was absent at Almora, and Colonel Colin Troup, who had been a captive in the Afghan war of 1842, was in command. There was a large European settlement at Bareilly, comprising many civil and military officers and their families, as well as other European and Eurasian residents. On 21st May Sibbald returned from Almora and harangued the troops. On the 29th, a body of mutineers belonging to the 45th Regiment arrived from Firozpore, won over the 18th Regiment then stationed at Bareilly, and two days after the great outbreak took place. The English bungalows were fired, and every white man who appeared was shot down. The brigadier himself was one of the first to meet this fate. It was determined to retreat to Naini Tal, and Troup arranged the movement with the officers of the 8th Irregular Cavalry. Those officers, like so many at that time, seem to have had a pathetic confidence in the loyalty of their men; so much so that Mackenzie, the officer in command of that regiment, persuaded Troup to let them face the rebels of the 18th. When confronted with that force, the sight of the green banner of Islam was too much for the Mussalman soldiery; they wavered, and in a few moments deserted and went over to the mutineers. They then turned the guns on the remaining regiment, the 16th, and compelled them to join in the rebellion. Four of the officers escaped from the ground, but were killed by some villagers. The commissioner, with three other civil officers, escaped to Naini Tal, but the four judges all perished, together with many business people and their wives and children. Khan Bahadur Khan, descendant of Hafiz Khan (who fell in 1774 in the Rohilla war), was proclaimed Nawab or viceroy, and gave orders that all Christians should be killed. The bodies of the victims, it is said, were dragged naked through the town and thrown at the foot of the Nawab's standard. The superintendent of the jail, Dr. Handsborough, fought manfully against the fearful odds, and defended himself all through Sunday, but at last was taken, brought to the Nawab, and slain before him.

These scenes of violence and terror are now matter of ancient history, and it is not likely that they will ever recur. Yet it is not without profit to recall them, on occasion, and to remind ourselves that the great calamity of 1857 was, under Providence, the means of the awakening of our countrymen to a deeper sense of responsibility towards India, and it is from that time that the serious work of the evangelisation of that land has been pursued with new energy and zeal.

Many of the mutineers on the suppression of the outbreak took refuge in the Himalayas, especially in Nepal. Sir Henry Ramsay used to tell of a tragic incident that befell in Garhwal at that time. The officials had received orders to track down and destroy all such runaways, and on one occasion a dozen of them had been surrounded and taken. Sir Henry himself had no liking for the task of executioner, but a European named Lyall, who was with the party, had no such squeamish feelings. The prisoners were made to stand along the edge of a cliff overhanging a river, and Lyall with his revolver sent one after another to his account, each man toppling over the height as he received his death-wound. One only of the number escaped, not having been mortally stricken, and got off by swimming to the other side. Sir Henry himself acted with great promptitude when the disaffection threatened to extend to the hill province. For days he went about with the key of the Government Treasury in his pocket, and when two faqirs arrived in the Almora bazaar to preach sedition, he had them hanged out of hand.

After leaving Bareilly and travelling about forty miles, we reach the Tarai, which here hardly presents the appearance that it shows in other portions of its extent, being cleared and fairly cultivated. The Tarai, or "fresh greenery," as the name implies, is properly the belt of grassy swamp about ten miles broad which runs parallel to the foot of the Himalayas, at a few miles distance from the outermost range of hills, before the thick jungle at the base of the mountains is reached, extending several hundred miles, below Garhwal, Kumaon, and Nepal. It owes its origin to the marshy nature of the ground, from which sluggish streams ooze and flow lazily or stand in stagnant pools. Tall reeds and grasses, higher than a man on horseback, cover the soil. Here and there a wretched village or collection of mud huts may be seen. It is a pestilential region, and the Tarai fever is one of the most fatal forms of malaria. During the hot and rainy months of the year it is dangerous for any European, or indeed for natives who are not indurated to it, to pass the night there. Lady Canning, the wife of one of the viceroys, is said to have contracted a fatal illness by so doing.

Another ten miles, and we enter the forest belt called the Bhabar, which has formed part of Kumaon from earliest times, and immediately skirts the mountains. The latter are clearly visible now, presenting a massive wall of forest-clad slopes and heights rising steeply from the vast plain which we have been traversing so long. At this part there is no gradual break-up of the ground or lower foot-hills, but the outer barrier springs at once to a height of from 6000 to 9000 feet above sea-level. We are passing now through thick tropical forest, in which the sal tree figures largely. The watercourses have entirely disappeared. There are no pools or streams, except where one of the greater rivers flowing down from the mountains pursues its wide sandy course. The numerous sharply-cut ravines, however, show that in the rainy season there are many fierce torrents, and these gullies reveal the fact that the ground consists of a vast collection of loose boulders, with a thin deposit of earth on the top, sufficient, however, to support a great growth of forest trees. It is in fact a tract in which all the water sinks deep down, till arrested by a bed of hard clay, and reappears farther on, in the marshy Tarai. The explanation of these peculiar features is that probably in former ages there was a great sea covering what is now the plain of Upper India, and washing the foot of the Himalayas, and that its level has been raised by volcanic agency and the action of rivers carrying down vast quantities of soil from the mountains. The Bhabar is supposed to represent the colossal beach of this ocean, and consists of loose stones and fragments of rock which have fallen down from the great cliffs above, and been worn and scattered by the breakers of the prehistoric shore. Thus the Bhabar, when left in its natural condition, is a dry belt of land which swallows up all the minor streams coming down from the mountains and gives back none of its waters until the Tarai is reached. Human art and industry, however, have been at work to remedy this condition, and we find, from earlier reports and descriptions of the country, that it was the custom of the people to harness several of the mountain streams and distribute them canal-wise over the Bhabar. This was done on a much larger scale by Government in the days of Sir Henry Ramsay, when the surplus waters of the Bhim Tal and other lakes were conducted by dams and sluices to the level below, and so the Bhabar has been to a great extent cleared and cultivated. Large numbers of the Kumaon villagers leave their fields and homes in the highlands to spend the winter season in the Bhabar, with their live stock, and there they till their fields and fodder their cattle on the abundant herbage, at a time when all is dry and parched in the hilly tracts.

The Bhabar and Tarai are not without historical interest, as a recent observer[1] has pointed out: "On either side, in the recesses of the forest, lie ruins of ancient towns and villages, and of temples, Buddhist and Brahmanical—vestiges of the ancient kingdom of Govisana, visited by the Chinese pilgrim Hiouen Thsang in the seventh century A.D., and said to have

[1] Lieutenant-Colonel L. A. Waddell, of the Indian Medical Service, writing in the *Pioneer*.

been laid waste by invading hordes of Pathans, Gurkhas, and others; though it may also be that the Mahamari or 'great death' (plague), which for centuries has lurked within the outer Garhwal hills, may have contributed to turn it into a wilderness, a favourite haunt of tiger. Latterly the forest became the retreat of wild Rohilla and other Pathan freebooters. The village of Chorgaliya or 'the Robbers' Gully,' to the east of the railway, preserves the memory of those not very distant days. Indeed, this part of the country is still notorious for highway robbery."

This enjoys the distinction of being one of the best regions in the world for big game. Tigers and leopards are plentiful, and wild elephants are also found. Pythons of great size are sometimes met with, wrapped round forest trees, or lying gorged with a repast of a deer swallowed whole. Sportsmen travel through the thick jungle and long grass mounted on elephants, a traveller on foot being immediately lost owing to the high growth of vegetation around him. His Majesty King Edward, when as Prince of Wales he visited India in the seventies, enjoyed the sport of this region under the guidance of Sir Henry Ramsay, then Commissioner of Kumaon.

After a rather tedious run (if "run" it can be called when the train takes over five hours to travel sixty miles, with lengthy stoppages at small stations), we reach Kathgodam (the name means "woodstore"). Here is the terminus of the little railway, and we have now to adopt some other means of conveyance up the forest-clad hillsides, rising high and steep at a short distance from the station. The choice is presented us of either a journey by "tonga" (light mail-cart) to Naini Tal, the beautiful summer station of the United Provinces Government, with its hotels and villas clustered round the deep-set lake, along the gradually sloping "cart-road," or by horse or "dandi" to Bhim Tal. The dandi or "jhampan" is the mode of being carried usually adopted by ladies. As most people nowadays are aware, it is a boat-shaped seat, with a pole at either end resting on the shoulders of carriers. It may be borne by two strong men only, if the distance is short and the occupant's weight not too great, but is more conveniently fitted with cross-poles and carried by four "jhampanis." Horses, or sturdy Bhutea ponies, may be had at Kathgodam, if one is not provided with a mount, at fixed prices for the varying distances of places in the hill-country. The Bhutea pony is an excellent animal at its best, very sure-footed and by far the most suitable carrier in the hills. Whether riding or walking, and I have done both many times, the journey to Almora is a most pleasant one. As a rule deliciously cool breezes are encountered on the slopes and heights, and as one rises higher and higher a feeling of exhilaration possesses the mind, the lungs are filled with pure, sweet air, and a sense of liberation is felt, after the dead level of the Indian plain. Below us, as we ascend the zigzag road, are deep gorges filled with subtropical growth, and above us are high fir-clad peaks, while if we turn and look backwards we see the great hazy plain below, stretching as far as the eye can reach, its greenery intersected by the white lines of one or two wide river channels.

Our baggage has to be carried on the backs or heads of coolies, whose services are obtained at Kathgodam. The coolie plays an important part in our life among the Himalayas, being the only means of transport, unless we hire mules, which are not generally used except by the military and some of the native traders on the main roads. A system of forced labour, if such it may be called, still prevails in Kumaon, the owners of land being obliged to supply coolies at the summons of Government when required, as a condition of their tenure. The coolies are of course paid at fixed rates, and the inhabitants of a village can thus supplement their gains from land cultivation. One class of coolie is the Dotiyal, from Doti on the eastern or Nepal side of Kumaon. He is one of the sturdiest carriers to be found in the world. He is said to be a meat-eater, the ordinary Kumaoni being a vegetarian, except on rare occasions. The Dotiyal carries his load, be it box, bag, or anything else, on his back, supported by a rope passing round the forehead. The strength and endurance of these men are marvellous. They will frequently offer to carry a double load on condition of receiving double pay, and one was pointed out some years ago as having distinguished himself by carrying a piano to Almora on his back unaided! The proper load of a coolie, as laid down in Government rules, is 25 seers or 50 lb.

To one whose home for many years has been among these grand mountains, there comes the peculiar attachment that has been so often noted in highlanders. There is an inexpressible pleasure in looking up once more to the massive heights and feeling the mountain air against one's cheek after long absence. The natives have a proverb that those who have once lived in Kumaon are never happy elsewhere. How many weary white faces of European men and women and children have brightened with renewed life and hope as they approached the great mountains, leaving behind them the burning plain of India with its shimmering pall of summer heat! They have "looked up to the hills whence cometh their help," assured that a healing balm will renew their jaded mind and body as they sojourn on those breezy heights. To the European in India "going to the hills" means holiday and joy and health.

To give the reader some idea of the scene that greets a traveller when he has climbed the first few miles and reaches the top of the outer lofty range, I will quote the words of Sir John Strachey in an article written for the *Calcutta Review* more than fifty years ago: "Let us suppose that we have ascended the first range of hills that rises above the plains, in Kumaon, to the lofty peak of Cheena, which overhangs the lake and station of Naini Tal. From this point, the elevation of which is about 8700 feet, an observer can obtain an admirable general idea of the structure of this part of the Himalaya. Our horizontal distance from the foot of the hills is only about five miles. We look down over the beautiful wooded mountains of the Gagar range, covered thickly with oak and pine, mingled with the gorgeous rhododendron, to the Bhabar forest, which lies almost at our feet, 7000 feet below, and beyond to the Tarai and the great plain. Turning to the north, we have before us a scene which the painter and the poet can alone describe, but which can never pass from the mind of one who has once beheld it. A chaotic mass of mountains lies before us, wooded hills, and deep ravines, and dark blue ranges, rising one above another; and behind all, piled up into the sky, the snowy peaks of the great Himalaya. He who has seen this view, or the still finer ones that are to be obtained from other parts of central Kumaon, may feel quite satisfied that he has seen the most sublime and astonishing of all earthly spectacles."

The writer of the above words, which revive in one's mind the impressions of many wonderful landscapes seen at early morn or dewy eve in different parts of the province, has omitted to mention one of the main charms of the scenery from the point of view which he describes, namely, the several lakes, whose shining waters, of lovely turquoise hue, glance up from the depths of their glens in the neighbourhood of Naini Tal. Far below at one's very feet is the lake of Naini herself, a goddess whose restored temple stands at the water's edge, memorial of ancient belief in a tutelary deity of the wild remote valley, which was "discovered" in the early forties by an adventurous Englishman, and thereafter became one of the gayest and most crowded of Indian hill-stations; memorial too of the terrible landslip which slid down from the precipitous hillside on the 18th of September 1880, overwhelming some forty Europeans, and carrying the old shrine into the depths of the lake. For two days rain had been falling in torrents, to the extent of 25 inches, and there was thus an enormous amount of water in the hills surrounding the lake. A steep slope nearly 1000 feet high rose behind the Victoria Hotel. During the morning of the fateful day a slight slip occurred behind the hotel, crushing some outhouses and burying about twenty Indians and one English child. The civil functionary and several military officers, with all the police and military available, repaired to the spot and set to work to extricate the dead and wounded, when (to quote a graphic account of the catastrophe) "in a moment the whole precipitous cliff overhanging the spot fell with a tremendous roar, burying at once the hotel, the soldiers, the assembly rooms below, the library, orderly room, road, and garden. Almost every person in the buildings and grounds was entombed. The place shook as with an earthquake, and the waters of the lake were driven to the south part of it in an immense wave, while vast clouds of dust rose from the falling masses like volumes of smoke after a terrible explosion."

These landslips are not infrequent among the Himalayas, the slopes being in many places precipitous and immensely high, and the rainfall so heavy as to load the soil and rocks beyond the point of stability. It is probable that all the lakes of Kumaon and Garhwal owe their origin to land-slides. Only a few years ago a huge fall of the kind occurred at Gohna in Garhwal, when the side of a mountain fell down during the night, to the terror of the inhabitants of the village near by, and blocked up a valley and stream. This in a few days formed a lake several miles in extent. Engineers were sent to render the accumulation of waters as safe as possible. A large dam or "bund" was erected, and precautions taken to warn the people of the lower valleys in case of a sudden burst of the pent-up waters. The bund was broken through in a few weeks, and a mighty flood rushed down to join the Alakananda river far away, in its course overwhelming and destroying the old town of Srinagar. Warning was effectually given to the people below, and it is reported that only one person perished, a wandering yogi who had not heard of the danger, or hearing had defied it. The Gohna lake still remains, though it shrank considerably at the time of the outburst.

As we are now making our way to Almora, the ancient capital of Kumaon, we leave the well-made cart-road that leads to Naini Tal and Ranikhet (where thousands of British soldiers live during the hot months), and turn into a bridle-path that takes us over a suspension bridge across the Gola river, and mount steeply by a zigzag road on the other side of the ravine. We mount over 3000 feet within a distance of five miles, obtaining at every few yards wider and finer views of the mountains and valleys about us and the far-stretching plains behind us. If the season be autumn, early in November or so, we meet great numbers of villagers going down with their families and household goods to winter in the Bhabar. Some characteristic touches of native life are to be observed. The wives of the men, especially if they have passed their youth, are seen carrying fairly heavy loads and walking before or else behind their lords and masters, who never walk *with* them, but always at a little distance. This is the invariable etiquette, except occasionally in large cities or among Christians who have adopted some European ways. Nothing appears to excite more ridicule among Hindus than the sight of a European walking side by side or, still more, arm in arm with the partner of his joys and sorrows. We notice now and then, however, a young and comely woman—someone's wife she must be, for practically all women are married in India—

mounted on a mule or pony, seated usually on some portion of the household stuff. Chubby infants are also seen tied up and supported on the baggage animals, or seated astride of their father's or mother's side as the latter walk along; and occasionally one has met a sturdy highlander carrying his infirm old father on his back, as erst the pious Aeneas bore Anchises from the walls of burning Troy. Another amusing sight sometimes met with is that of a babe a few days old carried in a basket at the mother's back. The men generally have tall muscular frames, and well-formed Aryan features.

A different class of travellers on this road at the same season of the year are the Bhoteas from the snowy regions in the north of the province, bringing down their loads of wool, etc., to the depôts at the foot of the hills. They drive before them long strings of sheep and goats, each loaded with a double pannier of cloth (karboja) protected with leather. These traders carry on a constant interchange of goods between Tibet and the lower hills and plains, crossing the lofty passes of the Johar and Darma valleys. From Tibet they bring chiefly salt and borax, and take back grain, cloth, etc., which are necessaries of life to the inhabitants of the barren plateau of Hundes. The approach of these droves of laden animals is announced by clouds of dust, by the peculiar whistling of the drovers, and by the noise of numerous little bells tied to the necks of the animals, the tinkling of which sounds pleasantly along the forest roads.

About seven miles from Kathgodam we turn a corner of the road and come suddenly on Bhim Tal, a beautiful sheet of water surrounded by high wooded

A DAK BUNGALOW

THE PĀNCH CHULE PEAKS

hills, and just over a mile in length and a quarter of a mile broad. Its waters are of a bluish green and very clear. We can observe fish occasionally leaping up; these are the Mahseer or Indian salmon. At the end nearest the plains we cross over a strong masonry embankment with sluices for letting out the flow of surplus water to the Bhabar—part of the engineering works for irrigating the waterless tract at the foot of the hills. Opposite this is a small wooded island about a hundred yards from the shore, and adding greatly to the beauty of the lake. We also notice the temple with a wooden "chhatri" or canopy at the top, standing at the southern end of the lake—built by a Kumaon raja, Baz Bahadur Chand, in the seventeenth century, and dedicated to Bhimeshwar, one of the many epithets of Siva.

The end of our march comes when we reach that famous institution in India, the dak bungalow, or rest-house for travellers. These places are kept up by Government and provided with simple furniture, at a fixed daily charge for occupation. There are two classes of these rest-houses in the hills—those having a Mohammedan cook or "khansamah" in charge, who can furnish the traveller with meals at short notice, usually by the sudden death of a fowl; and those which have no cook, and where the traveller must provide his own food. This being one of the most frequented roads, the dak bnngalows are all of the former kind. The building here stands on the lakeside in a charming situation, and is a favourite resort of fishermen on short leave from the plains.

There are other lakes in the neighbourhood, off the main roads, but known to enthusiastic anglers, such as

Sat Tal, Malwa Tal, and Naukachiya Tal or the Nine-cornered lake, regarding which the natives have a tradition that if anyone can get into such a position as to see all the nine bays of the lake at once, he will meet with some great stroke either of good or bad luck before the year is out. It has been remarked that an individual would have to possess a very powerful squint in order to do so.

Early the next day, for travelling under the semi-tropical sun is always best done in the fresh hours of the morning, even in the hills, we take the road northwards skirting the side of the lake, and make for our next stage, Ramgarh. We observe that at the upper end of the lake there is a plain of considerable extent, evidently part of the former bed of the lake, and where true peat may be dug out of the ground. A large camp of Boer prisoners was stationed here for some months in 1901–02, and in passing the place one used to meet serious-looking bearded men walking out in twos and threes talking quietly together. There were also not a few quite young boys gambolling about the camp. There must be many, now repatriated to South Africa, who retain a vivid remembrance of the Himalayan lake and its dark forest-clad mountains.

Leaving the valley of the lake, after a few miles of ascents and descents we reach the pass over the Gagar range, the highest point we shall have to surmount in our journey, and having an altitude of nearly 8000 feet. As we mount upwards to the pass the chir or pine tree (*Pinus longifolia*), with its long feathery tufts of leaves, gives place to thick shady ilex (*Quercus dilatata*) and giant rhododendron, which in its season is clothed with magnificent red flowers. A

Himalayan rhododendron forest in full bloom is a sight never to be forgotten. Above 7000 feet the vegetation of the Kumaon hills seems to be chiefly oak and rhododendron, and the great dampness of the climate during the rainy season (July to October) causes the gnarled spreading branches of the oaks to be covered with a wonderful growth of ferns, mosses, and delicate creepers.

Our day's travel is diverted here and there by the sight of the monkeys, running up the stems at our approach, or breaking away in droves over the tops of the trees with a crashing noise. The monkeys are of two kinds in the Himalayas—the large long-tailed Langur with whitish body and round black face surrounded by a hoary beard (rather reminding one of the portraits of Ibsen), and the little brown monkey with its young ones clinging to its back or sides as it swings out of the way and scrambles up its "family tree."

At the top of the Gagar pass, we find a kind of stone floor by the roadside, with certain religious emblems about it, marking it as a place of some sanctity. Near by there are strips of cloth tied to the twigs of the trees, rags torn from their clothing by pious coolies as they pass that way, and left as an offering to the spirit or divinity of the spot. We often notice these "rags of superstition," as they may literally be called, on mountain passes, or in dark and eerie corners haunted by demons, or at places where some crime or sudden death has happened in former days, and which may be supposed to be under the influence of the wandering and perhaps malevolent spirit of the departed. The mind of the Indian peasant is shadowed by infinite dark fancies of this kind.

In clear weather there is a magnificent view of the snowy range from the point we have now gained. From September to March the peaks are usually visible. I shall never forget the impression of this scene for the first time, as I stood here on a clear, bright day in November 1888, and beheld the "snowy summits old in story," soaring upwards from the shadows of the dark gorges at their feet—a fairy unsubstantial scene, a glory of delicate shade and colour, which one could hardly recognise as solid reality.

After a suitable pause to enjoy the scene, we descend for some miles through thick shady forest, where in winter the snow lies on the path, and even in summer the air feels cool and wet. Such forests as this are the home of many wild animals; the "khakar" or barking deer, a beautiful slender-limbed creature, the "gurral" or Indian chamois, the wild boar, and occasionally a bear or leopard, not to mention the Himalayan partridge ("chakor"), and pheasants of different kinds, the finest of which is the "monal," with its splendid blue tints, perhaps the most beautiful of birds.

Water flows abundantly on all sides as we pass down this forest slope, and we are never far from its refreshing sound. Channels made out of split logs form a picturesque little aqueduct which conveys an abundant supply of water to the village and rest-houses lower down the hill, which we reach after a steep descent. The remainder of the way to Almora is a series of climbs and descents, mostly through forest, and does not present any features of great interest. A last long and hot climb, from the suspension bridge over the Sual river, leads up to the Almora ridge. We pass under Granite hill on the right—a mass of boulders strewn about and heaped in fantastic shapes, and a little farther on is the Leper Asylum conducted by the London Mission. We pass its modest gateway by the roadside, but the settlement itself is so embowered in trees that we do not notice it until we are ascending the slope beyond, and then looking back we can see its neat rows of whitewashed barracks and little church and other buildings laid out on the side of the hill. Another mile, and we reach Almora.

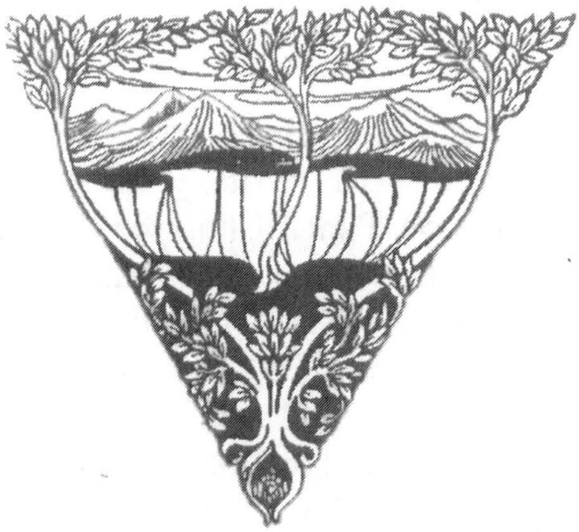

CHAPTER II

ALMORA

NESTLING among the lower spurs of the great Himalaya, and surrounded by range upon range of higher mountains fading into the blue distance, is the town of Almora, the ancient capital of the kingdom of Kumaon. Far away to the north stands out the wonderful line of snowy peaks, towering up into the sky to a height of 25,000 feet, and showing their well-defined peaks—the sharp wedge of Nanda Devi, highest mountain in the British Empire; Trisul, the trident of Mahadeo; Panch Chule, or the five fire-stalls of the gods, as they are called; and on the western extremity the square mass of Badrinath. These are the famous snowy summits, the sacred guardians of the Indian peninsula, and the home of the greater gods. On the sharp peak of Nanda Devi may be seen at times what looks like a wreath of smoke, which devout Hindu sentiment has supposed to be the sacrificial fire of some favoured worshipper whom the god has permitted to reach the very summit, and which the prosaic Briton has sometimes supposed to be the crater of a volcano, though more probably its smoke-like appearance is due to the feathery snow being blown aslant from the summit. For the English observer is the interest of science, for the children of nature is the poetry of superstition, the romance of a wild, often terrible, and at times beautiful mythology.

The town lies along the ridge of a hill a little over 5000 feet above sea-level, and surrounded on three sides by deep valleys through which flow small rivers, the Sual and the Kosi, that go ultimately to join the Ganges. On the north-east the ridge runs up to meet the higher hills. There are forests on the upper part of most of the surrounding ranges, but for a few miles around Almora there is a general absence of trees, said to be due to the practice of the Gurkhas, who were wont to lay waste the forests round any fortress occupied by them, to guard against being surprised by an enemy. Yet Almora nowadays no longer deserves the character given to it by good Bishop Heber, who visited it in 1824, and in one of his hymns speaks of

"Bleak Almora's barren steep."

The Forest Department is rapidly contributing to remove this reproach from the neighbourhood, and the young plantations of pines on the nearer hillsides are beginning to give quite a sylvan aspect to the landscape around Almora. In the daytime the deep ravines about the town, and the vast slopes of the mountains all around, seem to show nothing but wild forest, scrub, and barren rock, with here and there patches of cultivation; but when evening comes and fills the great hollows of the hills with shadow, innumerable points of light shine out, revealing the site of tiny hamlet or forest lodge or shepherd's hut high up on mountain face or by riverside. The view is one of great vastness, like most Himalayan landscapes, the only feature lacking to complete its beauty being water. With lakes or large rivers to add charm to the scene these expanses of vale and mountain in the Himalaya would be sublimely beautiful. As it is, the English residents of Almora have planted a bench at the end of the Mall road, overlooking a pathetically thin streak representing the Kosi stream far down in the gorge below, and have called the place "Brighton Corner."

During the rainy season (from July to October) the valleys and hillsides around assume the most lovely verdure, covering every foot of ground, so that the eye is delighted with delicate and endlessly diversified greenery, which appears to outline in clearest colour every fold and dimple of the hills. The "rains" in Almora are more endurable than in most other hill-stations, owing to the scarcity of the rainfall. There is hardly a day when one cannot get out for some hours at least, while Naini Tal, only thirty miles distant, remains bathed for weeks at a time in soaking mist and rain, the average annual rainfall there being ninety inches as compared with thirty at Almora. The cause of this marked difference is the fact that Naini Tal stands on the outer range of hills, considerably higher than the inner hills adjoining it, and catches the rain-clouds, which are thus to a large extent exhausted before reaching Almora. The latter place is situated on a ridge of moderate elevation in the midst of a vast amphitheatre of higher ranges, and is thus protected on all sides from excessive showers. This dryness of climate as well as of soil makes it a suitable place for persons suffering from lung complaints, and during the last few years it has acquired a considerable reputation, there having been some wonderful cures. The winter, however, is too trying and changeable for such patients. A great desideratum is a hospital or convalescent home for consumptives, where all cases might be received and properly treated.

During the months of May and June the thermometer at Almora usually stands at something between 80° and 90°, so that it is not a very cool place in comparison with many other hill-stations. In those months, too, the air is filled with a thick dust-haze from the plains, which effectually conceals even the nearer hills, and renders a view of the snows at fifty or sixty miles distance quite out of the question. Almora in fact is not, properly speaking, a hill-station. It is an old native capital, adopted as the headquarters of the administration on the annexation of Kumaon by the British Government, and a military station for a battalion of Gurkhas. The town was founded about 1560 by one of the Chand rajas of Kumaon named Kalyan Singh, who removed hither from the older capital Champawat, to the east of Almora. The legend runs that one day the king was hunting on the Almora hill, which then bore the name Khagmara, and was covered with dense forest. A hare suddenly started up before him, and he began to pursue it, whereupon it was transformed into a tiger, and on reaching the top of the hill disappeared. The king consulted his Brahman astrologers concerning this strange event. They all accepted it as a most favourable omen, and counselled the king to found his capital on the spot where the tiger had disappeared. The site was accordingly examined, and a large crowbar was driven into the ground. It sank so deep that the astrologers declared it had pierced the back of the Seshnag, or great serpent, which the Hindus suppose to support the universe (like the Midgard snake of Norse mythology), and they accepted the fact as a token that the king's dynasty should endure for ever. But the king, impelled by curiosity, insisted on the bar being dragged out of the ground, and, sure enough, the point of it was seen to be stained with blood. Thereupon the astrologers in wrath declared that as a punishment for the raja's presumption and unbelief, his descendants should reign but for a few generations. This prophecy was fulfilled, for the Chand dynasty had often to be renewed by borrowing a scion from the original royal stock in Jhusi, owing to failure of heirs or wholesale extermination of the royal family in Kumaon.

There appears to have been a fortress of some kind at Almora from earlier times, named Khagmara Kot, where the predecessor of Kalyan Singh, his adoptive father, was treacherously slain by a Khassiya chief, on whom Kalyan Chand took sudden and terrible vengeance at Ramgarh.

The name Almora is said to be a variant or corruption of Kilmora, the native word for the red sorrel, which grows abundantly on the hill.

Almora, like more famous cities, has a West and an East end, and the West is the fashionable quarter, inhabited by the civil officials and the officers of the 1st Battalion 3rd Gurkhas, who, with their amiable ladies, mainly constitute the pleasant English society of the place.

The native town consists mostly of a "bazaar" nearly a mile in length running along the top of the ridge, and paved with stone—in parts with the solid underlying rock. Half-way down this long street is an elevated piece of ground, on which stands the Kucherry or Government offices, occupying the site of the old fort, the last defenders of which were the Gurkhas in 1815, when the place was captured by the British. In the midst of the buildings surmounting the mound is an ancient Hindu temple with its images, sheltering under the wing of Imperial rule, and a standing witness to its tolerance. The Almora bazaar is a rather picturesque one. The houses are adorned with carved wooden fronts, the lower storey forming a shop or an open verandah supported on pillars. One of the oldest houses, with low round pillars, was built by Narayan Sah, steward and business-man of the kingly founder of Almora, who himself laid its foundation-stone. The house is still inhabited by the Sah's descendants.

Farther down the bazaar we come to an assemblage of public buildings, including the Tahsil or revenue offices, hospital, and Ramsay College, a mission institution of handsome and solid aspect, erected in 1871.

The northern slope of the Almora hill is occupied partly by a number of large houses inhabited by Brahman families. The Hindu joint-family system leads to a remarkable extension of the household, as many as a hundred people, young and old, representing various branches and generations of the family, often residing in the same barrack-like domicile. The Brahmans of Almora were originally immigrants from the plains, who came hither in the service of the Chand rajas at different times. They have multiplied largely, and having availed themselves of the educational advantages of the place, have monopolised the different branches of the Government service and thriven greatly.

The proportion of Brahmans to the general population is unusually large, forming about half the inhabitants of the town, who number about eight thousand.

The people of Almora, leaving out the Khassiyas or agricultural population, may be roughly divided into four classes: the Brahmans; the Baniyas or traders (also immigrants in former times), living in the bazaar; the Mohammedans, few in number and including some merchants in the bazaar and domestics in European service; and the artisans or Doms, who have a quarter to themselves on the southern side of the hill, and form a distinct community here, as they do everywhere, even in small villages of the province. The Doms represent the aborigines of Kumaon, and claim to have been in the country before either Khassiyas or immigrants from the plains were known. Their own tradition is that they were the drummers of Siva when he came to take up his residence in the Himalayas. They are generally of a darker and lower type than the caste Hindus, and in earlier times were kept in strict subjection. They were, in fact, slaves of the Khassiyas and Brahmans, and were passed from hand to hand like chattels, or were attached to the soil like the serfs or *adscripti glebæ* of feudal Europe. No Dom was allowed to wear a garment reaching below the knee, and the punishment for touching the "hukka" or tobacco-pipe of a Rajput or Brahman was instant death. There can be little doubt that the Doms are the remnant of a primitive race who occupied the land from earliest ages before the advent of Aryan and Scythian settlers. They seem to have few traditions, but their religious cults have largely influenced the later settlers in Kumaon. Their occupation is that of masons, carpenters, wheelwrights, and day-labourers, occupations which caste Hindus consider menial and degrading. Their habit of eating almost anything, even the flesh of dead cows, is regarded with abhorrence by the stricter castes.

The Doms are widely scattered over North India, and have acquired a European interest from being in all probability the source of the Gipsy race. The name "Romany" assumed by the Gipsies has often been supposed to refer to Roumania, but is more likely to be the word "Domani," the feminine of Dom. (The D in this word is pronounced almost like R.) The Gipsies are known from this language to be of Indian origin, and have been identified with a tribe of Doms near the Indus, who at some time must have been driven out by an invasion and sent on their long wanderings.

There is yet another class to be found in Almora, as well as in all towns of North India, namely, the Sweepers or "Mehtars." The latter is a Persian word meaning "prince," and is a sample of the flattering titles commonly used by Indians in addressing one another, and by which the wheels of social life are pleasantly and inexpensively kept oiled. The Sweepers do the menial work in the bazaars and in the houses of Europeans, and, like the Doms, have no particular rules about eating, taking broken meats from the tables of their employers. It is now impossible to determine their origin. They are most likely descendants of conquered races, and drift-weed of tribes that have at various periods lost status and been reduced to servitude. The study of North Indian history, with its continual wars, invasions, massacres, and migrations, presents a kind of racial kaleidoscope, in which the revolutions of the wheel of change have raised one to cast down another class or tribe in rapid succession, while the wholesale enslavement of captives which prevailed in former days often thrust whole communities to the bottom of the social fabric, so that racial origin does not always or necessarily correspond to dignity of caste. No country can with less propriety be styled "changeless" than India, as regards stability of race. The enduring element is the caste system under Brahmanical influence, but its constituents have continually been changing. The caste system has tended to become more and more unalterably fixed in later times of peace, and it may even be asserted that the permanence of British rule, which everywhere accepted the exact *status quo* as a rule to abide by, has contributed to add fixedness to caste, which in ancient times was more or less flexible. The Sweepers are said to have a curious religion of their own, with a species of priests or religious guides, few in number, called Lal Gurus, or "red priests," because they wear a red robe. They go about visiting the various scattered communities on tours of visitation, and gathering the Sweepers together address homilies to them. One of these discourses was once overheard. The Lal Guru informed his attentive hearers that they were certain to go to heaven, as they could overcome obstacles which would effectually prevent all other classes from gaining everlasting bliss. There were, he said, three rivers to be crossed on the way to Paradise. The first was of cow's blood, which would stop the Hindus; the second of swine's blood, which would bring the Mussalmans to a halt; and the third river was of filth, which would turn back the Europeans, with their sanitary fads.

The Ayahs, or domestic nurses, employed by Europeans, are the wives of Sweepers, and are the only class of women who can be got to act in that capacity.

The chief occupations of the people of Almora are Government service, ordinary trade and barter, and, we may add, education. There is a strong desire for education, and there are two high schools in the town, since the Government started a school of its own in addition to the mission one. The scholars, however, are drawn from all parts of the province. In addition to these, there are elementary free schools, and a Normal School for the training of teachers in the small village primary schools maintained by Government throughout the district. The traveller in Kumaon will sometimes come on a group of boys squatted under a spreading tree or under a thatched shed, going over their lessons in a noisy monotone, as they sway their bodies backwards and forwards, with the pandit sitting meditatively in the midst. This is a rural primary school, attended by the boys of a few surrounding villages, where they obtain a knowledge of the "three R's" in their own Hindi tongue. The curriculum in the high schools closely resembles the corresponding standard in Britain; and as practically all such schools receive Government aid, and are inspected by the Education Department, the course of study is strictly laid down, and the same system of examination serves for all—the University Matriculation and School Final examinations being the conclusion of a high school course. The medium of instruction in the higher classes is English, and the ordinary school subjects are taught, with the exception that Sanskrit or Persian (one of these, never both) take the place of Greek and Latin as classical languages. The Almora boys show great readiness in acquiring knowledge, and for several years have passed the examinations well and taken high places in the lists. This proficiency is no doubt due to the hill climate, which ought to give them superior energy. As an Indian educationist of some experience, I can testify that the Indian student is nowise lacking in mental powers. There are causes which go far to explain the somewhat unsatisfactory results of Anglo-vernacular education in the country, and they are causes more clearly visible to the practical workers in the field than to the theorists whose opinions are mostly heard on the subject. The attempt to make the student do his thinking in a foreign language, has naturally the effect of repressing originality and encouraging methods of cram, which is still further fostered by the hard-and-fast rules of the Education Department, which prescribes "courses" and attempts to lay down the whole scheme of school teaching with the minutest particularity. This may be a help to indifferent or incompetent teaching, but hampers the real teacher. The home life of the boys, again, often seriously militates against a studious tone. They are married men at an absurdly early age; and with the cares of a household often on their shoulders, they can scarcely be expected to enjoy the calm atmosphere necessary to student life. Many of them suffer from ill-health and physical weakness, for India is a tropical country, and the race is not a sturdy one. Great numbers of students are very poor. It is the poor, in fact, who seek knowledge, in order to make a living. Insufficiently fed and clothed and lodged, the body languishes and the brain misses that nourishment that is essential to healthy and vigorous thinking. Yet, with all these adverse conditions, the achievements of Indian students often strike one with admiration. Scotland herself cannot show greater marvels of dogged persistence and patient heroism than the story of many an obscure Indian scholar. It is a common charge against Indian education that there is no "pursuit of knowledge for its own sake." This phrase has indeed become almost too familiar. It may be asked how many European students who have a living to make, with perhaps several helpless beings dependent on them, and a difficult foreign language to master before they can even begin to see their goal in sight, would be found to cherish this wonderful but exceedingly rare "love of knowledge for its own sake." Education not being compulsory in India, most students are struggling youths who have to make their living. The rich either do not study, or pursue knowledge in their own way and in accordance with their native tastes, as might naturally be expected. The imposition of a foreign language as the medium of all higher education has cast somewhat of a blight on the national genius Had the native languages been allowed a fair chance they would in all likelihood by this time have developed some worthy literature and scientific phraseology of their own, instead of remaining in their undeveloped condition.[1] A further result of "English" education in India is that it has led to an idea that the aim of school and college life is to get Government service—only that and nothing more. This notion has been

[1] The tendency at present (especially in Bengal) is to encourage training of scholars in the vernaculars, and to have a limited number of higher institutions where students who have shown special fitness may pursue English studies. As yet, however, this is a new idea, and has not taken very definite shape.

fostered, indeed created, by Government itself making school and university examinations the test and qualification for its service. The result is that English education is regarded simply as a means of obtaining employment in some Government office, and there is almost a total absence of the much desiderated "love of knowledge for its own sake" in connection with our schools and colleges. A still further result is the growth of a class of English-educated men whose numbers are vastly in excess of the requirements of Government, yet who have worked only with the object of winning a post under Government, and consequently consider themselves ill-treated and deceived if they cannot succeed in their object, pursued often, as it has been, under such discouraging circumstances and with such amazing persistence. An official in Kumaon recently declared that he could not leave his house without finding an "Entrance pass" standing under every tree along the road, with a petition in his hand for employment in a Government office.

It is too late in the day now to attempt to reverse entirely the policy of English education, adopted half a century ago under Macaulay's influence. For good and ill it must remain, and the best must be made of it, as indeed Lord Curzon's Government is seeking to do by its careful inquiry into the conditions of secondary training, and by its recent University Act. But still the conviction remains with many of us that education conducted generally in a foreign tongue must fail to bring out the best that is in the scholars, and must remain more of a formula than a real eliciting of the natural powers of the mind. The difficulty in the way of employing the native languages for purposes of instruction is the very practical one that the Government and its Education Department is a foreign importation, and the impossibility of obtaining officers and teachers of the best Western training who are at the same time proficient in those languages. But it appears reasonable enough to hope that in course of time these conditions will remedy themselves, through the growth of a body of native *savants* of patriotic spirit who will make modern knowledge a common possession of the Indians, instead of a monopoly of the "English-educated." When this knowledge is led to flow in its natural channels, as a part of the speech of the people, it will be much more widely diffused, and will become the source of a real national progress. Then, if ever, there will be the love of knowledge for its own sake, and the confusion which has led to education being regarded as merely a purveyor of bread will become a thing of the past. The love of knowledge was once strong enough in India, and may be so again. The anxiety to obtain Government service will no doubt be modified in time, as other openings for the employment of talent are found. It is a mistake, however, to suppose, as many Europeans do, that crowds of youths are being educated by the Government and the missionaries almost in spite of themselves, and taken out of their natural hereditary rank and calling. The boys who attend high schools and secure English education are after all only a small percentage of the population, and are mostly the sons of Brahmans, Kayasths, etc., who are really dependent on clerical and official work for a means of livelihood. The remedy for the surplusage of educated men in India is not to restrict education, which no civilised Government can do, but to develop and revive the trade, resources, and manufactures of the country so as to furnish other and varied avenues of employment for all the available ability in the land.

Part of the Almora hill is occupied by the fort—Fort Moira, as it is called, after one of India's former viceroys, the Earl of Mayo—and the lines of the Gurkha battalion. These sturdy little men, as all the world knows, are among the best fighting material in any army. They are recruited in Nepalese territory, or rather on the borders of Nepal, whither they come to join the British colours, drawn by the attraction of the service. Their native officers are also from Nepal, but belonging to the true Gurkha race, and of a taller physique and more Hindu-like appearance than the private soldiers.

Thus it will be evident that the population of Almora, while fairly homogeneous for an Indian city, contains a good many elements of variety and interest.

The northern slope of the Almora hill is a good place for observing the ingenious way in which the steep hillsides of Kumaon are utilised for cultivation, and converted from arid rocky declivities, swept bare by rain-torrents, into fruitful fields and gardens. This is done by erecting a series of loose stone walls, and levelling up the soil within them so as to form a series of flat terraces from 10 to 20 feet wide. As many as fifty or more of these terraces can in some places be counted, descending one below another to the bed of the stream below. Without these it would be impossible to grow any corn in the hills. The lowest terraces of a slope, or those in which a spring flows, are most highly prized, as they can be irrigated and left under

View of Almora (Showing the Terraces)

water for the growth of the better kinds of rice. Rice is said to have a hundred different species here, each of which has a native name, and I have seen a complete list of these names somewhere. In Kumaon rice is a luxury but seldom enjoyed by the poorer classes, the staple food of the people being "madua," a species of millet. There are two harvests in the year, called Rabi and Kharif respectively. The former is chiefly wheat, sown in the winter and reaped in March; the other consists of madua, sown in the spring and reaped in October. The wheat is mostly sold, the madua being kept for home consumption. It is a poor cereal.

The salubrity of Almora secures a general exemption from the serious diseases that sometimes lay waste the country districts. The Mahamari, a disease closely resembling bubonic plague, if not precisely the same in its nature, is said to be indigenous in the Himalayas, and sometimes breaks out in alarming fashion in some of the neighbouring villages, though its habitat is chiefly Garhwal. It affects places where the people live in dark stone huts and amid filthy conditions. On the appearance of plague, the inhabitants of the village at once take off the roofs of their houses to let in the sunlight and air, and betake themselves to the jungle, where they remain in discomfort for some weeks. This remedy never fails to be effectual in stopping the outbreak, and has been tried with success in recent epidemics of plague in Indian cities. Sir Henry Ramsay used to say that the plague was often observed to run in lines, attacking some villages and leaving others, off the line, intact, which might be due to the course taken by infected rats. Cholera seldom attacks the town of Almora, though in 1903 there was a severe outbreak, in which the town shared with the province generally, and some hundreds were carried off. The cholera generally takes its rise from the vast gathering of pilgrims at the Hardwar fair, and spreads from there as a centre.

The Leper Asylum, situated about a mile to the south-west of the town, has already been mentioned. It is laid out in neat rows of whitewashed barracks, in a fine grove of Australian gum, deodar, and fruit trees. It was originally started by Sir Henry Ramsay, Commissioner of Kumaon for a long term of years, who was known as the "King of Kumaon," as indeed he was, in the old non-regulation days when the commissioner had a free hand in the administration of the province. When a young man holding a subordinate rank in the Kumaon Commission, he noticed the number of wandering and destitute lepers in the district, and had a few huts erected for their lodging. He maintained these poor creatures for several years, when a grant of some Government tea-gardens was obtained for their support, and the asylum was placed under the charge of the Rev. J. H. Budden, of the London Missionary Society. In the encouragement of education, and in philanthropic work generally, Sir Henry was ever active and generous, and was an example of that fine old school of paternal despots whom changing conditions have nowadays ruled out of existence.

The disease of leprosy is sadly prevalent in Kumaon, especially in its eastern portion and the adjoining district of Doti in Nepal. The cause of this affliction, the most terrible to which humanity is liable, is still obscure. It affects mostly the poor and those who live in unwholesome conditions, with scanty and bad food, though the wealthier classes are by no means exempt. One is aware, of course, that the disease is a specific one, with a bacillus of its own. There can be no reasonable doubt, in spite of some medical theorists, that the steady isolation of lepers in asylums, and the segregation of the sexes therein, is a practical way of diminishing and finally exterminating leprosy. This method proved successful in several European countries in the Middle Ages, and if consistently followed in India would, in the course of a generation or two, almost cleanse the land of one of its worst scourges. An interesting fact is that in the course of some thirty-five years about fifty children of lepers, brought to the asylum at different times, have been removed from their leprous parents and brought up in the Mission Orphanage, and of that total number only two or three have become lepers, which would seem to prove that the disease is not hereditary, though there may be predisposition, as in some other maladies, and that it is got by actual contagion rather than self-developed.

Almora, though it cannot claim to be one of the most beautiful of Himalayan stations, has a certain charm of its own, especially to old residents, and has inspired a local rhymester to sing its attractions.

ALMORA.

The hills are all around thee,
O Almora!
The mighty mountains bound thee,
O Almora!
And the skies are blue and bright
In that land of shimmering light,
Where thou gleamest soft and white,
O Almora!

The snowy heights look o'er thee,
O Almora!
Like the steps of heaven before thee,
O Almora!
To their pure and peaceful breast
Thy meek glances are addrest,
And the grandeur of their rest,
O Almora!

Sweetest breezes blow athwart thee,
O Almora!
Gentle winds of summer court thee,
O Almora!
Roses bloom nigh all the year
In thy golden atmosphere,
And all flowers to thee are dear,
O Almora!

When the evening falls upon thee,
O Almora!
And the crown of peace lies on thee,
O Almora!
Down the valleys far and deep,
Where the starlit shadows sleep,
Lights of distant hamlets peep,
O Almora!

How should e'er my heart forget thee,
O Almora!
In my memory I have set thee,
O Almora!
And the little hillside grave,
Where the wind-swept bushes wave—
There a charge to thee we gave,
O Almora!

Before concluding this chapter, some reference may be permitted to the work of the London Missionary Society, which has been established in the province, with Almora as its centre, for over half a century.

Founded in 1850 by the Rev. J. H. Budden, it has developed in many directions. The work was at first entirely supported by the contributions of several godly officers at that time living in the province, led by Captain, afterwards Sir Henry, Ramsay. The Leper Asylum, Ramsay College, orphanages, churches, schools, and dispensaries conducted in the district by the members of the mission, male and female, represent the result of half a century's labour, and the presence of some three hundred Christians in the town and neighbourhood proves that the effort has not been wasted, even from a statistical point of view. The effect of the teaching and preaching that have gone on during that period has no doubt been deep and, let us hope, enduring in its impress on the lives of many hundreds, and our trust is that a much greater harvest will, in God's good providence, crown the labours of the years that are past and yet to come.

CHAPTER III

HIGHLAND FAIRS

IN all agricultural countries, especially where communication is difficult, and where the land is cut up by mountain or water, the need is felt for periodical meetings at convenient centres, where exchange and sale of commodities may take place. A district like Kumaon holds many valleys which are absolutely dependent on such meetings for their supply of common necessaries, and consequently fairs or periodical markets are numerous. There are two kinds of these. The weekly assemblages, corresponding to "market-day" in an English provincial town, are called "Penth." They are of an ordinary kind, and have no religious associations. The great annual fairs are known by the name of "mela," and are always connected with religious ideas and customs. They very often centre round some famous local shrine, which reaps an extensive harvest at the annual festival. Business, pleasure, and religion are cheerfully combined in these junketings, which are doubtless the chief oases in the monotonous lives of the Indian peasantry. It is at the melas that one can best see the general population, men, women, and children, in their holiday apparel and merriest mood, and there the missionary can reach, by the spoken or printed Word, thousands of people who are otherwise never brought in his or her way.

The best known and one of the largest fairs in Kumaon is held at Bageswar, twenty-seven miles north of Almora, in the month of January, and is frequented by Almora traders, on barter or money-lending intent, and by the Bhotiyas from the snows, as well as by a great multitude of people from the surrounding villages. The scene is a river valley between high wooded hills. The little town of neat and solidly built stone houses lies on both sides of the rocky Sarju river, connected by a handsome modern suspension bridge; and a short distance below, another stream, the Gumti, joins the former. The junction of two rivers is always a most sacred spot in India, especially if they be tributaries of the Ganges, and it is this junction which makes Bageswar so holy that it is often called Uttara Baranasi, or the Northern Benares. The priests of the place, indeed, declare that the day is not far distant when Bageswar will outrival even the original Benares in sanctity, and will be the great place of pilgrimage for Northern India. It is perhaps natural that these gentlemen should have a *penchant* for their own particular shrine, and a desire to see larger crowds attending it.

At the junction of the rivers stands a large temple with its conical tower. The peculiar shape of the Indian temple, by the way, is said to represent the original thatched hut of the aborigines, consisting of a cluster of long bamboos tied together at the top and covered with leaves or thatch. The temples exhibit a similar form, constructed in stone. Here is the shrine of Bageswar or Vyagreswar, the "Tiger Lord," an epithet of Siva. Tigers are not unknown in the river valleys nowadays, and in former times may have seriously infested the neighbourhood. I remember a few years ago coming on unmistakable traces of a tiger not far from Bageswar. These tigers are not, as some people suppose, always immigrants from the plains, but are indigenous, and indeed have a distinct character and appearance of their own. The hill tiger often looks larger than his brother in the Indian plains, owing to the greater thickness of his fur. Leopards are also found in most parts of the province, and these are called "Bagh" or tiger, almost indifferently.

The temple as it now stands was erected by the Kumaon raja, Lakshmi Chand, about 1450 A.D., but there is an interesting Sanskrit inscription there of a far earlier date. It is written on a stone slab, which has unfortunately been injured, especially in the part where the date should be. The inscription is evidently a relic of the age of the Katyuri rajas, and records a grant of some land to the temple of Bageswar. The translation of the concluding words of this lengthy inscription runs as follows:—"Bhudeva was king of kings, a zealous worshipper of Brahma, an enemy of Buddha Sravana, a lover of truth, rich, beautiful, learned, continually engaged in religious observances; whose eyes were beautiful as lilies, and quick, the palms of whose hands were like young blossoms, whose ears were often troubled by the sound of the jewels of the crowns of rajas who bowed before him, and whose weapon destroyed darkness, whose feet resembled the colour of gold, who granted pensions to his favourite attendants." The gist of these remarks, from the

Corner of a Village Fair in Kumaon

writer's point of view, probably lay in the last clause. The inscription is probably some eleven centuries old.

At the great Utraini mela, held in January, from fifteen to twenty thousand people are brought together, and goods to the value of three lakhs of rupees (£20,000) are said to change hands. The chief articles of merchandise are: ponies, goats, sheep, furs, yak-tails, musk-pods, borax, salt, horns, books, shoes, fruits dried and fresh. The Bhotiyas bring down excellent ponies, which breed in a wild or semi-wild state over the Tibetan border, and are sold at prices from 150 rupees (£10) upwards; and great quantities of skins and fur of leopard, snow-leopard, bears, foxes, etc., can be picked up. Rewards are given by the Government officers for skins of wild beasts, especially bears and leopards, and then the skins are for sale.

The religious part of the mela consists in the bathing that takes place before daybreak on the appointed day. On the previous day great numbers of villagers from the surrounding district come pouring in with their wives and families, many of them dragging logs and branches of trees from the jungle, with which they make bonfires on the slopes around, the weather being cold at that season. All night they camp round these innumerable fires, singing and chattering. I remember that on one occasion when I was staying in a small tent outside the dak bungalow, the noise, combined with the pungent smoke from so many burning logs, rendered sleep entirely out of the question. At the earliest light of dawn a hush falls over the scene, and the whole multitude steps down to the river, where they wash away their sins for another year by plunging in the cold waves of Ganga, and then set out on their homeward journey.

The curios and rarities still to be picked up at Bageswar have long had a reputation in India. Raja Lakshmi Chand in the beginning of the seventeenth century is mentioned in some old memoirs as bringing a present, to gain admission to the imperial presence, "beautiful strong ponies, several hawks and falcons, numerous pods of musk, and whole skins of the musk-deer with the musk in them. He also presented various swords and daggers"—no doubt the "kukris" or heavy curved knives common still in the hills. "This raja is the richest hill chief, and it is said there is a gold mine in his territory." It is rather remarkable that a gold mine was very recently (1903) opened in the neighbourhood, though not much has yet been heard of it. From time immemorial gold washers have made a scanty living from the sands of several of the Kumaon rivers, especially the Pindar river.

Bageswar lies in a low valley, and in summer is so hot and unwholesome that the greater part of the inhabitants migrate to more salubrious places. In fact, many of the winter residents are Almora merchants, whose chief business there is attendance at the two fairs, and trafficking with the Bhotiyas.

I shall now give a few extracts from Pandit G. D. Uprety's notes on the fairs in Kumaon, which he has kindly shown to me. They will be interesting to readers of a practical turn of mind, and they exhibit the chief material elements of the very simple Himalayan conditions of life.

The fair next in size and importance to that of

Bageswar is the Thal mela, held at the temple of Baleswar in April, when over twelve thousand people are assembled. In addition to the common articles of sale, the following are to be had: Borax, woollen cloth, furs, tea, sugar, sugar-candy, boxes of reed and bamboo, soap, musk-pods, yak-tails, medicinal herbs and roots, bitumen, horns, wax, rikhtiti (the gall of bears), lac, claws of leopard and tiger.

Amongst articles sold at different fairs, I note the following: Milk, curds, vessels of brass, copper, zinc, and iron, treacle-cakes, baskets, tobacco, wooden bowls, earthen jars, iron bars for ploughs, hoes, sickles, hemp ropes, cords, and bags, skin sieves, umbrellas made of leaves (these always stay up), chillies, turmeric, ginger, native musical instruments, beds, dyes, lamps, peacock fans and plumes, live deer, bear cubs, live leopards and monkeys, fireworks.

All kinds of places are used as sites for the melas. The deep cave of the mountain known as Dyari is the scene of a fair lasting one day, at which fruit, vegetables, and grocery are the chief commodities.

Two or three fairs are held on the anniversary of some battle, and after the business is over, the people amuse themselves by throwing stones at each other, in the fashion of the Bagwali described in another chapter.

At most of the fairs gambling is practised, and at many it has become a serious abuse.

CHAPTER IV

BYWAYS IN KUMAON

A PLEASURE-TRIP which has of late years attained some fame among Anglo-Indians is that to the Pindari glacier in Kumaon—all the more so that it can be made without any great trouble or expense, not even a tent being required. Some twenty years ago, rumour has it, a certain Lieutenant-Governor of the United Provinces, having a surplus at the end of his financial year, resolved that it might be profitably spent on making accessible some of the glorious scenery of the Kumaon Himalayas. He accordingly planted staging bungalows, at convenient distances, right up from Bageswar to the glacier from which the Pindar river issues, a total distance of over eighty miles from Almora, and thus made all lovers of nature in her grandest manifestations lasting debtors to his generous thoughtfulness. The reformer may exclaim that this is not the way that the tribute wrung from the Indian sons of toil ought to be spent, but one may venture to opine that if State funds had never been less uselessly employed, there would be but little cause for complaint.

Leaving Almora at its eastern end, the traveller setting out on the conquest of "the Snows" passes the neat Gothic church of the London Mission, standing on the very mound from which the British troops in 1815 delivered their last volley of shot and shell against the fortress of Almora, but now a home of peace and praise to God. Here on the night of the 25th April, the British forces held their ground, and on the Hiradungri hill farther away, against a desperate sortie of the Gurkhas from the fort and town, assailing them in front and rear, close on a hundred being slain. We proceed onwards under the pine-clad height of Hiradungri, passing a small temple and native "sarai," where (or rather close by, in a small "dharmsala" or travellers' lodge, which has now disappeared) one of the Chand rajas of Almora, after losing a battle against the famous Harak Deb in 1788, was confined for a time and afterwards put to death.

We now ascend the gradual slope of the Kalimatiya hill, which faces the town with its large bare outline, destitute of trees on this its southern face. Two or three European bungalows, outposts of the Anglo-Indian occupation, are seen on the right, where farther away the well-wooded height of Simtola rises. At the very top of the Kalimatiya hill, built on a rock, is an old temple and monastic lodge, where, tradition relates, a most renowned sorcerer and sage of olden times, Sri Ballabh Upadhya, once resided. So great was the supernatural power of this worthy, that he used to burn iron bars in his kitchen instead of wood.

The blackness of the soil near the summit of the hill is said to be due to a great sacrifice which one of the rajas kept going for months there. A more prosaic explanation of the name of the hill, which means "black earth," and of the fact itself, is that it is owing to the presence of graphite or plumbago in the soil, which has been tested by experts, long ago, and found to be of very fair quality. This same Sri Ballabh, who lived many centuries ago, was the ancestor of a great many of the Pande Brahmans in the neighbourhood. He was a great professor of Tantric formulæ, by virtue of which he could (so it is believed by his descendants) work many miracles.

The view on either side of this high ridge is grand beyond description. To the westward and southward stretch the deep valleys of the Kosi and its tributaries, opening out from the low plain of Hawalbagh, and the vast panorama is closed in on all sides by noble forest-clad ranges of mountains, many of which are over 10,000 feet high. The depth of the valley beneath one's feet seems immense, and villages down below show nestlike on the sides of the declivity. I remember once seeing from this height a great cloud of locusts flying over the abyss far below, and the sunlight shining through their bright filmy expanse, of terra-cotta hue, was a most strange and beautiful sight. On the other side, to the north, is a view of the snowy range, which Sir John Strachey has described as one of the finest to be obtained anywhere, rising above and beyond the dark oak-forests of Binsar. The road from this point turns northward and passes under the slope of the Binsar range, through thick forest, until it reaches a river valley, and then again begins to ascend. Gananath, among broad grassy lawns and forest slopes, is the scene of a battle in 1815, when the brave Gurkha leader, Hastidal, was shot dead, shortly before the capture of Almora.

O the charm of these forest paths! The sunlight

falls, tempered by lofty foliage, between the tall, straight stems of the pines on the hillside slopes, or at higher elevations one climbs or descends among gnarled leafy oak and rhododendron, the earth everywhere clothed with fern and moss and creeper; moist, cool dells and emerald banks on every side tempting the eye to linger on their beauty. The scent of sweet wildflowers and thyme mingles with the resinous odour of the pines, and bright blue sky and glorious sunshine overarch all the fair scene, near and far. It is indeed an earthly paradise! A village here and there is passed, near some clearing in the forest, where the peaceful Kumaoni pursues the even tenour of his way from generation to generation, and the voices of his little ones are heard in the depths of the woods, as they vary their occupation of minding the goats and cows, by shrill cries and jödels. Now and then a drove of monkeys breaks away over the tree-tops, startled by the traveller's approach, or a partridge rises noisily beside the path. When, with some toil, we reach the summit of a lofty range, a wondrous scene expands on every side! How pleasant to sit down on some fallen trunk under cool shade, and drink in the freshening breeze, while the eye strays from vale to vale and from distant range to range, and nature does her healing work on the unquiet heart of man.

> The sunlight sleeps in all the vales;
> A snowy cloudlet floats on high;
> A white-winged bird serenely sails
> Between the mountain and the sky;
> A light wind stirs the nearer leaves,
> And childish voices come from far—
> Scarce other sound the stillness cleaves;
> No hint of worldly noise to mar

This perfect hour of nature's rest,
In dreamy mood as here I lie
Upon the mountain's grassy breast,
And faintest breezes wander by.

Oh might this peace for ever stay!
This refuge in the heart of God!
This shelter from the heat of day
In pathways by the world untrod!
Yet 'tis enough! new strength is won
From out this space of hallowed calm:
Sweet nature's remedy is done,
And on my spirit falls the balm
That bides through days of forced unrest
And is the anodyne of strife—
Well armed with peace and deeply blest,
Go, Heart, to meet the clash of life!

A long and very steep descent through grand pine-forest takes us down to the valley of the Sarju, and after traversing the level valley for about two miles we reach Bageswar, with its bazaar, suspension bridge, and dak bungalow standing close by the side of the clear, fast-flowing river. This we may consider the last outpost of civilisation, the last place where we shall be able to obtain ordinary food and have it cooked for us by the servants of the dak bungalow. Beyond Bageswar we must depend on our own supplies, and take our own "*chef*" along with us, who, if he is an active and handy man, will get on ahead and have his fire lighted and his kettle boiling by the time we reach the end of our day's march. As the coolies have to be changed from day to day, we have applied for a "chaprassi" or Government messenger at Almora, who goes into the villages *en route* and arranges for the services of the required number of men to act as carriers to the next stage.

As a general rule, the villagers lend their services

readily enough, at a fixed rate of four annas per stage of ten miles or thereabouts; but when harvest or other field-work claims their attention, it is sometimes difficult to tear them away from their home interests, and all the authority of the dreaded chaprassi has to be exerted to drag the unwilling men to their burdens. This system of *corvée* has its disadvantages; but without it, travelling among the hills would be well-nigh impossible. The land in Kumaon is held on the express condition that coolies must be supplied for travellers and Government officers, and the advantage is in most cases a mutual one. Where villages are inhabited by Brahmans, however, there are somewhat bitter complaints, as carrying work is considered derogatory by them. Such is the case at the first stage from Almora, the Brahman occupants of which are said to have been compelled to take up agriculture, by the tyranny of one of the old rajas.

From Bageswar we travel for several miles up the right bank of the Sarju, at first along a road shaded by bamboos and other semi-tropical vegetation, for the valley is low and hot, but afterwards among the usual pines and hazels and maples. The river is an interesting and fair companion on our upward way, flowing sometimes in broad shallow rapids, bright and sparkling, at other times gathering its waters in dark deep pools under lofty overhanging rocks, which the path skirts or climbs as best it may. At one point we come on a black swirling pool named Balighat, where a strange and fearful scene was enacted about a hundred and fifty years ago, when the redoubtable minister Harak Deb caused a great number of Brahmans, his enemies, to be tied up in sacks and hurled into the seething waters. This river valley is flanked on both sides by steep heights, which at times descend close above the stream, at other times retire, leaving fairly level spaces where some little cultivation is seen, though the road from Bageswar to the glacier is rather singularly lonely, and but few human habitations are met with. Such people as there are, are mostly engaged in rearing sheep. After following the river for about fourteen miles we reach the village of Kapkot, where is a small dak bungalow situated a little above the river, affording views of the river valley upwards and downwards and a peep of one of the snowy peaks above the nearer hills. Round about here considerable game is to be found by a sportsman who will spend a few days in the neighbourhood. Goral or Himalayan chamois; kakar, a kind of antelope; and a little farther, at Dhankuri, the splendid monal pheasant, are found. The Sarju River, especially near Bageswar, abounds in mahseer or Indian salmon, which are often of a large size, though not by any means easy to get the better of. Snaring, line-fishing, netting, and even, it is said, poisoning, are freely resorted to by the people, and one often comes on a netting party at work in these Kumaon rivers, sweeping both small and large into their net. The wonder is that any fish are left. To make up for this wholesale destruction, however, pious pilgrims and others, at Bageswar, are in the habit of throwing little balls of paste into the water, containing the name of the god Rama on a slip of paper. It is believed that some merit is acquired for every one of these pellets swallowed by a fish, just as for every verbal repetition of the name of the god. Hence the usual salutation of villagers to each other is "Rama,

Rama," by the constant repeating of which the good Hindu piles up stores of merit, as well as satisfying the claims of politeness. I have even heard men repeating the names of deities as they went along the road, no doubt with the same idea. A wayfarer with whom I once walked a mile or two, in the intervals of conversation kept repeating "Narayana" with great gusto. This is part of the widely diffused superstition in India that there is virtue in mere words and sounds, on which the whole of the Tantric magical system, and a good deal of European sorcery and witchcraft, were founded.

Our next day's march is through fine forest and mountain scenery to Lwarkhet, which is inhabited by Bhoteas. Half-way to this place we pass the turning of the road leading to Milam, a journey which I have afterwards to ask the obliging reader to make with me before the end of the chapter. There is nothing to relate about Lwarkhet, where we spend the night, except that it is half-way up a long ascent which we complete the following day, and arrive at Dhankuri, 10,500 feet, at the top of a high range facing the snows, and justly famed for its magnificent views of the snowy range, which here stand out in their full height and grandeur, without any obstacle between them and the eye of the beholder. The little dak bungalow stands among fine forest not far from the summit, in truly Alpine scenery and climate. The great ridge on which it is placed is a watershed running down from the towering mass of Nanda Devi (over 25,600 feet), and dividing the streams which flow into the Ganges westward from those which feed the Sarda and Gogra eastward, and only reach the Ganges at Patna, a thousand miles distant. The site of the Pindari glacier, with its river, the Pindar, forming a dark line below it, can be seen from here. The scene is almost terrible in its frowning height and bewildering vastness. Peaks that seem to pierce the very zenith tower above great stretches of snow, diversified by ice-falls and crevasses and black jutting crags, while streaks of white that mark the course of great glaciers here and there descend into the dark gorges at the foot of the mountains.

From this point I will transcribe from a diary which I wrote during a visit to this place some ten years ago. I may premise that there were four of us in the party, a lady and three men, and that we did the trip in the simplest possible style, the lady only being provided with a "dandi," carried by four or five of the cheery, sturdy highlanders of this northern part of Kumaon, who differ considerably in character and physique from those living in its more southern quarters. The glacier is about twelve miles from here, in the midst of glorious scenery. The lofty hill of Dhankuri is covered with forests of oak, cypress, and rhododendron, and carpeted with every variety of flowers, ferns, and mosses, and abounding with wild strawberries, of which we have lately eaten gallons. The view from the top of the range is as a rule visible only in the early morning, as during the day clouds invariably collect and conceal the higher summits. From this place we descended into the valley of the Pindar river, which the road now follows up to its source in the glacier. The rest-houses on the way, three in number, are situated at convenient distances, but are very small for our party of four, as they contain only two small rooms. The Pindar is a glorious river, filling the whole gorge with its roar. There are waterfalls over the cliffs above the river, some of which are over 400 feet in height, and can be seen far aloft falling over still higher precipices—in some cases the whole cascade with its various leaps being not less than 1200 feet in perpendicular descent. The mountain scenery as we approached the snows was simply stupendous—no other word can describe it. From the river-bed we looked up to mountains rising sheer from the bank to a height of 8000 feet above the river, and 16,000 above sea-level, clothed with forest about half-way, and ending at the top in terrific battlements and walls of bare rock. Then above all this, glimpses of the snowy peaks soaring into the very zenith, as it seemed, at a height of 25,000 feet. But words and figures can give no idea of the glories of such a scene. They are truly "the wonderful works of God," and among the grandest sights on the earth.

Descending the mountain from Dhankuri, we noticed the soil turned up a great deal by wild boars in search of roots. This forest is also a favourite haunt of bears, which are sometimes ugly fellows to meet. A young officer some years ago saw a bear here and fired at him from below, wounding him only slightly. The brute rushed at his assailant and, seizing him, flung him down the precipice into the Pindar river hundreds of feet below, where his body was found by a search-party some days afterwards. The poor lad (he was only twenty-one) is buried in Almora churchyard.

At Khati, some ten miles from the glacier, we met with a heavy shower of hail. We were told that the crops of millet, which grow scantily there, have been ruined for the last seven years by hail, and that coolies are sometimes actually killed by the heavy fall.

The next day we reached the travellers' lodge at Dwali, beautifully situated at the junction of the Kaphini with the Pindar, on a rising knoll with a raging torrent on either hand. A continual roar and bluster of waters kept us awake half the night. Here we were at an elevation of over 8000 feet, with great mountains to right and left, clothed with dense forest except on the left side, where the mountain-sides are so steep that hardly anything can find foothold. On that side are numerous waterfalls, some of them descending from rock to rock for over 1000 feet. Words cannot describe the grandeur of these towering fortresses of rock, clothed as they now are with the loveliest verdure, and adorned with foaming cascades and lightly spraying waterfalls, some of which seem to disappear in mid-air and form again lower down the mountain-side. The vegetation is wonderful; every variety of tree and plant seeming to grow at one elevation or another, in successive zones. Maiden-hair ferns of the finest species grow in fronds of a foot long. Oak, pine, cypress, yew, rhododendron, laurel, holly, ivy, innumerable creepers and ferns and mosses, blackberries, wild strawberries, red currants of very large size, chestnuts, walnuts, maples, rowans, birches, hazels, Scotch thistles, strange fruits and flowers of which none of us know the names, are seen on every hand.

Phurkia, the last stage, is about four miles from the glacier. Here is a quaint little rest-house shaped like a small ark, with a very steep roof on account of the winter snow, and containing only one room and a dressing-room. This is the second bungalow that has been built here, the former one having been swept away by an avalanche. The elevation, 9900 feet, makes one glad of a good fire. The path from Phurkia leads up a rather narrow and desolate valley over ground strewn with boulders. A cave is passed which tradition declares to have been once inhabited for a time by the great hero of the age of the Mahabharata, Bhima, famous for his Herculean strength and prowess. The first sight of the glacier is a little disappointing. It appears to be a great slope of dirty snow coming down between two huge mountains, and between high banks of moraine rubbish, and ending off suddenly in the valley. All around are the great snow peaks, over 20,000 feet high. To the right rises the sharp cone of Nanda Kot. The river rushes out of a kind of cave or mouth below the glacier, of considerable size at its very birth. Closer examination shows that the lower mass of the glacier at this point consists of rocks mixed with ice, or rather a mass of ice covered by stones and mud. The great debris-heap on the left side of the glacier being reached, a steep and rather difficult path leads down the inner side of this, and then a smaller moraine ridge is reached, immediately overlooking the glacier. Here we halted and prepared some hot coffee. The water we got from melted lumps of ice, which was everywhere within an inch or so of the surface of the pebbly ridge on which we were seated. Although we were now on ice, and at an elevation of about 12,000 feet, our chief sensation was one of heat, for the sun was shining very fiercely. The glacier could now be seen in its true proportions. It appeared to be about three miles long by half a mile broad, and consisted of two parts, meeting more than half-way up its course. Farther up it could be seen that the glacier descended in steep irregular steps or terraces, lower down spreading out in a broader yet still fairly steep expanse of ice, the moraine ridges on either side being well defined.

Punoo, a Bhotea, who had accompanied us from Lwarkhet as guide and factotum, now came to the front, and the coolies who had carried the "dandi" converted themselves into Alpine guides. Good ones they were, too, and very plucky and helpful on the ice. We had ropes, a plank seven feet long, and ice-axes, though I cannot say that we found our paraphernalia of much use. We now stepped on to the lower part of the glacier, consisting here of pure ice crested with a little gravel, and almost level. Little runnels of ice water ran over and under the crisp frozen surface, and here and there were curious mouths or crevices in the ice, filled with water, and showing the blue ice underneath. Even these little holes were five or six feet deep, though the aperture was only a few inches square. After crossing this first portion of the glacier we came to the more formidable part. The ice began to rise in great humps or hummocks, with crevasses half-full of water between, and the only way of getting forward was to walk along the top of these hummocks, which were often narrow, and slippery under foot, with the help of the ice-axe to form steps. The coolies helped us over the difficult places skilfully enough, making steps in the ice with their axes, and clinging with their bare feet to places where you would hardly think a cat could walk. One crevasse that we passed alongside of seemed to be of immense depth, as stones thrown into it were heard falling and rebounding for a long time. The ice caverns and pits were very beautiful, showing depths of clear blue ice. Far above, in front, an immense flight of icy stairs reached many hundreds of feet above us, the higher terraces being crowned with fantastic pinnacles and pillars of ice, some of which looked exactly like statues. These were the ice-tables, formed by a cap of stone resting on ice and preventing it from melting immediately below, until at last a pillar is made. Above the whole scene, on three sides, rose the mighty snow peaks, close at hand. Having proceeded about half a mile and got well within the glacier, and finding progress stopped by impassable crevasses and ugly holes, Punoo informed us that Sahibs never came so far, and the coolies began to chatter and mow with (most likely pretended) dread of the Devi, whom they declared to inhabit those regions. We therefore returned, finding that coming *down* a steep ice-slope is very much harder than ascending it.

From the head of the Pindar valley there is a path by which it is just possible to reach one of the glens of the Milam valley to the east, but as this pass is 20,000 feet above sea-level and by no means easy, it may readily be supposed that few are daring enough to attempt it. One of the first commissioners of Kumaon, Mr. Traill, is said to have accomplished it, and to have been the first to do so. Since then it has only been tried by one individual, a German named Boeckh, about 1893. This gentleman called upon me while passing through Almora, and I was able to help him by sending a few supplies from time to time. He was a real mountaineer, who had ascended nearly all the Alpine heights in Europe, but said he was tired of them, as one always found someone "talking shop" at the top of them. What he yearned for was "pure nature" and solitude. He certainly must have found it at Phurkia, where he stayed for some months climbing and photographing, and living only on "chapattis" or meal-cakes cooked for him by a rough hillman. After his return to Europe he sent me a book he had written in German, with excellent views of the snows.

The journey to Milam, near the Untadhura pass into Tibet, is interesting, though the scenery cannot compare with that on the Pindari route. After leaving Kapkot, the next stage, it will be remembered, above Bageswar, the traveller turns off to the right and makes for the valley of the Goriganga or White Ganges, by way of Shama, Tejam, and Girgaon. A tent must be taken on this route, there being camping-grounds at the places named. Tejam is prettily situated in the valley of the Ramganga, a river which afterwards joins the Sarju in Eastern Kumaon. At this place the small stinging fly called the "mora" is particularly troublesome at times. I remember that when camping there in the month of May, my hands were in a few minutes streaming with blood. The fly is of minute size, and seems to attack almost exclusively the hands, and the bare feet of natives, who often suffer greatly from the irritation on the upper part of their feet. The sting causes blood to flow, and then a small black pimple of extravasated blood forms under the skin. The mora is certainly one of the worst of flying pests, though fortunately it is confined to a few places in the province.

A long and toilsome ascent takes us past the village of Girgaon to the summit of a lofty ridge, whence one can overlook the comparatively wide and extensive valley of the Goriganga. There are several villages of the Bhotiyas scattered about it, which have separate names, but are included under the general name of Mansiari, the whole valley right up to Milam being known as Johar. The Bhotiyas are a prosperous class of traders, conducting the carrying trade between Tibet and Northern India over the lofty passes. They lead a migratory life, but have homesteads at three different points on the road leading downwards into Kumaon. Their summer residence is at Milam and the neighbouring villages, right up among the snows, and only a few miles from the pass of Untadhura. About September they remove to this lower part of the valley, and in winter their wives and children reside still lower down, in the vicinity of Tejam, whilst the men of the family are busy buying and selling at Bageswar, Almora, and in the plains of India. There is, of course, a settled agricultural population in the Johar valley, who are in a manner the serfs of the Bhoteas. Farther to the west there is a more populous settlement of Bhotiyas in the Darma valley, leading to a pass into Tibet which is much lower and easier than the Untadhura pass. The traders of that quarter, however, suffer the disadvantage of having to pay tribute both to the Tibetans and the Nepalese, the former of whom still claim a kind of suzerainty over the Bhotiya tracts on this side the British border. The Lhassa Government has never yet acknowledged the right of the British to this strip of territory, and still reckon it as part of their dominions. Indeed, it is most probable that the transfer of ownership, though it occurred so long ago as 1816, has never yet been reported to the Lhassa Grand Lama and his functionaries, so obstinate is the ignorance of that strange and benighted power. The pretence of rule over the Bhotiyas takes the somewhat unpleasant form of yearly dues, which are paid by the traders, still under the name of land-tax, though they are really taxes exacted for the privilege of trading in Tibet. Every year at the beginning of summer, when the snow melts sufficiently to allow of crossing the pass, the Tibetan local official, named the Jong-Pen, visits the valleys inhabited by the Bhoteas, or sends his emissaries, to find out if any infectious disease is prevailing, and if not, gives permission for the traders to enter Tibet. They carry their goods, consisting chiefly of grain, cloth, and other necessaries, on the backs of sheep and goats, or else of "jibbus," which are a cross between the Tibetan yak and the cow, and very hardy and useful pack-animals, being able to resist cold and fatigue much better, it is said, than the native yak. The Tibetans barter borax, skins, salt, gold, precious stones, and other articles, for the necessaries of life that are brought over the passes into their barren country. Ponies are also a chief article of commerce; and being great sheep-breeders, the Bhotiyas sell the fleeces to the agents of the Cawnpore Woollen Mills at the foot of the hills.

The road from Mansiari up to Milam is about thirty miles long, and in the proper season not more difficult than most tracks of the kind. On my visit to the valley some years ago, I was so ill-advised as to attempt it early in May, before the snows had melted, and even before any of the Bhotiyas had gone up the valley. The consequence was a good deal of discomfort, including such minor incidents as having to climb up among the cliffs by out-of-the-way paths, plunge through waterfalls, cross by snow bridges over the river again and again, and at times to wade through the icy water. Bridges over tributary streams, consisting of a single log, are not pleasant episodes of the day's march. At that time, too, a precipitous cliff by the riverside in one spot had to be negotiated by means of an artificial gallery consisting of logs resting on iron bars driven into the face of the rock; and when, as sometimes has happened, one encountered in the middle of this narrow footway a long drove of sheep laden with their panniers of merchandise, and was compelled to *straddle* over them in order to let them pass, the experience was more laughable than agreeable. Our little tent having been one night blown down in a storm of wind and rain, we had to seek shelter in a low cave at some distance, out of which the gnats and stinging flies had first to be driven by burning twigs.

The deep cleft of the Goriganga, through which we pass on this route, really takes us beyond the great chain of snowy peaks into the tract on the farther side. At one point on the road, not far from the village of Martoli, a glorious view is obtained of Nanda Devi (25,600 feet) at a few miles distance up a side valley. The whole stupendous mass of the mountain rises before the eye, every single black rock jutting out of its snowy vesture clearly outlined, and the vast peak towering into mid-heaven. It is a sight never to be forgotten! Otherwise, there are few glimpses of the higher snows to be obtained on the road, as the valley lies too low beneath their shoulders to afford a view of the summits.

At Milam the valley is wider, with the glacial river flowing at the bottom, and surrounded by high hills, some of which are crowned with snow, affording pasturage to a few flocks of hardy sheep. The vegetation is very scanty, though potatoes are grown near the village, introduced, so report says, by Sir Henry Ramsay many years ago. The aspect of the scene is stern and desolate in the extreme. It strikes one, indeed, as the dreariest landscape one has ever dwelt upon, though not without a wild grandeur of its own. The village of stone huts is a fairly large one. Near it are some of the Tibetan sacred walls bearing slabs inscribed with Buddhist texts, which pious Tibetans circumambulate as a religious exercise. Flocks of white snow pigeons fly about the valley, the flesh of which afforded us a welcome change from our scanty diet. At a small lake some few miles up the glen of the glacier there are a few wild duck to be had. Bears are in plenty, and at night their approach is made sufficiently known by the hideous concert of the large fierce Bhotiya dogs, which strike one as being removed by a very few generations from the wolfish stage.

The Milam glacier is much larger than that at the source of the Pindar, but does not lend itself to exploration as well as the latter, nor is its appearance so interesting. It pours out the headwaters of the Gori in a large stream, rendered milk-white by the particles of limestone ground up by the glacial action upon the rocks. Hence the name of the White Ganges given to this river. The water contains a large solution

THE PASS INTO THIBET BEYOND MILAM

A VILLAGE ON THE WAY TO BAGESAR

of lime, which makes it undrinkable even at Mansiari, thirty miles lower down.

The road to the pass turns off to the right a short distance before the village is reached. Milam itself is over 11,000 feet above sea-level, and the road into Tibet has twice to cross passes over 17,000 feet. A few miles from Milam, on this road, beautiful specimens of ammonites and other fossils were last year found embedded in the fine black shale, by Colonel L. A. Waddell, proving that this lofty land was once the bed of a great sea, before the upheaval of the Himalayas.

The London Missionary Society has stations, with schools and one or two dispensaries, at some of the places mentioned in this chapter, namely, Kapkot, Mansiari, Milam, and Bageswar. The hope is entertained that at some time, through the agency of the Bhotiyas, who know the Tibetan language and have free access into the "Forbidden Land," the gospel will be carried there.

CHAPTER V

A CHEQUERED HISTORY

IN prehistoric times the forest-covered mountains of Kumaon and Garhwal were doubtless occupied by tribes of a low type of culture resembling the Kols and Gonds of Central India, or the Bhuksas and Tharus still inhabiting the skirts of the Himalayas. These aborigines lived by the chase, and on the edible roots, herbs, and fruits that are still so abundant and form no small part of the food of the people. They may possibly have practised a rudimentary agriculture, consisting in burning down a patch of forest and sowing a few grains of millet, then passing on to another ground, leaving the original field fallow for six or ten years, as is even now done in the Tarai and some other places. The Doms are the remnants of those thinly scattered races, who have left no memorial of their early occupation of the land, unless some curious cup-shaped markings on the rocks at Debidhura and elsewhere in the province, not unlike similar traces to be found in Britain, and probably belonging to the pre-Celtic race there, may be attributed to them.

At one time it was maintained, by Benfey and also by Weber, that the Indo-Aryans for a while sojourned in Tibet, and that they must have entered India by the passes over the Himalayas into Kumaon; but subsequent study of the Veda showed that such a course was out of the question, and that the Aryans must have advanced through the north-west passes and gone down the valley of the Indus.

From allusions in the Vedas, including the Hymns and Brahmanas, and in the Mahabharata, some portions of which are believed to be as old as the Vedas themselves, we find that the people of Northern India in the earliest historical period (variously reckoned as lying between 2000 and 800 B.C.) were divided into three classes: (1) The Aryans, who formed a united community in the Panjab and Doab, or tract between the rivers Ganges and Jumna; (2) other Aryan tribes which had become separated from the "Aryans" proper, and were regarded by them as Mlechchha or outcasts because they "saw no Brahmans"; and (3) the aboriginal tribes. The names of these Aryan tribes who had become lawless and fallen away from Brahman orthodoxy are given in several places. The fact, of course, was that the Brahmanical system had grown up after the separation of the tribes; but the Brahman writers, in the Veda, Mahabharata, and Code of Manu, describe them in terms of theological odium as having proved unfaithful to an original institution. The Brahman writers habitually describe such people as having sunk to the condition of the aborigines, and apply the same name of "Dasyu" to both, at the same time (though only in some instances) distinguishing their origin. This confusion of Aryan and non-Aryan tribes in the Hindu Scriptures has given rise to much misapprehension. The Mahabharata gives a long list of northern frontier tribes whom it calls Dasyu, yet acknowledges to belong to the Kshatriya or Aryan warrior caste. It is clear, in fact, that these tribes, such as the Sakas (Scythians), Yavanas, Kambojas, and Khasas, were regarded as having the same origin with the Aryans to whom the Brahmans belonged. The Khasas in a passage of the Mahabharata are expressly mentioned as among "degraded Brahmans, contemporary with Prajapati (the Creator). They have no Veda, no Vedic ceremony, nor any sacrifice." The Khasas are here mentioned along with tribes inhabiting the Panjab, and seem at first to have had a more westerly location than Kumaon. Another tribe, inhabiting Kashmir and Garhwal, was the Nagas, who are often referred to as actual serpents. The name borne by them (Naga = snake) and their practice of snake-worship probably account for this strange idea. In old Buddhist sculptures and pictures they are sometimes represented in a form combining serpent and human features (see Rhys Davids' *Buddhist India*, ch. xii.). Snake-worship, as we shall see, is still very common in Kumaon and Garhwal.

This is not the place to attempt to reproduce the long and elaborate argument (*Himalayan Districts*, vol. ii.) by which, from many negative premises, the conclusion has been drawn that the Khassiyas, the agricultural population of Kumaon, are to be identified with the Khasas, a warlike tribe, of Aryan or Scythian blood,[1] who seem to have been at one time widely spread beyond North-Western India, and to have become broken up by invasion and conquest and the

[1] It seems still doubtful whether the Scythians were Aryans or not. Dr. Isaac Taylor, in his *Origin of the Aryans*, distinctly says that they were.

innumerable revolutions of history during the last two thousand years, so that some of their descendants are now Mussalmans in the far north-west, while others have become Buddhists in Nepal or Assam, and the Khassiyas of Kumaon have forgotten their origin and adapted themselves to their Hindu neighbours and settlers, and are now an ordinary Indian community, sufficiently orthodox to be unmistakably Hindu. The interesting fact is pointed out that the ruling dynasty in Kumaon for several generations was called the Katyuri, and the people the Khasas; while in far-off Kabul for a long period the name of Katura or Kator was given to the reigning family, ruling over an Indian race named Kho or Khosa, who are still the oldest inhabitants of Chitral and other districts. The names Kashgar, Kashmir, Hindu Kush are referred to the same source.

The foregoing statements must, of course, be taken with a certain reserve. No community in India at the present day can be said to be identically the same as any tribe or race of antiquity, as is evidenced by the ethnological researches of recent years and the results of anthropometry. During the period named, India has resembled a great smelting-pot, into which races and tribes have been thrown together and subjected to every kind of intermixture, until now the resultant is something very different from anything belonging to the remote past.

The writer referred to sums up his conclusions about the Khassiyas of Kumaon in the following words, the essential correctness of which is being yearly confirmed by modern research :—

"The time has passed for attributing to the small

immigration of the Aryans that has given us the Vedas, the origin of all the races who are to-day assumed to be of Aryan blood, and even for holding that all so-called Rajputs are of Aryan descent. Many of our Rajput clans can be traced back to Bactrians, Parthians, and Scythians, when the facts now accumulating are closely examined. We have seen already how the Aryan writers themselves acknowledge that in many cases all the castes had a common origin. Many of the purer race did not accept the advanced ideas of their priest-led brethren, and are accordingly contemptuously classed amongst the outcasts because "they knew no Brahmans." The Aryan immigrants themselves found on their arrival in India that other members of their race had preceded them. These, from admixture with the so-called aborigines, had degenerated from the primitive type in customs, and perhaps also in features. Their religion also was affected by this union, for the Pasupati cult had its origin amongst the non-Brahmanical tribes, and from this sprang the terrible forms of Siva which have taken such hold, in comparatively modern times, of the popular religious thought of India. The influence of the Vedic Aryans is better shown in the language and literature of modern India, and in the modifications of the physical characteristics of the various tribes with which they have come in contact." As Huxley says: "The Indo-Aryans have been in the main absorbed into the pre-existing population, leaving as evidence of their immigration an extensive modification of the physical characters of the population, a language, and a literature."

The history of Kumaon and Garhwal in early times is

not clearly distinct from that of Northern India as a whole. The inhabitants also, as they now exist, may be said to belong to wider divisions of population. Those dwelling in the lower hills between the snowy range and the plains are practically Hindus, and enjoy what is really an Indian climate, with the same seasons and climatic conditions as prevail in the plains below. There is a hot, dry season from April to the end of June; a rainy season lasting from July to the middle of September; and an autumn and winter of clear, bright weather. During the year the temperature of this lower Himalayan region varies from 90° to 50° F. But we have also to include in the province the country known as Bhot, inhabited by the Bhotiyas, a tribe of Mongolian or Tibetan affinities, whose proper habitat is the snowy tract lying beyond the first range of high peaks, and extending up to the watershed where the headwaters of the great rivers take their rise. The climate there differs widely from that of the sub-Himalayan hills, and the conditions of life resemble those of Tibet, which it adjoins.

From what is elsewhere said about the fame and sacredness of the land, and the consequent large influx of Indo-Aryan visitors, we can well understand that the population must have become Hinduised from very early times, notwithstanding their remoteness from the main centres. The physical aspect of the Khassiyas of Kumaon is distinctly Aryan, their language is an almost pure dialect of Hindi, and there is little ground for the assumption that they have been mixed to any large extent with Mongolian tribes.

In the Tarai, the tract running along the foot of the hills and now covered by jungle, there are found many ancient remains, showing that there must have been an extensive population living in towns and possessing a high degree of civilisation. The Nepal Tarai is now known to have been inhabited by the Saka tribe (of Scythians), to which the Buddha's family belonged, while the whole country from the snows to Benares was included in the Kosala kingdom in the sixth century B.C. The Buddhist Pali Scriptures, the Jatakas, etc., recently translated, prove that there was a powerful though simple type of civilisation prevailing in those Aryan village communities. They possessed mote-halls for the transaction of public business, rest-houses for travellers, reservoirs, roads, and public parks. The headman or "raja" was a kind of consul, who looked after the communal rights and duties in the republic. Of such a kind was the commonwealth in which Sakya Muni was born. We know that in his lifetime and for some while afterwards a great struggle was going on between Kosala and the rival kingdom of Magadha, which resulted in the supremacy of the latter. Megasthenes, the Greek Ambassador at the Court of Chandragupta, King of Magadha, at Patna, about 300 B.C., shows Magadha (Behar) as the ruling power over all Northern India, having absorbed Champa, Kosala, and other free kingdoms, and ruling even the distant Panjab through viceroys. Chandragupta, King of Magadha, was succeeded by his son Asoka about 270 B.C. The latter was a pious Buddhist, who adopted the method of recording the precepts of his religion on rocks and pillars, so as to spread its tenets and provide enduring memorials of the Buddhist faith and of his own efforts to propagate it. At the village of Kalsi in Garhwal there is a rock, about ten feet high and the same length, one side of which has been smoothed, and bears an inscription, which is also carried on to another side. It was discovered in 1860, the natives having been accustomed to call it Chitrasila or the "picture stone," from the figure of an elephant inscribed on it. The writing was covered over at that time with moss and incrustations; but on clearing these away, the inscription appeared quite fresh and new. It was found to be an edict of Asoka, in more perfect preservation than any in India. (So far, thirty-four of these inscriptions have been discovered.) It mentions the names of five Greek kings, Antiochus, Ptolemy (Philadelphus), Antigonus, Magas, and Alexander. Thus it has been possible to fix the date at about 253 B.C.[1]

There is other evidence also of the spread of Buddhism in the Himalayas during Asoka's reign. The Ceylon Buddhist chronicles give the names of missionaries sent to Kashmir, to Gandhara (Kandahar), and to "the Himalayas." Five missionaries (a leader and four assistants) were sent to the Himalayan region, and three are named as Majjhima, Kassapa-Gotta, and Dundhubhissara. When the brick-built mounds or "topes" at Sanchi in Central India were opened by Cunningham, some funeral urns were found with inscriptions, and one of these bore the legend "of the good man Kassapa-Gotta, the teacher of all the Himalayan region." On the inside of the urn is written, "Of the good man Majjhima." In another tope was an urn inscribed, "Of the good man Gotiputta, of the Himalaya, successor of Dundubhissara" (Rhys Davids' *Buddhist India*, p. 279). It seems to have been the custom among Buddhists to

[1] For a full description of this inscription, see M'Crindle's *Ancient India*, ed. 1896.

distribute portions of the ashes of holy men to different places, where they were treasured by the community, and topes were built over them. The Himalayan region referred to no doubt denotes particularly Nepal, Kumaon, and Garhwal, the part of the mountains nearest to Asoka's kingdom of Magadha, the modern Behar. It can hardly have included Tibet, where tradition assigns 640 A.D. as the date of the introduction of Buddhism. There can be no doubt that Buddhism was once prevalent in the Himalayas. In Kumaon there are many traces of its existence. There are remains of temples without idols, walls of monasteries, and houses of the Buddhist period. I am told that these temples are venerated by the villagers, who commit their cattle and fields to their care, and call them "Baudan." Nepal is even now the only part of Hindustan proper where Buddhism in any form still holds its own.

Hwen Thsang.

Before considering the history of Kumaon and Garhwal as taken from internal sources, it will be well to refer to the evidence of the Chinese Buddhist pilgrim Hwen Thsang, who in 634 A.D. passed through Northern India, and has left an itinerary of his travels giving most important facts regarding the condition of the country at that period. His statements, whenever capable of verification, have been found remarkably accurate. Selecting only what is of local interest for our purpose, we find that he describes a city called Mayura or Mayapura, near to the present town of Hardwar, and tells how he journeyed thence to Brahmapura in the hills, 300 li or 50 miles to the north. The kingdom of Brahmapura, says Hwen Thsang, was 666 miles in circuit, "surrounded on all sides by mountains. The capital is small, but the inhabitants are numerous and prosperous. The soil is fertile, and seedtime and harvest come at regular intervals. Copper and rock-crystal are produced there. The climate is slightly cold, and the people are rough in their manners; a few devote themselves to literature, but the greater number prefer the pursuit of commerce. The inhabitants are naturally uncultivated, and there are followers of both the Buddhist and Brahmanical faiths. There are five monasteries, within which reside a few monks, and there are some dozen temples of the gods. The followers of the different Brahmanical sects dwell together without distinction. To the north of the kingdom, in the midst of the great snowy mountains, is the kingdom of Son-fa-la-na-kiu-ta-lo (Suvarnagotra), where gold of a superior quality is procured, and hence its name.. From east to west this kingdom has its greatest extension, but from north to south it is narrow. For many centuries the ruler has been a woman, and hence it is called 'the kingdom of the queens.' The husband of the reigning sovereign has the title of 'king,' but does not meddle in affairs of state. The men occupy themselves with war and husbandry. The soil is fertile, and is favourable to the growth of a poor kind of barley, and the people rear large numbers of sheep and ponies. The climate is icy-cold, and the inhabitants are abrupt and turbulent in their manners. This country touches on the east the country of the Tibetans, on the north is the country of Khoten, and on the west is Son-po-lo."

The city of Brahmapura evidently lay in Garhwal.

Mr. Atkinson was of opinion that its site is to be found at Barahat in Tihri or independent Garhwal, which is exactly fifty miles north of Hardwar and in every respect agrees with Hwen Thsang's description. There, also, are many remains of temples and ancient buildings, and it is traditionally known as the seat of an old monarchy. There is a great brazen trident of vast antiquity, and bearing inscriptions of Nepalese Buddhist rajas who had visited the place in the twelfth century and found the trident there, showing that at that period Buddhism was still a flourishing religion in Nepal and professed by some of its leading chiefs.

The kingdom mentioned by Hwen Thsang as existing to the north of Garhwal among the snowy mountains is evidently that of Suvarnagotra, or the "golden country." For a long time it was supposed that he was romancing when he described the Amazonian constitution of this kingdom, but his account has now been ascertained to rest on a basis of solid fact. The kingdom evidently lay across the Himalayas in the valley of the Satlej, where there are still famous gold mines among the sandy hills, which have simply to be scooped out to obtain the gold. Old fables met with in Megasthenes and elsewhere speak of "gold-bearing ants" in that region, which may refer to the appearance of the vast sandhills and the dark figures of men employed in digging in them. (The reader is again referred to M'Crindle's *Ancient India.*) The Amazonian kingdom of the north is mentioned in the Vishnu Purana, and Wilson in his famous translation of that work says that it is usually placed in Bhot, and is an allusion to the custom of polyandry.

But Mr. Atkinson refers us to the Chinese "Sui" annals, of which a report was given in the Journal of the Asiatic Society by Dr. Burnell. This chronicle describes a tribe in Eastern Tibet known as the Nu-wang, who always had a woman for their ruler. The female sovereign held her court in a palace nine storeys high, and was attended by hundreds of women. The men confined themselves to fighting and cultivating the land. Gold, copper, cinnabar, musk, yaks, and horses, with salt, are mentioned among the products of the country, and they were great traders with India. At the funeral of the queen, "several tens of the great ministers and relatives were buried at the same time." From the year 742 A.D. they adopted male rulers, and a few years later the kingdom was absorbed by Lhassa.

Thus Hwen Thsang is again justified, and the kingdom of the Amazons, regarding which so many wild legends were current in the ancient world, is seen to have had a real existence, in Tibet. The details as given by the Chinese traveller are in every respect correct, and suggestive of modern conditions in the same regions. Thus, only a few weeks ago, I was offered a fine rock-crystal for sale in Almora, and when I inquired where it had come from, the very district described by Hwen Thsang was named. The Tibetan or Bhotiya ponies are still much sought after, and are a common article of commerce, while the trade in salt and gold still goes on over the Indian border.

Hwen Thsang's account shows Buddhism and Brahmanism as still dwelling side by side, and apparently on fairly friendly terms, in the Himalayan region. The fact appears to be that to some extent Buddhism died a natural death in India, owing to the failing of its early impulse and its growing admixture with superstitious elements. The Northern Buddhists began to assimilate their beliefs to those of their neighbours, and to reverence the Hindu gods as powerful dispensers of boons, alongside of the incarnations of Buddha. The degraded Tantric rites connected with Siva worship were also taken into their system, together with the elements of the Yoga theosophy, and all the darker features of aboriginal cults. Indian Buddhism when it perished was no longer worth preserving; indeed, it differed in no essential from the surrounding cults, and therefore opposed no strong or united opposition to Brahmanical aggression.

It is time, however, that we addressed ourselves to a closer study of the internal history of Kumaon and Garhwal, for which the foregoing remarks have served as a background and preparation.

Hwen Thsang's account already quoted shows us a flourishing Hindu kingdom in Garhwal, and from other records there is evidence of the widely extended dominion of the rulers of Garhwal and Western Kumaon during the period from 400 to 700 A.D. Hwen Thsang's description also proves that Buddhism still flourished in the Himalayas.

Between that date, however, and the time of Sankara Acharya, important religious changes must have taken place, because all local traditions testify to the complete removal of Buddhism from Kumaon after Sankara's strenuous campaign against it. It is difficult to determine when Sankara lived. Indian writers, with characteristic uncertainty, assign all kinds of dates. His own particular Brahman followers in the south of India say that he lived two thousand years ago; others give the beginning of the Christian era or the fourth century as his period. Colebrooke refers him to 1000 A.D. The general testimony of modern scholars is in favour of the seventh or eighth centuries, soon after the visit of Hwen Thsang. Weber, in his *History of Indian Literature*, says "about the eighth century."

The vexed question as to the mode in which Buddhism passed from India is one of great interest, and we can study it with reference to the Himalayan region perhaps better than any other. In Southern India, Kumarila Bhatta was the champion of Brahmanism, and Sankara in the Himalayas. The traditions of Nepal, as given by Dr. Wright, cast light on the subject, and they show that there is after all much truth in the ordinary view that there was a great deal of conflict, and that Buddhism, in some quarters at any rate, was suppressed by force. This view has been strongly contested of late, especially by Professor Rhys Davids, who, with reference to a statement that the followers of Buddha were persecuted and slain, exiled or made to change their faith, and that by this means Buddhism was driven out of India, says (*Buddhist India*, p. 317): "I do not believe a word of it. The misconception has arisen from an erroneous inference drawn from expressions of vague boasting, of ambiguous import and doubtful authority. We must seek elsewhere for the causes of decline of the Buddhist faith; and they will be found, I think, partly in the changes that took place in that faith itself, partly in the changes that took place in the intellectual standard of the people." But what is to be made of a statement like that about to be quoted from Dr. Wright's *Nepal*, due not to the boasting of Brahmans, but to the tradition current among Buddhists or people of Buddhist sympathies themselves? The Nepalese and Kumaon traditions agree that Sankara came to the Himalaya and drove out or suppressed Buddhism by force. He found a curious intermixture of the two religions, Buddhist or Bauddhamargi priests officiating in the temples of Pasupati (Siva), and "all the four castes" following the religion of Buddha. Some were professed monks and nuns (Bhikshus and Bhikshunis), while others were household professors of the religion (Grihasthas).

"Some of them," says Dr. Daniel Wright, quoting from Nepalese traditions, "were put to death. Some who would not allow that they were defeated were also killed. Wherefore many confessed that they were vanquished, though in reality not convinced that they were in error. These Sankara ordered to do Hinsa (that is, to sacrifice animals), which is in direct opposition to the tenets of the Buddhist religion. He likewise compelled the Bhikshunis or nuns to marry, and forced the Grihasthas to shave the knot of hair on the crown of their heads when performing the 'chara-karma' or first shaving of the head. Thus he placed the ascetics and the householders on the same footing. He also put a stop to many of their religious ceremonies and cut their Brahmanical threads. There were at that time eighty-four thousand works on the Buddhist religion, which he searched for and destroyed. Having thus overcome the Buddhists, he introduced the worship of Ṣiva in place of that of the religion of Buddha. . . . Sankara thus destroyed the Buddhist religion and allowed none to follow it, but he was obliged to leave Bauddhamargis in some places as priests of temples, where he found that no other persons would be able to propitiate the gods placed in them by great Bauddhamargis."

What Sankara did in Nepal, he did also in Kumaon and Garhwal. He drove out the Buddhists and restored the Brahmanical religion, aided by the princes who were worshippers of Siva and Vishnu. No doubt great tracts of land had passed into the possession of the monasteries, as in other Buddhist lands, and the same motives that actuated many of the nobles of England and Scotland at the time of the Reformation must have been at work on the minds of the hill rajas. The Buddhists were driven out of the ancient shrines of Siva and Vishnu at Kedar and Badari, and Sankara established disciples of his own there and in many other places in the Himalayas, and preached the efficacy of pilgrimage to these holy places. Thus, as Mr. Atkinson points out (ii. 466), the constant influx of Brahmanical pilgrims in Kumaon and Garhwal prevented a relapse into Buddhism, and powerfully affected the religious tone of the people, while Nepal, being more inaccessible and practically cut off from communication with the plains, retained its admixture of Buddhism to a much greater degree.

The Katyuris were for many centuries the rulers of Western Kumaon and Garhwal. Their earlier capital was at Joshimath in Garhwal. From there they seem to have been driven by religious quarrels between the followers of Siva and Vishnu, not long after the time of Sankara, to make their headquarters at Katyur in Kumaon, a valley about twenty miles west of Almora. Early Sanskrit inscriptions exist in temples of Kumaon and Garhwal recording grants of land made by the rajas, whose capital is called Kartikeyapura, from

Kartikeya, a god. It is a question whether the resemblance between Katyur or Kator and the name of the city is accidental, or whether the dynasty took its name from the city. One of the inscriptions is on stone at the temple of Bageswar, and mentions the names of a number of sovereigns of the Katyur dynasty, and their wives. Five inscriptions are records of grants engraved on copper, still in the possession of the holders of the lands therein mentioned. One of these includes a most interesting list of the different classes of inhabitants of the capital, more especially the officials of the royal court. It is interesting as a proof of the advanced and complex state of society in an Indian kingdom of that age, about 700 to 900 A.D. (The date is determined from the use of the Kutila style of writing employed at that period.) It is probable, however, that the Kumaon kingdom did not itself contain all these officials and classes. Elephants and camels are mentioned, which would hardly be kept in the hills; and the enumeration of tribes with which the list ends, named as subjects of the king, could never have applied to Kumaon. The probability is that the long list is a copy of some formula used in one of the larger Hindu kingdoms of the plains. The Katyur dominions doubtless at one time extended far into the plains; and in inscriptions in the plains the empire of one of its kings, Deva Pala, is said to have extended from the Mahendra mountain to the Himalaya.

The site of the ancient Kartikeyapura is in the valley of the Gumti and Sarju rivers. An old legend relates that there was an earlier town there called Karbirpura, near the present village of Baijnath, and that the materials were used in building the new city.

There are still extensive ruins and remains, but until lately the neighbourhood was one of the least populous in Kumaon, and more than half the existing villages were deserted, owing to the unhealthiness of the place. The Chand rajas, who reigned at Almora, are said to have been in the habit of offering criminals the option of suffering punishment or exiling themselves to this valley, where they were certain to die before long. There are now several tea-gardens in the vicinity, and the place is more prosperous and healthy than it was half a century ago. The sites of ancient capitals in the East are generally very unwholesome, and this was no doubt the reason that in former times absolute rulers often ordered complete deportation of populous communities to another site.

The cause of the decline of the Katyur kingdom is not clearly known, but it seems to have been due in part to the oppression of the later rajas and their general unfitness for rule. An interesting tradition is told regarding the later days of the kingdom, under the rajas Dham Deo and Bir Deo, who finally brought on the downfall of the dynasty. "The revenue of the country was collected in kind, and it was customary to give out a part of grain brought into the raja's treasury to be ground for the use of the household. Each village took its turn to prepare the flour, as a customary due to the state. The servants of the raja, however, used to measure out the grain in the slightly indented *bottom* of the 'nali' (a measure) turned upside down, but still called the grain given out 'a nali.' When the people brought back the grain ground, the raja's officer spread at the foot of a great stone seven mats, and then mounting on the stone scattered the flour in the wind. The heavier particles fell on the mats near the stone, and none but the very finest reached the seventh mat. Then coming down, he collected the flour from the seventh mat and told the people to take away the rest, as it was not fit for his master's use. Of this fine flour, moreover, they were obliged to give a quantity equal to the nominal weight of the grain that had been given out to them from the raja's stores. The raja used also to seize their sons and daughters as slaves, and the taxation was on no system. In order to provide themselves with water from a favourite spring some twelve miles from the palace, the Katyuris stationed slaves along the road, who remained there night and day and passed the water from hand to hand. Bir Deo still further shocked the prejudices of the people by marrying his aunt. He used to fasten iron rings on the shoulders of the litter-bearers and pass through them the poles of the 'dandi' (litter), so that the bearers might not be able to throw him down a precipice; but, wearied with his tyranny and profligacy, two men were at last found patriotic enough to sacrifice themselves for the good of the people. They reflected that they themselves were ruined, their children were taken as slaves, and life was not worth living: so one day being pressed into service as litter-bearers, they flung themselves and the raja over a cliff, and so perished. After the raja's death dissensions broke out amongst his family, and each seized on a portion of the kingdom for himself, whilst the countries beyond Kumaon and Garhwal that had once paid tribute to the Katyuris threw off their allegiance."

In another chapter some description will be given of the worship paid to these Katyuri rajas and their relatives by the common people of Kumaon. The explanation they give of the oppression of Bir Deo is that the Katyuris grew weary of dominion, being highly religious men, and longing for peace and retirement, they set about making themselves as unpopular as possible, so that the people would no longer wish to be ruled by them!

After the break-up of the kingdom, members of the Katyuri family established themselves in various centres as independent rajas. Thus there was one at Askot, another to the east in Doti, another in Kali Kumaon, another in Barahmandal (the country around Almora), others in Dwarahat and Katyur itself. These principalities are sometimes spoken of as Khassiya kingdoms, and it is possible that in a few instances a Khassiya family succeeded in establishing a local chieftainship, but as a general rule the rajas were members of the Katyur royal house. Their descendants yet remain in the province. They were not exterminated by the Chand rajas, it is said, because the latter wished to take wives from among them. They married daughters of the Katyuris, but never gave their own daughters in marriage to them. The Katyuris were thus compelled, says Mr. Atkinson, to take wives from the small Thakuri rajas in Nepal, or even of late years to intermarry with the wealthier Khassiya families. One of the chief kingdoms for a long time was that of Doti on the Nepal border, which ruled over or took tribute from a considerable part of Kumaon, and often came into conflict with the Chand rajas. The smaller chiefs in Kumaon and Garhwal seem to have occupied fortresses on hilltops, whence they harried and laid under tribute the surrounding country, something like the "free barons" of the Rhineland in former ages.

The Chand Rajas of Kumaon.

A branch of the Katyuri family seems to have been established during the period from 800 A.D. onwards at Sui near Lohaghat in Eastern Kumaon, where the ruins of an old temple of the sun-god are still to be seen in a grove of lofty deodar trees. Some memorials of these Katyuri chiefs in Eastern Kumaon yet remain, in the form of ruined temples, Chabutras, and wells, and especially low stone pillars.

At some time, which it is not easy now to determine, a scion of the Lunar dynasty (Chandrabansi or Sombansi) at Jhusi, an old city on the Ganges opposite Allahabad, came to the hills and settled in Kumaon. There are various conflicting accounts of this event, but on the whole it is probable that the adventurer was named Som Chand, and that he married the daughter of the Sui raja, and afterwards succeeded his father-in-law, or perhaps supplanted him. The date of Som Chand's arrival in Kumaon is very uncertain, but from calculations based on different extant lists of Kumaon kings, it was probably in 953 A.D., though it is possible that the Chand rule began at a much later date.

Som Chand is said to have received a plot of land fifteen acres in extent from his father-in-law on his marriage, and to have built there a house which was called Raj-Bungi, or the royal fort, and which was afterwards named Champawat. For some centuries the Chand rajas appear to have been more or less subordinate to the raja of Doti, like the Khassiya

An Almora Temple

chiefs around them, and in the beginning of the thirteenth century they were simply heads of Mandalas or circles under the Doti raja. It is likely that the family had small beginnings and gradually raised itself to power over the neighbouring chiefs. Local tradition in Kumaon represents Som Chand as a very important personage, who immediately on his arrival in Kumaon took over the whole region and reigned like his later successors, but this is far from probable. At that time there was no kingdom of any large extent, and the Chands had to carve out their dominion gradually, like many other more famous royal houses of whom we read in history. A legend, told to me recently by a Brahman of Almora, relates how Som Chand on his journey to the Himalayas was one day lying asleep on the ground when a cobra came and shaded his head from the sun with its extended hood. The inevitable Brahman who accompanied Som Chand, seeing this striking portent, just as inevitably foretold that he would become a great king. The Hindu imagination loves to embellish the scanty records of national history with stories like this; and there are certain hoary traditions of remarkable similarity told about nearly all their famous heroes.

At the period of which we are now writing, Kumaon appears to have been split up into very minute subdivisions. The general use of the title "raja" to denote what in other countries would be regarded as simple landholders or lords of manors, sometimes gives a wrong impression. Every "patti" or group of a few small villages had a chief of its own who owed allegiance to some greater chief, in a kind of feudal system.

From earliest times in Kumaon there have been

two great factions, which under one form or another have continued their struggle down to the present day—an example of intense and long-continued strife to which it would be difficult to find a parallel, except perhaps in that of the Guelfs and Ghibellines in Europe. According to one story, the coming of the Chands themselves was due to the action of the rival factions, in despair of any settled government; it having been at last agreed to call in an outsider from the plains as ruler. It was these same parties that caused the ruin of the Chand kingdom at the end of the eighteenth century, and enabled the Gurkhas to conquer the country. As usual, the quarrel had an insignificant source. The two parties were named the Maras and the Phartiyals, and their headquarters were the villages of Kot and Dungari respectively, whose rivalry was probably the *fons et origo* of the ancient strife, and in which the same spirit is said to be maintained to the present day. Som Chand is reported to have brought Brahmans from the plains as his courtiers, the civil administration being committed to the Joshis and the religious duties entrusted to the Bishts and Pandes. At the time of his decease his kingdom (subject to Doti) included Kali Kumaon and some of the neighbouring tracts, if tradition can be believed. His successors continued to extend the bounds of their kingdom, until there came a powerful uprising of the Khassiyas, whose chiefs usurped the rule for a period of about two hundred years (fourteen kings of this new Khassiya dynasty are enumerated in an old list). During this interregnum the Chands retired to the Tarai at the foot of the hills. It may be mentioned that Indra Chand, the fourth in descent from Som

Chand, is said to have introduced the silkworm into Kumaon, from Tibet or Nepal, and the manufacture of silk flourished for some centuries, until it was destroyed by the Gurkhalis.

Weariness of the Khassiya rule led to the recall of the Chands in the person of the youthful Bir Chand, who led an army against Som Pal, the last Khassiya king, and slew him.

Kumaon having lost by Mohammedan invasions the tract at the foot of the hills, which is so indispensable to the hill-people for pasturage and cultivation in the winter, the Chand raja, Gyan Chand (1374–1419), made a journey to Delhi to petition the Mogul emperor for its restoration, or more probably he went to visit the emperor when the latter repaired to the Tarai to hunt. He was well received, and while hunting had the good fortune to shoot at and kill a large vulture (Garur) while it was flying high in the air carrying a snake in its talons. The emperor was so pleased with this feat that he then and there granted him the Bhabar and Tarai, and ordered that he should henceforth bear the name of Garur, wherefore he is known in the local annals as Garur Gyan Chand.

In the brief reign of Udyan Chand (1420), which lasted only one year, the kingdom extended right up to Almora, and from the Sarju in the north to the Tarai in the plains. Like a certain Scottish monarch, he was "a sair king" for the royal house, for he spent great sums on restoring temples, and during his year of rule remitted all the taxes of his subjects. He must have been extremely popular.

The little principality of Shor near the Kali river long remained independent, until it was annexed by the Chands. Its rulers, the Bam rajas, seem to have pursued a more enlightened policy than some of their neighbours, by assessing the land and making a record, a kind of Domesday Book. This work was entrusted to an officer named Jainda Kiral, who entered the land records in a series of books, kept in a muniment room in the raja's palace. The people had no great liking for these records; and once when the faithful Jainda was absent bringing some refractory villages to order, his enemies resolved to destroy the obnoxious volumes. They accordingly brought news to Jainda's wife that her husband had perished in battle, and succeeded in persuading her to be *Sati* for him. They represented that the most acceptable deed that she could perform for her departed lord would be to burn herself on a funeral pyre together with the record-books which he had valued so much, so that he might take with him into the next world all that he held most dear. The poor woman gave ear to their dissembling words, and ascended the pyre with all the settlement records of Shor, which were thus burnt to ashes, while her husband's enemies looked on with grim delight.

Another legend has special interest as referring to Almora, which at that time was in the possession of a Katyuri chief who had his fort, called Khagmara, on the Almora hill, which was then otherwise uninhabited. A Brahman, named Sri Chand Tiwari, coming from Champawat crossed the Swal river and ascended the Almora hill, passing by the garden of the raja. There a gardener gave him a lemon to refresh him. Sri Chand declined to eat the lemon, saying that there was another lemon inside it. The fruit was cut open, and lo! it was so. The fact was told to the raja, who sent for Sri Chand and asked him to explain the omen. The Brahman told him it meant that he should shortly lose his kingdom. The raja, to avert the threatened evil, handed over his lands to Sri Chand and fled northward, when his kingdom was promptly seized by a neighbouring chief, and finally annexed by the Chand raja.

Bhishma Chand (1555–1560) was troubled by various rebellions in his kingdom, and feeling the need of a more central capital, fixed on the old Khagmara fort (Almora) as his future headquarters. While he was staying there, a Khassiya chief who lived in a fortress near Ramgarh (between Almora and the plains), made a sudden attack on Khagmara by night, and slew the aged king. His adopted son, Kalyan Chand, was then absent, fighting against Doti; but he at once returned and exacted the utmost vengeance from the murderers, putting a great number of the Khassiyas to death. He established Almora as his capital, and took all the land that did not already belong to Sri Chand Tiwari, as just related.

The Kumaonis have a somewhat boastful tradition to the effect that Rudra Chand (1565–1597), on the Tarai being invaded by one of Akbar's generals, led a force there and expelled the Mussalmans. Complaints were made to the emperor, and an army was sent to encounter Rudra Chand, who, seeing the futility of a regular battle, proposed that the matter should be settled by a personal combat between two champions of the respective armies. This was agreed to, and Rudra Chand himself fought with a Mohammedan officer, and gained the victory after a long and fierce struggle. The emperor thereon invited him to Delhi and made much of him, employing the raja and his hill-troops in his war against Nagor, and making a formal grant of the Tarai to Rudra Chand. Rudra Chand is said to have appointed the emperor's favourite Hindu counsellor, the famous Birbal, as his family priest, and the descendants of Birbal, tradition states, were wont to visit Almora right up to the end of the Chand rule, to collect their dues from the raja. The Mussalman historians, says Mr. Atkinson, do not give such a flattering picture of this visit to Akbar. One of them relates that in 1568 "the raja of Kumaon arrived at Lahore from the hills for the purpose of paying his respects. Neither he nor his ancestors (the curse of God on them!) could ever have expected to speak face to face with an emperor. He brought several rare presents, and amongst them a Tibetan cow (yak) and a musk-deer, which latter died on the road from the effect of the heat. I saw it with my own eyes, and it had the appearance of a fox. Two small tusks projected from its mouth, and instead of horns it had a slight elevation or hump. They said that there were men in those hills who had feathers and wings and could fly, and they spoke of a mango tree in that country which yields fruit all the year round. God knows whether it is true," adds this chronicler, with scepticism quite of the modern brand.

Rudra Chand built the fort in Almora on the site now occupied by the public offices. He greatly encouraged learning, and during his reign the pundits of Almora are said to have equalled those of Benares and Kashmir. The story is told of him that on his return from Delhi he was in great haste to reach home, and pursued his journey even by night. Riding in the dark along one of the mountain paths, his bridle broke, and his groom, in the obscurity of the night, picked up a snake, with which he mended the bridle. When day broke, the raja discovered the strange circumstance, and taking it as a good omen, rewarded his groom with a grant of harvest dues from all the villages in the kingdom.

During the reign of Lakshmi Chand (1597–1621) certain villages or groups of hamlets were required to supply stated departments of the royal household; for example, a line of villages extending from Almora to the snows were under obligation to pass on snow to the capital for the raja's table. Every bit of land was assessed and taxed, so that a custom grew up, and still prevails in many villages, of growing fruit and vegetables on the housetops, those being the only places left untaxed. This king made many attempts to conquer Garhwal, between which and Kumaon a never-ending strife went on for ages, renewed in each reign. On one occasion, when he had to beat an ignominious retreat from Garhwal and was being carried along hidden under a washerwoman's bundle of clothes, he overheard a rustic say that his bad fortune was due to his neglect of religion, and, struck by the charge, he proceeded to found temples at Almora—the old ruined temple of Lachmeswar—and at Bageswar; but he never made any real progress against the Garhwal kingdom, the most that he achieved being to plunder some part of it in his last expedition.

His successor was Dalip Chand, who had twenty-one sons. Bijai Chand, the next king, was murdered in the palace by one of his ministers after reigning for one year only. After his death the two factions, the Maras and Phartiyals, each set up a candidate for the throne. The Maras succeeded in reaching Almora first with their favourite, Tirmal Chand, and had the accession ceremony performed; and the other party, reaching the ford over the Swal river below the town at the same hour, on learning the state of affairs, scattered and fled. The new king began his reign by punishing the murderers of his brother, Bijai Chand. Two of the ministers who had plotted against his life were blinded (the most common punishment in those days), and a third was permitted to go to Allahabad on condition that he put an end to his life under the sacred fig tree there, "where suicide was lawful."

A list of the duties of the king's chamberlain in this reign has been handed down, which, for its quaintness and the light that it throws on the household arrangements of an Indian raja in olden times, is worth transcribing. It runs as follows:—

"1. He should see that the cook did his duty well. 2. He should have no dealings either with Maras or Phartiyals. 3. He should tell the raja everything he saw and heard. 4. He should not tell lies. 5. He should not repeat anything heard or seen in the palace. 6. He should taste everything used for the raja's food. 7. He should never allow the cook to be out of his sight. 8. He should constantly move about and threaten the servants, whether there was cause or not, so that none might become careless. 9. He should never allow other than the regular servants to have anything to do with the raja's food. 10. He should not allow these servants to perform any other duty. 11. He should only enter the Darbar at the prescribed times, and not go in and out as if it were a private assembly. 12. He must never speak of poison, opium, or bhang, nor touch them. 13. He must remain with the raja at his meals, and always treat him with due respect and no familiarity, watching his countenance for any signs indicating his wishes. 14. He must never hold friendly intercourse with the people of Kali Kumaon or Shor, or members of the Katyuri family, or junior members of the reigning family, nor enter their houses. 15. He must address the women of the palace with the greatest respect; and when duty led him toward the female apartments, he must always proceed with downcast eyes and speak in a low voice. 16. He must never speak of spells (mantras), as they are only used for evil purposes, nor cut his nails, nor shave himself (ill-omened acts) within the limits of the palace." From these directions it would seem that the life of a Kumaon raja in the seventeenth century was surrounded with as many terrors, real and imaginary, as that of a Russian Czar nowadays, and required almost as much protection.

Tirmal Chand having no son, began to look round for an heir. A rumour was current that Baz Bahadur, the son of his brother Nil Gosain (who had been blinded by some wicked courtiers of Bijai Chand, who had attempted to kill off all his brothers, before he himself was murdered), was living. The tradition is that when this Nil Gosain was blinded, the women of his zenana were taken over by Bijai Chand, and a jealous concubine of the raja took the boy and threw him over a precipice, where he was found uninjured by the wife of a Tiwari Brahman and brought up as her own child. On inquiry being made, the Brahman's wife denied all knowledge of the matter; but on being reassured by the raja, who declared his innocent intentions, she produced Baz Bahadur, who was then formally adopted as the raja's heir, and succeeded to the kingdom in 1638, reigning until 1678. He settled the government efficiently, obtained a "farman" from the Emperor Aurungzeb, invaded the country of the Huniyas to the north,—who had persecuted the Hindu pilgrims to the holy lake of Mansarovar and Mount Kailas,—assaulted their fortress of Takhlakhar, and made the Huniyas promise to give free passage to the pilgrims, as well as to the Bhotiya traders. Good fortune attended him in all he undertook. While absent in the Bhotiya country, the Garhwalis invaded Kumaon and recovered their lost territory; but immediately on his return, Baz Bahadur sent a force by way of Lohba, which drove the Garhwalis back on their capital Srinagar, where a peace was signed. The news of this victory, as I have often heard from the Almora people, was flashed thither by lighting beacons on the hills all the way from Srinagar; and the custom of lighting grass bonfires, called "khatarwa," on the hills around Almora is still continued, and takes place on a certain evening in October. Baz Bahadur is even said to have carried his conquering arms into the plains, and to have plundered the city of Nagina. It was he who built the interesting temple on the Bhim Tal lake which the traveller notices on his way to Almora from the plains.

The raja's end was a sad one. He suspected his son of plotting against his life, and exiled him to Gangoli in Kumaon. At the instigation of a Brahman counsellor he seized and blinded many of his best

A Bazaar in Kumaon

friends and followers, and then, finding out the deception that had been practised on him, strove to make amends by presents and gifts of land to their families. Becoming at last a moody and suspicious tyrant, hated by his subjects, he drove away all his old servants, and died neglected and alone at Almora in 1678. He had endowed and built many temples; and on one of his expeditions to Garhwal he carried off the image of the goddess Nanda, which he placed in a temple at Almora, with a train of flower-girls and female slaves to attend upon it. This temple was at first in the precincts of the fort, but was removed by Mr. Traill to its present site. Probably this removal is the origin of a wild and absurd story which has been told me more than once by natives of the place, to the effect that Mr. Traill, the early Commissioner of Kumaon, was struck with snow-blindness on a visit to the north of the province; and believing that it was due to the displeasure of the goddess Nanda Devi, whose home is among the peaks, he vowed to build her a temple, which vow he fulfilled on his return to Almora, and was delivered from the curse.

Wars between Kumaon and Garhwal occupied the next few years. At one time the army of the latter conquered nearly as far as Almora, but in 1709 the tables were turned by the capture of Srinagar, the Garhwal capital. This was in the reign of Jagat Chand. His successor, Debi Chand, was a weak ruler. Like his ancestors, he made raids into Garhwal, but was defeated and lost much of his territory on that side. The story goes that on one occasion he set out on an expedition against Srinagar, but thinking better of his intention, halted half-way, and spreading a hill near

8

his encampment with carpets, he called the summit Srinagar and took it triumphantly, afterwards giving the place the name of Fatehpur, or "city of victory." He had in his treasury the immense accumulations of previous kings, amounting to thirty-five million rupees. With this money he proposed to pay off all the debts of his subjects and, like Vikramaditya, establish a new era to be called by his name. He spent about ten millions in this wild attempt, but gained nothing by it, as most of the money found its way into the hands of the Brahman money-lenders, who were thus furnished with means to pursue the course of ambitious plotting and interference which they carried on for nearly a century after. This weak and probably somewhat demented prince actually attempted to take part in the policy of the Mogul Empire, and supported a rival candidate to the imperial throne, named Sabir Shah, who collected an army of Rohillas, but was defeated. The raja himself took a force of hillmen to fight the great Mogul's army, but was deserted by his general, an Afghan, and the Kumaonis fled back to Almora. He was murdered in a pleasure-house which he had built in the Bhabar at Kota for his winter residence, it is said at the instigation of some traitorous counsellors, who gave out that he had died of snake-bite.

The next king was a puppet of these same ministers, and was after three years murdered also, in his palace at Almora (which had been newly built in 1685 on the site now occupied by the Ramsay College). The raja of Katehir was the father of the murdered king who had been set up by these counsellors, and when they asked him to supply another son, he declined, saying, "My children are not goats that they should be sacrificed in this manner." The ministers then made so bold as to instal the bastard son of one of the late raja's female slaves as raja, though he was only eighteen days old; and they assumed the regency as before. But this was too much for the Kumaonis. The members of both factions united in resistance, and searched for a member of the Chand family to carry on the succession. They found a man named Kalyan who was living in poverty in the Tarai, and, bringing him to Almora, installed him as raja.

This Kalyan Chand (1730–1747) was really a peasant elevated to the throne by a strange turn of fortune, and his character and attainments were not such as to fit him for his position. He was distinguished rather by low cunning and pitiless cruelty than by any royal qualities. Beginning his reign by taking vengeance on the murderers of his predecessor, and in constant danger of plots, he proceeded to exterminate all the remaining members of the Chand family. These Raotelas, as they were called, throughout the length and breadth of the land were slain or exiled. The raja had a system of espionage which led to the worst excesses. One member of a family, it is said, had only to denounce the others as concerned in some plot against the raja, to get the whole family property into his hands. On one occasion news of an extensive intrigue amongst the Brahmans came to the ears of Kalyan Chand, and in a frenzy of fear he ordered that all the accused should be seized and blinded. Seven vessels filled with eyes of Brahmans (such is the tradition) were placed before him. His favourite summer residence was Binsar, where he built the temple of Mahadeo, now in ruins. One of the Chands named Himmat Gosain, whom he had blinded, raised an army against him, and a battle was fought at Kashipur below the hills, in which the raja was victorious; but realising that he had raised up many enemies by his cruelty, he began to dismiss his former advisers and take counsel with more enlightened men, such as Shib Deo Joshi, to whom he committed the charge of the Tarai, and Hari Ram Joshi, who had charge of Almora. His enemy Himmat took refuge in the camp of the Rohilla chief, Ali Muhammad Khan, but Kalyan Chand sent emissaries who took his life. Ali Muhammad, in a great rage, thereupon invaded Kumaon. The raja was too stingy to send supplies or men to his minister Shib Deo, who was consequently unable to resist the Rohillas. The latter carried all before them, and in 1743 occupied Almora itself. Kalyan Chand fled to Garhwal and placed himself under the protection of the raja of that country. The fierce Mussalmans went everywhere in Kumaon, defiling the temples by sprinkling cow's blood upon the altars, breaking the noses of idols, and seizing and melting down images and ornaments of gold and silver. It is said that the great temple at Jageshwar, the most ancient shrine in Kumaon, about twenty miles east of Almora, escaped pillage owing to swarms of bees which came out and drove back the plunderers. The raja of Garhwal at last interfered, and agreed to pay three lakhs of rupees to the Rohillas on behalf of Kalyan Chand. After staying for seven months in the hills, where many of them died owing to the unsuitable climate, they left Kumaon. Kalyan Chand soon after went to Delhi to complain of the Rohillas, and was well received by the emperor (Muhammad Shah), who granted him a fresh lease of the Tarai. It is said that in order to appear at court with suitable presents the raja had to borrow the jewels from the Jageshwar temple, the only one left intact by the Rohillas. In his last days Kalyan Chand was afflicted with blindness, a punishment, as was naturally believed, for his many cruelties. His son, Dip Chand, succeeded him, and for many years had a prosperous reign, during which the kingdom rose to perhaps its highest pitch of greatness, which was due to the able administration of Shib Deo Joshi, the chief minister of the state for a long period. He, however, was not unopposed in his plans, and powerful disaffection at times showed itself. Battles were fought, and Shib Deo with difficulty maintained his influence. Hearing once that the Daniya Joshis, a clan of Brahmans, were concerned in a plot to overthrow him, he had the ringleaders seized, tied up in sacks, and hurled into the seething pool at Balighat, on the Sarju river above Bageswar—a punishment which for a time struck terror into the hearts of his enemies. In 1764 he was called to Kashipur in the Tarai by news of a mutiny among the soldiers there, who demanded an increase of pay. On repairing thither, he and his two sons were murdered by the soldiery. The death of this shrewd and determined statesman marked the beginning of a rapid decline in the prosperity of Kumaon. The rule over the Tarai was never afterwards effectually held, and internal troubles so distracted the mountain province that no stable government can be said to have existed until the invasion by the Gurkhalis, who sought to justify their interference by pointing to the disturbed state of the country.

THE GURKHAS IN KUMAON.

Nepal, up to the middle of the eighteenth century, had been divided into a number of petty chieftainships. About that time the raja of Gurkha, a small state to the north of the Nepal valley, began a career of rapid conquest, which in a few years made the Gurkhalis masters of the greater part of what is now called Nepal, together with some of the eastern and northern portions of Kumaon. The race was a pure Hindu one, which at a previous period had migrated from a country far to the west of Nepal. The Gurkhalis appear to have followed a well-laid plan of aggression with great determination, and had not their career been arrested by the necessary resistance opposed to it by the British rule in India, it seemed at one time probable that the dominion of these hardy mountaineers would extend over the whole of Northern India. From 1778 onwards Ran Bahadur Sah was the raja of Nepal, and during his reign the aggressive policy of the state was pursued vigorously. Knowing the distracted condition of Kumaon, the Nepal Darbar in 1789 resolved on invasion, and early in the following year two forces were sent into Kumaon, with the result that after some doubtful engagements the country was conquered and Almora was entered. The leading spirit in Kumaon at that time was Harak Deb Joshi, who for some years had acted as a king-maker and dictator in the hills, and now, in despair of any settled government, is said to have thrown in his lot with the Nepalese, and assisted them in the invasion of Garhwal. The invading army had to be recalled from that quarter owing to a Chinese invasion of Nepal, and Harak Deb was taken thither by the Gurkhalis as a kind of hostage. He made his escape before long and fled to Johar, near the Tibetan side of Kumaon. After making a settlement with the Chinese, the Gurkhalis returned to Kumaon. Very heavy taxes were imposed, including a poll-tax. For some years previously mercenaries from the western hills had been employed in Kumaon by both factions there, and many of them had married and settled in the land. The Gurkhas, suspecting their loyalty, had a census made of all such persons, and on a certain night they were all put to death. This Kumaon St. Bartholomew's Day was called the Mangal Ki Rat, or "Tuesday night," and the phrase is still used to denote any great atrocity. In 1804 Garhwal was annexed by Nepal. From that date to 1815 the administration of Kumaon was in the hands of the Gurkha Bam Sah. Meanwhile the Nepal raja, Ran Bahadur, who was more or less mad, had been deposed in favour of his son Vikram Sah, and had gone to live at Benares as a pensioner of the British. There he met with Harak Deb, who had been trying in various quarters, including also the British Government, to get help for the Kumaonis. After a while Ran Bahadur returned to Nepal at an opportune moment and again became king, but in 1807 was assassinated.

The rule of the Gurkhas was oppressive in the extreme, though Garhwal suffered more severely than Kumaon. A story is told that once when a new tax was imposed in Kumaon, the demand was not immediately answered by the villagers, whereupon orders were issued to the headmen of 1500 villages to repair to Almora and hold a conference with the governor on the subject. On their arrival they were all massacred in cold blood, as a warning to the population. Many families fled to the plains, and many more, as in Garhwal, were sold as slaves at the foot of the hills. We can hardly wonder that the term "Gurkhiyani" is still used in Kumaon to describe any act of cruelty and oppression. At the same time it would be unjust to regard the Gurkhalis in a wholly unfavourable light. From time to time attempts were made by the Nepal Darbar to institute a regular and stable system of administration and taxation, and these plans only failed because the conquered country was entrusted to a number of military governors and officers who had little notion of settled government. Bam Sah at Almora and Hastidal in Garhwal, however, were men of good character and intentions. The Nepal forces in Kumaon consisted mostly of men raised in the country itself, acting as a kind of militia in co-operation with the Gurkhali troops. The Gurkhas themselves are described in an old report by Mr. Fraser, a British official in Kumaon, as "veteran soldiers, with a fearlessness of danger and much of the true and high spirit of a soldier—that setting of life at nought in comparison with the performance of duty, and that high sense of honour which forms his most attractive ornament and raises his character to the highest. They are cheerful, patient of fatigue, industrious at any labour to which they are put, very tractable and quiet, and from what has fallen under my own observation and knowledge, not cruel. This, however, is a somewhat dubious part of their character; in various situations they have behaved in different ways; even as a nation their character seems various and unsettled. The individuals must exhibit a greater

variety still." The foregoing description probably suits most of the more forcible Eastern nationalities, and is not inapplicable to-day to Nepal, as well as to the Gurkhas who form such a valuable part of our Indian army.

The British Invasion in 1815.

For many years, from before 1800, the Nepalese had pursued a system of wanton aggression against the territories of the East India Company, extending on their frontiers for hundreds of miles along the foot of the Himalayas. It is said that as many as two hundred villages and large tracts of land had been taken over; and in spite of repeated protests and much negotiation between the Company and the Nepal Darbar, no redress was obtainable, and the Gurkhalis, evidently thinking that the forbearance of the British was due to fear, became yearly bolder and more overbearing. The evidence collected in *Himalayan Districts* and in Prinsep's *Transactions* shows clearly enough that it was in no merely Jingo spirit that war was at last resolved on. The proverbial last straw had appeared in an attack on a British police station, and the murder of its officer, combined with an attempt to destroy British troops and subjects in another quarter by extensive poisoning of wells. It was determined to push on the war rapidly and effectively from the first, and several points were selected for simultaneous attack—no less than four bodies of troops entering the hills at different places. It cannot be said that the campaign shed any great glory on the British arms. The Gurkhalis probably never had more than 5000

men in the field, while the British had over 20,000. The force that acted against Katmandu accomplished nothing. The commander of another force, General Gillespie, was shot dead in the attack on the fort of Kalinga, the brave garrison of which, being reduced by famine, at last cut its way out and made good its escape. The account given by Mr. Fraser of this siege is full of interest. During the siege the Gurkhas had shown the greatest pluck, cheerfulness, and courtesy to the British wounded and prisoners. "The confidence they exhibited in the British officers was certainly flattering; they solicited and obtained surgical aid; and on one occasion this gave rise to a singular and interesting scene. While the batteries were playing, a man was perceived on the breach, advancing and waving his hand. The guns ceased firing for a while, and the man came into the batteries; he proved to be a Gurkha whose lower jaw had been shattered by a cannon shot, and who came thus frankly to solicit assistance from his enemy. It is unnecessary to add that it was instantly afforded; and when discharged from the hospital, he signified his desire to return to his corps to combat us again, exhibiting thus a strong sense of the value of generosity and courtesy in warfare, and also of his duty to his country, separating completely in his own mind private and national feelings from each other, and his frank confidence in the individuals of our nation, from the duty he owed his own, to fight against us collectively."

The worthy and somewhat didactic Mr. Fraser, being an old Anglo-Indian, probably was acquainted with the well-known power of the Oriental to "reckon up" the character of those he has to deal with; and certainly he

is right in thinking that the story proves the almost pathetic confidence in the honour and humanity of British gentlemen, which is the surest bulwark of our rule in India. The fort of Kalinga was razed to the ground; but two monuments mark its site—one to General Gillespie and the others who fell in the assault; and the other "as a tribute of respect for our gallant adversary Bulbudder, commander of the fort, and his brave Gurkhas, who were afterwards, while in the service of Ranjit Singh, shot down in their ranks to the last man by Afghan artillery."

Another force which was acting in the east of Kumaon scattered itself too much, and its commander, Captain Hearsey, was taken prisoner and brought to Almora as a hostage. The proceedings so far had indeed been confused and fruitless; but General Auchterlony showed military qualities of a higher order, and, entering the hills near the Sutlej, by a series of skilful movements forced the Gurkhas to concentrate their forces. Kumaon itself was left almost unoccupied by the Gurkhas, and it was now determined to invade that part, as the key to the situation. It was known also that the people of Kumaon were greatly incensed against their Gurkha conquerors, and would be likely to welcome an invader who would rid them of their tyranny. A proclamation was circulated in Kumaon notifying the intention of the British Government to rescue the inhabitants from their oppressors, and a force of Rohillas and Pathans was raised for the invasion. The campaign is described at great length in *Himalayan Districts*. It must suffice here to note that a successful advance was made, with the help of the people of the country, who willingly co-operated, and after severe fighting in the outskirts of the town, Almora was entered and the fort surrendered on 26th April 1815.[1] A conference was then held between Bam Sah and Colonel Gardner, the British commandant of the force, and it was arranged that the Gurkhalis should evacuate Kumaon and retire beyond the Kali. Kumaon and Garhwal were then formally annexed to the British dominions, and peace was ere long made with Nepal, though only after General Auchterlony had advanced within twenty miles of Kathmandu and gained a decisive battle there on the 28th of February 1816.

Respecting Garhwal, it may be mentioned that the Gurkhas first raided it in 1791, and finally reduced it in 1803. They appear to have treated the Garhwalis with much greater severity than they showed towards the people of Kumaon. In the *Asiatic Researches* (vol. xi.) it is stated by a traveller that "at the foot of the pass leading from Harkapairi is a Gurkhali 'chauki' or post, to which slaves are brought down from the hills and exposed for sale. Many hundreds of these poor wretches, of both sexes, from three to thirty years of age, are annually disposed of in the way of traffic. These slaves are brought down from all parts of the interior of the hills, and sold at Hardwar at from 10 to 150 rupees." It is said that 200,000 people were sold as slaves in this manner, so that a vast number of villages became deserted, and few families of conse-

[1] It is a fact worthy of mention that elephants were used in this campaign to carry the mortars right up to Almora. When we consider the mountainous nature of the country and the condition of the roads, or rather their non-existence at that period, the feat almost rivals that of Hannibal in entering Italy.

A Brahman Official at Almora

quence remained in the country. The prices given for slaves at the foot of the hills were much smaller than those given for horses and cattle—less than half in fact. Those who could not pay the taxes and fines arbitrarily imposed on them were sold as slaves.

At the end of the war with Nepal, the Garhwal raja, Sudarshan Sah, was living in straitened circumstances at Dehra Dun. The part of Garhwal west of the Alakananda river was handed over to him by the British Government, and this is the raj of Tihri which is now held by his descendant.

The fate of many of the Gurkhalis who were left in the province, especially in Garhwal, or were unable to make good their escape, was in many cases a terrible one. Some who had married into local families cast in their lot with the Kumaonis and were spared, but great numbers were massacred, while others fled to the forests and lived on roots and fruits until they perished.

The story of the province since 1815 is part of the history of the British Government in India, and, as it presents few features of general interest, I must refer the reader who seeks for further information to the authorities from which this brief narrative has been constructed. The great names in the administration of the country are those of Traill, Batten, and Ramsay. Kumaon and Garhwal have remained peaceful and prosperous, rarely if ever suffering from serious famine. Roads have been opened in all directions, and the trade between Tibet, the hills, and the plains has greatly increased. The numerous public works afford a ready source of income to the surplus agricultural population, so that none need starve. Education has been spread; the standard of living has been remarkably raised. The people are sturdy, independent, and shrewd, a somewhat different type from the Hindus of the plains. They still remember the old times with some share of pride and affection, and love to tell of events in the days of the "Chand rajas." Do they ever regret them? An old and long-headed Brahman official once told me that the Indians really prefer a *personal* government, for its spice of romance, and the opportunity it affords to talent and intrigue, as contrasted with the impassiveness of too respectable British rule, with its "sceptre of lead." What they like, he said, is to feel that the poorest man among them may some day be lifted to the highest position in the state, if he has luck. Yet who will attempt to deny that under the solid administration of later times the people of Kumaon and Garhwal have been immensely better off and happier than they ever were before?

The importance of the Kumaon war is well shown in a recent article by Colonel L. A. Waddell (in the *Pioneer*, 26th September 1903), who writes: "The capture of the Nepalese stronghold (Almora) in 1815 was an event of much importance for British rule in India. At that critical and stirring time, shortly after the battle of Delhi in 1803, when General Lake had defeated the French-Mahratta confederacy in their scramble for the sovereignty of India, and secured the great Mogul throne to the East India Company, the Mahrattas were again actively intriguing with the Gurkhas and other native states for a universal campaign against the English, to sweep them out of

India; and the native states, with their troops ready mobilised on their frontiers, were eagerly watching the issue of our struggle with the Gurkhas, which at first was going disastrously against us all along the line from the Sutlej to Tirhut. With the capture of Almora, however, the tide turned in our favour, and its permanent annexation, as well as that of Sikkim, was forced on us as a measure of self-defence to cripple the dangerously aggressive Gurkhas, to hem them in and cut them off from intrigue with the adjoining hill states and Upper India. In acknowledging their defeat one of their generals is said to have remarked, 'Hitherto we have been hunting deer, but now we have been hunted by tigers.'

"The leading part in this Kumaon war, under General Auchterlony, was taken by that knight of fortune, Lieutenant-Colonel William Linnaeus Gardner, afterwards Lord Gardner of Anglo-Indian fame. He had formerly been in Scindhia's service, and afterwards raised the renowned Gardner's Horse. On the outbreak of the Gurkha war he was taken from the irregular police-patrol he was commanding, and appointed to raise a battalion of 3000 Rohillas. With these levies he entered the hills, and by a series of brilliant movements outmanœuvred the Gurkhas, forcing them to retire on Almora, and cutting off their communication with the Sutlej division of their army. Colonel Gardner's romantic career formed the subject of Thackeray's burlesque of 'Major Gahagan,' and to him has been ascribed the chief credit for the addition to the British Empire of the mountain province of Kumaon."

CHAPTER VI

AN INDIAN HOLY LAND

IT may appear surprising to some readers that the name of a holy land should be applied to the Himalayan province of Kumaon and Garhwal, yet there is no difficulty in proving its claim to the title. The great shrines of both the leading deities of modern India, Siva and Vishnu, the active partners in the Hindu Triad or Trinity, are situated within its bounds, and these places, Kedarnath and Badarinath, are the supreme objects of pilgrimage to devout Hindus. Beyond all other "tirthas" or holy places, either at Benares, Gaya, Prayag, or Puri, the mountain fastnesses, which are believed to be the dwelling-places of Siva and Vishnu, are regarded as sacro-sanct, and more merit is obtained by the long and toilsome journey to the snowy peaks than to any other of the numerous goals of pilgrimage throughout India. The very sight of the everlasting snows is said to bestow sanctity and bliss; nay, it is written in the Skanda Purana, "He who thinks of Himáchal, though he should not behold him, is greater than he who performs all worship in Kashi (Benares). In a hundred ages of the gods I could not tell thee of the glories of Himáchal. As the dew is dried up by the morning sun, so are the sins of mankind by the sight of Himáchal."

The great Indian epic, the Mahabharata, also many times refers to their sacredness, and connects them with the most ancient traditions of the Indo-Aryan race. Hither the five sons of Pandu, the royal house of Hastinapur in earliest times, retired to die when they were told that their power had passed to the sons of Kuru; walking in single file, clothed in dresses of bark, accompanied by their common wife Draupadi, and followed by their faithful dog, they ascended the mountain path. Their names and traditions of their wonderful deeds are still preserved in the names of many places in the province. Here they were visited by Krishna himself, who is said at another time to have performed penance for long ages on the great Mount Gandhamadana, the square castle-like mass of peaks now called by the name of Badarinath, which is seen so clearly from Almora, standing out at the western end of the snowy range. Here Siva by sacrifice and austerities gained supernatural power and divine rank above all gods, in the belief of his votaries, so long as the merits of his works shall last. Here, near the confluence of rivers at Bageswar, Siva was wedded to his consort Parvati, the "mountain-born," after obtaining the consent of her father Himáchal, a personification of the Himalayas. Here, among the snowy peaks to the far north, is Siva's throne on Mount Kailas, while Parvati dwells on the nearer range. On the hill named Kurmachal, from which the name Kumaon is said to be derived, near the old capital of the Chand rajas at Champawat, Vishnu descended in his tortoise (Kurma) incarnation to deliver the earth. Both deities are believed to be peculiarly present in and near their temples at Kedar and Badari, and the pilgrim advances under the snow-clad heights with bated breath, believing himself in the presence of his god. The very stones of those places are sacred, and are regarded as emblems of the deity. Where the Kosi river breaks through the mountain barrier and flows down into the plain of Upper India, and is joined by the Sita river, there has been from ancient times a beautiful grove of asoka trees, where Rama and his faithful Sita are said to have sojourned. As the Skanda Purana relates, "Sita was charmed with the beautiful forest, and said to Rama, 'It is the month Baisakh; let us stay in this wood, and bathe in the waters of the river.' So they abode there, and on their return to Ayodhya, the name of the place was changed to Sitabani, the grove of Sita."

It will thus be seen that Kumaon and Garhwal are specially consecrated to the great gods of modern India, and one of these deities, namely Siva, is probably of Himalayan origin. The pilgrim routes leading to Kedar and Badari are every year traversed by many thousands of pilgrims from all parts of India, including the extreme south. Distance, in this case, lends enchantment to the view, and the southern pilgrims are the most devout and often the most numerous. This religious resort is of no recent origin, but appears to have prevailed from earliest times, even before Siva was regarded as a national deity or adopted by the Brahmans as popular supplanter of their Vedic nature-gods. The explanation of the early sanctity appertaining to the Himalaya is not far to seek. When the Indo-Aryans were gradually advancing into India through the passes of the north-west, and invading the land southward in the Indus valley and eastward along and under the Himalayas, they must have carried with them affectionate memories of the snow-clad mountains and lofty uplands which had been their earlier home.[1] As they looked up from the hot enervating plains of India towards the Himalayan heights they must have seen there in imagination the ancient home of their race, where the spirits of their ancestors dwelt, and whither they might also pass at death to the "Fathers," in what has always been to the Hindus the sacred quarter of the north. The Himalayan mountains must have appeared to them as the grandest embodiment of the forces of nature that they had ever met with, and before long they came to be adored as the dwelling of the gods. Just as their kinsmen who lived in Greece had their Olympus, whose cloud-capped summits hid the assembly of the Hellenic deities from mortal eyes, so the Indian Aryans had their Himalaya, the sacred "Abode of Snow," hereafter to be known as the home of the later deities, whom the Brahmans laboured to identify with their own Indra, Agni, and Rudra. To these mountains, from earliest times, saints and sages found their way, to meditate in their solitudes among scenes of wild grandeur and beauty. In the Sanskrit Scriptures we read of many such Rishis and Munis, whose dwelling was among the mountains of Himavat, and whose names and memories still cling to peak and pool and river-bank.

The Himalayas appear to have been especially

[1] In one part of the marriage ceremony of the Hindus the husband and wife are exhorted to direct their thoughts to the great mountain of the north called Sapta Kula Parvata, or the mountain of the seven castes, the original home of their ancestors, the mountain being represented by a stone smeared with sandalwood oil.

favoured by Brahmanic settlers, and there is strong reason for believing that important colonies of Aryans were settled in the hills at an early period. It is probable that the first advance of the Aryans, after leaving the Indus region, was not down the course of the Ganges, but along the foot of the sub-Himalayan range, with diversions into the hilly tracts, which extend for a hundred miles from the snowy peaks to the plains. Thus the Vedic "Brahmana" Scriptures, most of which are of very old date, state that the sacred language (Sanskrit) was spoken in this part of the Himalayas with greater purity than anywhere else. We know that the Kashmir pandits farther west are some of the finest specimens of the pure Indo-Aryan race.

It is now well known that in the sixth and the seventh centuries B.C., Kumaon and Garhwal were included in the great Hindu kingdom of Kosala, which had its capital at Savatthi, a little to the east, over the Nepal border, and in Buddha's time was contending for supremacy with the kingdom of Magadha, in what is now Bengal. Kosala extended from the Himalayan snows to the Ganges at Benares, and its power is said by Dr. Rhys Davids, in his recent book *Buddhist India*, to have been founded on the superior energy and hardihood of the troops whom it drew from the hilly region to the north. The Buddha was born in this kingdom of Kosala at the foot of the Nepal hills, where his native place has recently been discovered and excavated. To Buddhists also the central sub-Himalayan tract is a sacred land. The Chinese pilgrim Hwen Thsang in 634 A.D. notes the existence of an important Hindu city named Brahmapura within the hills, and the site of this has been identified with the small town named Barahat in Tihri or Independent Garhwal. All this is evidence of the early importance and also sacredness of the country.

There is no doubt that this portion of the Indian Himalayas owes much of its repute for sanctity to its beneficent character, as the source of the mighty Ganges and dispenser of water to the thirsty plains below. In tropical countries water is the most prized and valuable of products. It is one of the chief factors in human life, and in a land like India it has been remarked that half of the conversation of the people is concerned with it. Hence we can understand the fanciful legends which have grown up regarding the origin and nature of the Indian rivers, and especially of the Ganges. Our province is cut up into a number of narrow valleys and deep gorges, each of which carries its contribution to form the great river. The main sources of the Ganges are in the glaciers of the snowy range, though the longest of its feeders take their rise beyond the first line of peaks, in the high ground between that and the more northerly range in Tibet, and burst through gorges of marvellous depth into the rolling hilly region of the sub-Himalaya. Kumaon and Garhwal is the gathering-place of all the headwaters of the sacred river, whether they flow south-eastward before turning towards Bengal, or go more directly south to join the main stream. In an eloquent passage of his famous article on India, Sir William Hunter describes the immense part played by the Ganges in the economy of the Indian people: "Of all the great rivers on the surface of the globe, none can compare in sanctity with the Ganges, or Mother Ganga, as she is affectionately called by devout Hindus. From her source in the Himalayas to her mouth in the Bay of Bengal, her banks are holy ground. Each point of junction of her main stream with a tributary has special claims to sanctity. The ancient legend relates how Ganga, the fair daughter of King Himalaya and of his queen the air-nymph Menaka, was persuaded, after long supplication, to shed her purifying influence on the sinful earth. The icicle-studded cavern from which she issues is the tangled hair of the god Siva. Loving legends hallow each part of her course; and from the names of her tributaries and of the towns along her banks, a whole mythology might be built up. The six years' pilgrimage from the source to the mouth and back again, known as Pradakshina, is still performed by many; and a few devotees may yet be seen wearily accomplishing the meritorious penance of 'measuring their length' along certain parts of the route. To bathe in the Ganges at the great stated festivals washes away guilt, and those who have been thus purified themselves carry back bottles to their less fortunate kindred in far-off provinces. To die and be buried on the river bank is the last wish of millions of Hindus."

At the foot of the Pindari glacier in Kumaon the river Pindar issues from an icy cavern, and is poetically said to flow from the matted locks of Siva. A legend tells how the river was at first confined to the sky, but the prayers of a certain sage availed to make it fall on Mount Meru, where it divided into four great branches, representing the Indus, the Alakananda (the source of the Ganges), the Oxus, and the Hoang-Ho. Siva, who was leading the life of an ascetic in the Himalayas at the time, is said to have retained the Ganges for ages in his long matted hair (the Jata of the ascetic) until at last it was permitted to fall on the mountains, since when the Ganges has been the most sacred of rivers, visited by the crowding myriads of India, who repair to her to have their sins washed away in her magic waters.

The mention of Mount Meru brings before us one of the most familiar ideas of Hindu geography or cosmogony. The region represented by this fabulous mountain and its related marvels is the great Himalayan plateau beyond the Kumaon peaks, partially known to the old Indo-Aryans, and invested by them with all the fanciful imagery of a terrene Paradise. As the theology of the Brahmans took more definite shape, it became needful to mark out the residence of the gods more clearly than before, and to indicate a "land of pure delight" to which the souls of the good might depart after death. What more natural than to point to the mighty ranges on the north, crowned with their white and glistering peaks, like pinnacles of some celestial palace, and to say, "There is the dwelling of the holy gods, and there your souls shall rest, where sorrow never comes, where 'the day is aye fair in the land o' the leal.'" "There," says one of the Puranas, "are the regions of Swarga (Paradise), the seats of the righteous, where the wicked do not arrive even after a thousand births. There is no sorrow, nor weariness, nor anxiety, nor hunger, nor apprehension; the inhabitants are exempt from all infirmity and pain, and live in uninterrupted enjoyment. The goddess never sends rain upon them, yet the earth abounds with water. In those regions there is no distinction or succession of ages, and Time is no more."

It may well be that some of the Aryans had penetrated through the icy barrier of the Himalaya and had wandered on the high plateaux of Tibet, which are almost rainless, owing to the exhaustion of the moisture brought by the Indian monsoon on the southern face of the range. Returning from that region of calm and clear air, they may have told their comrades of a land "where the goddess sends no rain"; and such impressions, mingling with the longing expectation of a blissful future which never wholly fades from the heart of man, grew up into the story of a Paradise beyond the snowy range.[1]

The early description of this dimly-known trans-Himalayan region in the Puranas is of interest, as showing us the extent of geographical knowledge possessed by the Indo-Aryans. It was regarded by them as the hub or centre of the universe. The world being in a chaotic condition, Brahma, it is said, formed seven great continents, separated from each other by seas of salt water, sugar-cane juice, wine, ghee or clarified butter, curds, milk, and fresh water respectively. The central continent was named Jambudwip, which was in the form of a lotus. This was the only one with which human beings are acquainted, the others indeed being declared to be illusory. In the midst of Jambudwip, which represents India and the countries to the north of it, there is a vast and glorious mountain called Meru, round in shape, and forming

[1] Compare Pindar's description of Elysium—

> Thee to the Elysian plain, earth's farthest end,
> Where Rhadamanthus dwells, the god shall send;
> Where mortals easiest pass the careless hour;
> No lingering winters there, nor snow nor shower.

the centre of the world-lotus. To the south of Mount Meru there are three ranges of mountains, the southernmost being Himavat or the Himalaya, adjoining Bharata (India). To the north of it there are also three ranges, the northernmost bounding the country of the Uttara-Kurus, which is regarded as a kind of heaven. Four great lakes are also mentioned, described at length in the Vayu Purana (See essay by Wilford in *Asiatic Researches*, vol. viii.) These may be the lakes on the Tibetan tableland, north of Kumaon, the best known of which are the sacred Mansarovar and Rakhas Tal, or they may include the great lakes to the north-east of Kashmir.

If we search for the origin of the idea of a central Mount Meru, it is probably to be found in vague early reports of Kailas, the mountain near Mansarovar lake, so much reverenced by Indians, and to which the long and difficult pilgrimage is still made by the more devout worshippers of Siva. It is said to be an object of great splendour and beauty. A traveller, quoted by Mr. Atkinson, describes how it rises straight out of a large grassy plain, separated from the other heights of the range to which it belongs by a deep ravine, and rising to a height of over 4000 feet above the plain, with a dome-shaped peak at one end, some 1500 feet higher. "The peak and upper ridge were well covered with snow. The stratification of the rock is strongly marked in successive ledges that catch the snow falling from above, forming irregular bands of alternate white and purple. One of these bands, more marked than the rest, encircles the base of the peak, and this, according to the Hindu tradition, is the mark of the cable with which a

Rakshas or demon attempted to drag the throne of Siva from its place. In picturesque beauty Kailas far surpasses the Gur-la or any other of the Indian Himalayas: it is full of majesty, a king of mountains. Through the ravines on either side of the mountain is the passage by which the pilgrims make the circumambulation. The circuit is performed in two days by those who take it easily, but with more exertion it may be done in one day."

I remember to have seen somewhere an explanation of several of the common epithets of Siva as being connected with this grand mountain, which seems to have been identified with his worship from very ancient times. He is generally represented in pictures as an ascetic with a serpent twined round his neck, and this is referred to the appearance of the lines of strata on the mountain, as just described. Again, he is spoken of as Nilakantha, the Blue-necked, an allusion to the dark band of colour of the rocky mountain-sides below the snow-line, though the popular explanation is different, and attributes it to his swallowing the poison at the "churning of the ocean." His matted locks, again, are thought to represent the icicles and snow-wreaths of the glaciers and peaks.

Taking into account the wonderful natural features of Kumaon and Garhwal, and their relation to the religious history of India, it is not surprising that we should describe it as an Indian holy land. The late Mr. E. T. Atkinson, in his *Himalayan Districts*, admirably expresses this aspect of the country in the following words:—

"The importance of the Kumaon Himalaya in the

history of religion in India is mainly due to the existence therein of the great shrines of Badari and Kedar, containing forms of Vishnu and Siva which still hold a foremost position in the beliefs of the great majority of Hindus. To them the Kumaon Himalaya is what Palestine is to the Christian, the place where those whom the Hindu most esteems spent portions of their lives, the home of the great gods, the 'great way' to final liberation. This is a living belief, and thousands every year prove their faith by visiting the shrines. The later devotional works are full of allusions to the Himalaya, where Parvati was born, and became the wife of Mahadeo, and wherever a temple exists the celebrant sings the praise of Kedar and Badari, where live Mahadeo, Nanda, Narayan, and Lakshmi. To many the fruition of all earthly desires is the crowning glory of a visit to the sacred tirtha, by which the sins of former births are cleansed, and exemption from metempsychosis obtained. Here are laid many of the scenes in the life of the deities; here Rama propitiated Mahadeo; there with his consort, Sita, he wandered through the asoka groves. Here Arjuna and Krishna meditated on the Supreme Being, and the Pandavas ended their earthly pilgrimage. Each rock and rivulet is dedicated to some deity or saint, and has its appropriate legend. Nature in her wildest and most rugged forms bears witness to the belief that here is the home of the great gods; and when, wearied with toiling through the chasms in the mountains which form the approach to the principal shrines, the traveller from the plains is told to proceed in respectful silence lest the god should be angered, he feels the 'presence.' And should the forbidden sounds of song and music arise, and the god in wrath hurl down the avalanche on the offenders, then the awe-stricken pilgrim believes that he has seen the god, terrible, swift to punish, and seeks by renewed austerities to avert his displeasure. All the aids to worship in the shape of striking scenery, temples, mystic and gorgeous ceremonial and skilled celebrants, are present, and he must indeed be dull who returns from his pilgrimage unsatisfied."

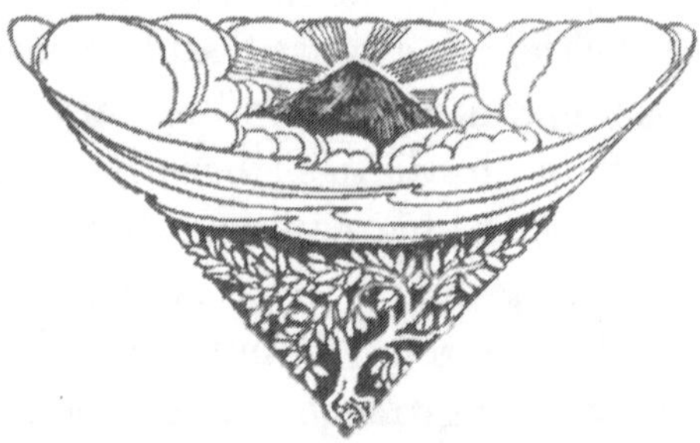

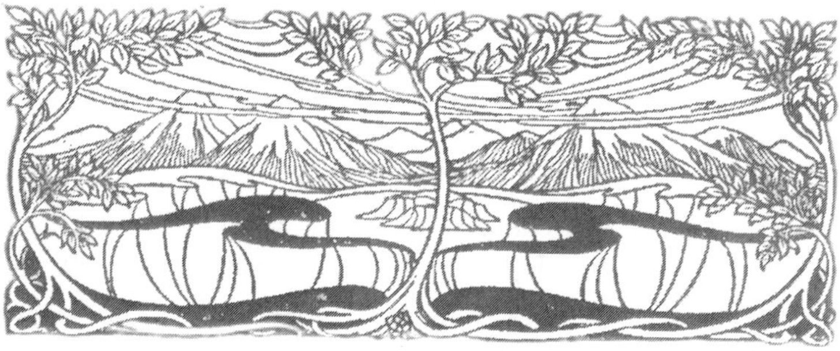

CHAPTER VII

KEDAR AND BADARI

AS we have already seen, the tract of mountainous country including the peaks of Badrinath and Kedarnath is regarded by vast numbers of Hindus as the holiest in India, and therefore in the whole world. It lies at the northern extremity of Garhwal, in British territory, and the authentic source of the Ganges is generally supposed to lie close to it, in the stream called the Bhagirathi which flows down from Tihri or Independent Garhwal. A glance at the map of the district, however, shows that neither this stream nor the Mandakini, which takes its rise in the glacier of Kedarnath, is so long as the higher branch of the Alakananda river, into which they flow as tributaries, and which has its source in the Rakhas Tal, close to the Mana pass, which crosses over into Tibet at a height of 18,000 feet, and lies about thirty miles to the north-east of Kedarnath as the crow flies. Yet it has always been the custom to regard the Bhagirathi as the true source of the Ganges. The question is now one of little general interest, but there was a time when the minds of the British in India were considerably exercised about it, as so many fabulous stories were current, and there was no ready access to the

Himalayan snows before the British occupation of Kumaon. In the eleventh volume of the *Asiatic Researches* we find an account of an expedition undertaken in 1808 by a Captain Raper to discover the sources of the Ganges, and an essay by the famous Colebrooke "On the Sources of the Ganges in the Himadri or Emodus." These are still well worth reading, and I have culled a good many facts from them for other portions of this work.

The twin peaks of Kedarnath and Badarinath rise at a distance of but ten miles apart, the former being 22,853 feet and the latter 22,901 feet above sea-level. Perhaps nowhere do the snowy summits appear grander than here. From a point a few miles down the valley of the Mandakini the two sharp peaks seem to pierce the very skies, and the white battlements, with their enormous slopes of smooth and shining snow, tower into the air in a wonderful manner. Travellers have dwelt enthusiastically on the scene. At the pilgrim's feet, edging the beds of snow which the pilgrim has to traverse at intervals, grow a profusion of pale rose-coloured auriculas and yellow primroses of delicious fragrance. He passes through primeval oak-woods, the gnarled boughs of which are festooned with long white moss, thick ivy, and beautiful festoons of creepers, while here and there are mingled great walnut, chestnut, maple, and hazel trees. As he mounts the steep, the woods become thin and scanty, but their place is taken by roses and syringa bushes of powerful scent. So strong is the fragrance of the flowers near the border of eternal snow, that travellers have sometimes been overpowered by it; and this, combined with the rarity of the air, producing a feeling of faintness, has no

Badrinath and Kedarnath Peaks in Garhwal

doubt contributed to the belief in the peculiar presence of the gods in such places. A native informant tells me that the pilgrims fortify themselves with large quantities of peppers and cloves to eat, as a safeguard and tonic against the strong scent of the flowers and the rarity of the air.

Strange sounds are also heard in that rarified atmosphere, the effect probably of distant avalanches and rendings of the ice and snow, but which superstition has fancied to be the voices of the gods, assembled for sport or council. The whole tract of Kedar is full of shrines and holy places, whose fame and efficacy is described in the Skanda Purana. Indeed, that precious collection of marvels has a special section or chapter devoted to this region. Parvati, the wife of Siva or Mahadeo, is represented as conversing with her spouse —a frequent device of introduction in the Puranas— and inquiring what are the fruits of visiting its sacred places and bathing in its waters. Mahadeo answers, "The place that you have spoken of, O goddess, is peculiarly dear to me. Brahma and the other gods are there; whoever dies there becomes one with Siva. If anyone desires salvation, he shall find it there; though his sins were as great as can be imagined, the virtue that accrues from a visit to Kedar is sufficient to cleanse them." In proof of this sin-cleansing potency of the region sacred to Mahadeo, stories are related of great sinners whose crimes were absolved by visiting it, even though involuntarily. A crow, for example, carried the bone of a deceased sinner, and dropped it there, whereupon the man's soul, though he had been guilty of the most flagrant crimes, was borne to heaven, and all his sins were forgiven. A hunter (who as a slayer of living souls is supposed to have forfeited future happiness) once threw his dog into the pool of Tungeshwar Kshetra. The dog on coming out shook itself, and some drops fell on his master. Such was the efficacy of even this partial sprinkling that both dog and man were carried off at once to the heaven of Siva. Bathing at the shrine of Kanwa near Badrinath releases even thieves and slayers of kine or Brahmans (sinners of the deepest dye) from the just penalty of their sins. The water of the Sailodak spring if applied to the eyes enables one to see hid treasure. "Whatever be a man's desire, he will obtain it by worship at Badari; and whatever may be his sins, they will be forgiven if he supplicate the deity through the priests of Badari and Kedar." However we may regard such undeserved remission, in which there is no mention of either repentance or purifying penance, the purpose for which these narratives have been strung together is obvious enough. One of the early Anglo-Oriental scholars is said to have detected his own pandit (or Sanskrit tutor) forging some new chapters to these books; and no doubt large portions of the Puranas, and especially this Skanda Purana, have but little claim to antiquity. At the same time, they are almost the only sources of information regarding the religious history of India, and embody a great mass of more or less reliable tradition.

The great pilgrim routes to Kedar and Badari are, first, the road passing from Hardwar, where the Ganges debouches from the hills, up the course of the Alakananda, by way of Srinagar and Rudraprayag; and secondly, the one that passes through Kumaon by way of Dwarahat and Karnaprayag. The journey by the latter route is one of endless variety and charm. At one time the traveller surmounts passes of great height, at another time winds along dark gorges, with occasional views of the great peaks, their silvery glory, bright against the deep-blue heavens, amply repaying him for the toil of the way. The richest vegetation is always to be found between the heights of 6000 and 10,000 feet. In autumn the ground in many places is covered with flowering plants—white anemone, columbine, and a kind of strawberry of delicious flavour that grows in great abundance, as well as the common *Fragaria indica*, resembling a raspberry. In a few places one still sees the "jhula" or rope-bridge, though these have been improved away on the main roads. They were once the only means of crossing rivers in the Himalayas. Two strong ropes of twisted grass are stretched across from cliff to cliff, and to these are attached shorter ropes supporting transverse pieces of wood, while over the latter are laid lengths of split bamboo, upon which the passenger has to walk. The track or footway is only about ten inches wide, and the whole affair swings about in an alarming fashion. In construction, however, it is evidently the forerunner and model of the modern suspension-bridge which has now replaced it. Another kind of bridge is called a "sangha," and consists of a couple of fir trees roughly thrown across the chasm. A sad story is told in connection with an obscure grave in the garden of a bungalow at Hawalbagh, the earliest European settlement in Kumaon, five miles from Almora, in the valley of the Kosi. Curiously enough, it has to do with the very route which we are describing in this chapter. It is taken from the interesting series of sketches entitled "Almoriana," by V.

"In 1827 a young girl, Miss Elizabeth Salmon, and an officer, whose name is given in an old account as Major H—, were travelling between Banjbagar and Ramni, about fifty miles north of Almora. They had to cross the Mandakini by a primitive bridge formed of two fir spars thrown across the river, with planks nailed down on them. In the middle of the bridge they stopped and began to amuse themselves by causing it to sway up and down with their weight. The bridge either broke or escaped from its anchoring, and the two were thrown into the swollen stream. The man was washed ashore at once and escaped; the girl, who a moment before had laughed and played above the roaring torrent, was carried down by it. Here (to Hawalbagh) she was brought and buried, and here till four years ago, when a village lout wantonly destroyed it, a marble slab fixed in the masonry of the tomb told her tragic story. Its fragments now lie in the verandah of the Old House, but the peach trees still surround, and the deodar still sweeps, her forgotten grave. And down below, the Kosi still runs babbling on, and the pine trees still wave on its far bank, and from among them comes, as doubtless it did seventy years ago, the plaintive song of the wandering cowherd."

A traveller who visited the holy ground so long ago as 1847,[1] yet whose account is still one of the brightest and most vivid, tells how one evening, about a score of miles from Kedarnath, and high up in the mountains, he and his company reached the lovely

[1] Dr. W. Hoffmeister, *Travels in Ceylon and Continental India.*

mirror-like lake of Durital. After walking round its shores they espied under an overhanging cliff a tent pitched, in front of which were seated some figures clad in robes of yellow silk. It was the Rawal or High Priest of Kedarnath, who had come out to meet their party and offer his respectful salutations. A few moments after, his approach was heralded by the loud discordant sound of long trumpet-like wind-instruments. Ere long, the Rawal appeared, a handsome man in the prime of life, with noble features marking him as a Hindu of the purest race. He distributed a number of presents, consisting of sweetmeats, cashmere shawls, yak-tails, musk, and a bowl full of rupees. Next day he led them to Ukhimath, where he resides, though it is some miles from the Kedar temple, his "chelas" or disciples taking duty in turn at the shrine among the snows. The dwelling of the Rawal of Ukhimath was then a large square building, with galleries surrounding a central court, and a "dewal" or temple. Both he and his associates are always from Southern India, and belong to the sect of Namburis in Malayalam. The reason of this anomaly is that the worship at this place was restored and organised by the famous Sankara Acharya, the apostle of revived Brahmanism, about 800 A.D., when he visited the Himalayas. In many places of the Himalayas he seems to have introduced his own countrymen and disciples as celebrants in the chief temples, and in no less than four of the five temples forming the Kedar establishment are Namburis of his own tribe in Malabar. He is said to have died at Kedarnath, though there does not appear to be any special memorial of him existing there. This remarkable man may be reckoned among the "worthies" of the province, owing to the important part played by him in its religious history, and his death within the sacred boundary of Kedar. Sankara Acharya must be regarded as one of the greatest spirits and most influential personalities of the world. There is, in fact, no one, with the single exception of the Buddha, in the range of Indian history who approaches him in greatness of mind. There have been monarchs, like Asoka or Akbar, whose names are better known, but Sankara by sheer force of intellect rose from a humble position to sway kings and empires and inaugurate vast religious changes throughout the length and breadth of India. The times were no doubt favourable. Buddhism had become a corrupt superstition, and no longer held the minds of men in thrall. The forces of Brahmanism, which had been kept in check by its great religious rival, were aroused, and the favour of the great was to a large extent secured by the new movement, yet it is simply amazing to read of the achievements of this young Hindu, who died at the early age of thirty-two, leaving behind him an array of literary works that might well have occupied three ordinary lives, and which all rank among the most valuable theosophical treasures of Sanskrit literature. His boundless zeal in preaching the dogmas of Brahmanism, reforming its sects, settling its disputes, defining its bounds, and organising its priestly constitution, in addition to founding a sect of his own, the tenets of which strongly resemble the philosophic theism of our own day, represents an amazing output of energy. The attraction that drew him from far-off Malabar to these northern mountains must have been their well-established sacredness as the home of the gods, especially of Siva, for whose worship he seems to have had a decided preference.

The glen of the Mandakini, along which the pilgrim road advances, is mostly narrow, wild, and precipitous. At the point where it bends to the south, a few miles from the source, it receives the waters of the Basuki river, the magnificent falls of which, 150 feet in depth, descend with deafening roar and angry spray. The path becomes narrower and more difficult, until it consists only of steps in the rock, from which the eye looks downward to the torrent at a fearful depth below. The sides of the rocky cliffs are bare, but crowned on the top with rhododendron, oak, and pine. The temples of Gaurikund are next reached, where are some hot springs, situated only a few yards from the river. The pilgrims are accustomed to bathe in the water, although in the chief pool it has a temperature of not less than 125° F. The more timid, especially the women, may be seen popping in a foot and quickly withdrawing it, while some of the faqirs, with heroic indifference to pain, stand in the bubbling waters, only betraying their sufferings by a most doleful expression of countenance. Three immersions are prescribed by religious custom, and the garments are next washed, with the recitation of many prayers.

From this point the road, still narrow and steep, winds along the ledge of rock above the deep glen of the Mandakini, ascending 5000 feet before reaching the temple that is the goal of pilgrimage. The river roars with hollow sound far below, often hidden from view, the tops of the cliffs and the slopes being clothed with noble forest. Then as the rocky path mounts yet higher and higher, the forest trees give place to stunted bushes, and the scene becomes more desolate and wild. A splendid waterfall is seen descending, in several cascades, over a precipice some hundreds of feet in depth; and then Bhimudiar, the last resting-place of the pilgrims on the road to Kedar, is reached. The valley rises more steeply after this is passed, and beds of snow begin to cross the path, covered in parts with fallen stones. The river itself at most seasons of the year is vaulted over with arches of snow, under which it pours its rushing stream. The ground, even here, is covered with vegetation—dwarf rhododendron, iris, and anemone give beauty to the slopes.

Suddenly the pilgrim finds himself in the vale of Kedar, encircled by mountains and high frowning crags. The valley is over 11,000 feet above sea-level. To the north rise great banks and heaps of darkened snow and rubble, and to the north-east is seen the lofty peak of Kedarnath or Mahapanth. Some hundred feet above the valley and its snow is the rock from which the river takes its rise. Its precipice is famed as the Bhairava Jhamp or "leap," from which pilgrims used to cast themselves, offering their lives to the god, until the practice was stopped by order of the British Government. We are told that formerly the immolation was celebrated with imposing rites. A musical procession accompanied the victim, and he was sent to his death with solemn prayer and song. In former times, also, it was no uncommon thing for pilgrims to give up their being to Mahadeo by climbing up among the snows until overcome by fatigue and cold, when they sank down, to sleep and wake no more. It is not impossible that the practice may still prevail, or, at any rate, that accidents of the kind may still occur to the fainting, weary pilgrims, many of whom are insufficiently fed and clothed, and whose fanaticism hardly knows any bounds.

The temple of Kedarnath stands in the bottom of the valley on a slight elevation of heathy ground. The beautiful violet auriculas so common in this region grow profusely round it. The building is neither large nor of great age, though the basement, and some capitals of pillars strewn near by, are evidently much older. It is popularly believed that the god Siva sometimes manifests his presence in visible form on the peak above, and that the snow-showers seen blowing from it are wreaths of smoke from sacrificial fires.

BADRINATH.

The great rival of Siva, the god Vishnu, though his special followers are not so numerous in the hills as in the plains of India, yet commands the worship of large numbers in the province, and his favoured dwelling-place at Badrinath is annually visited by large crowds of devotees from distant places. Indeed, a large proportion of the pilgrims visit both tirthas. There is very little sectarian animosity at present in North India, and orthodox Hindus, Brahmans at any rate, pay almost equal regard to the five deities of modern Hinduism—Siva, Vishnu, Devi, Ganesa, and the Sun.

The name Badari is said to be derived from "badari," the jujube tree, though that tree does not seem to grow near the temple of Badrinath. Wherever the worship of Vishnu prevails, the name is found, and evidently rests on some ancient, now forgotten, connection between the god and the tree. Thus there are four temples bearing the name in Kumaon, and an equal number in Garhwal.

The famed and original shrine of Badrinath stands not far from the river Alakananda in a valley about a mile broad, between two great peaks, the Nar and Narayan Parbat. One of the temples is said to have been built by Sankara Acharya a thousand years ago. It has a copper-plated roof and gilded ball. The antiquity of this temple is however very doubtful, as most of the ancient buildings in Garhwal have perished in the severe earthquakes that have again and again laid waste the province. In the account of the expedition undertaken in 1808 to discover the source of the Ganges (*Asiatic Researches*, vol. xi.), the tumble-down condition of nearly all the temples and other edifices at Barahat, Srinagar, and throughout Garhwal generally, is described, due to the great earthquakes of 1803. Here also is a hot spring; so hot, indeed, that the water has to be mixed with colder fluid from a neighbouring spring before it can be used for bathing. The efficacy of an ablution at this place (which has to be well paid for) is so great that from five to ten thousand pilgrims, mostly ascetics, visit it every year, and in the Kumbh season, every twelfth year, the number rises to thirty or forty thousand of all classes. The special sacredness of the twelfth year, when all melas or religious fairs appear to have fourfold popularity and efficacy, is because in that year the planet Jupiter is in the sign of Aquarius.

The "season" at Badrinath lasts only from June to November, as during the rest of the year the place is covered with snow. The high priest, as at Kedar, is called the Rawal, and there are always several aspirants for the office about him. They belong to the same caste as the Kedarnath Rawal—the Namburi Brahmans from Malabar. The services for pilgrims are of a severely simple character, consisting of the chanting of a short litany, bathing, and, in the case of orphans and widows, shaving the head. The following is Mr. Atkinson's description of the idol and his worship at Badrinath.

"The idol in the principal temple is formed of black stone or marble about three feet high. It is usually clothed with rich gold brocade, and above its head is a small mirror, which reflects the objects from the outside. In front are several lamps, always burning, and a table, also covered with brocade. To the right are the images of Nar and Narayan. The idol is adorned with one jewel—a diamond of moderate size—in the middle of its forehead; whilst the whole of the properties, including dresses, eating vessels, and other paraphernalia, are not worth more than five thousand rupees." (There must have been more formerly, as once some Garhwal robbers made their way across the snows in winter and carried off some 90 lb. weight of gold and silver vessels, but were seized and punished by the Garhwal Government.) "A good deal of ostentatious attention is paid to the personal comforts of the idol at Badari. It is daily provided with meals, which are placed before it; and the doors of the sanctuary are then closed, and the idol is left to consume its meals in quietness. The doors are not opened again until after sunset; and at a late hour, its bed having been prepared by the attendants, the doors are again closed until morning. The vessels in which the idol is served are of gold and silver; and a large establishment of servants is kept up, both male and female, the latter as dancing-girls and mistresses of the celibate priests. The only persons who have access to the inner apartments are the servants, and no one but the Rawal himself is allowed to touch the idol."

In this connection I may mention that a short time ago a native friend brought one of the oldest members of the priestly fraternity at Badrinath to visit me in Almora. The old man appeared to be of a free-thinking turn, and had given up all belief in idols and pilgrimages. He declared that he believed in a Supreme God and in doing good—the rest was nothing; and proceeded to recite some verses of his own composition to this effect which reminded one of the effusions of the famous Kabir.

The Rawals both of Kedar and Badari have authority over other foundations, Saivite and Vaishnavite, in Garhwal and Kumaon; they in fact exercise episcopal supervision over many temples, and have done so ever since the time of Sankara Acharya. A melancholy interest attaches to the Siva temple of Kamaleshwar in Srinagar, formerly under the Kedar Rawal's control. That town, with nearly all of its relics of antiquity, was swept away by the bursting of the Gohna lake a few years ago. At this temple, on a certain night of the year, it was customary for women who desired offspring to attend the services, each with a pair of small lamps alight on her upturned palms; and thus they remained before the god during the whole night, performing their ablutions in the morning, and presenting fees to the priest.

There are other minor tirthas of great fame and

sanctity, in addition to these described, such as Joshimath, Gangotri, Deoprayag, etc., but the accounts of Kedar and Badari will suffice to give some idea of the scenery and character of all.

The large number of ascetics (Yogis, Bairagis, and Sanyasis) visiting the shrines is accounted for by the fact that persons desiring to acquire merit or get rid of their sins by making the painful pilgrimage, forsake their ordinary avocations for the purpose, and adopt the dress and habits of the Indian devotee. Men or women, for instance, who have lost husband or wife or children, believing themselves to be under the curse of the god for some offence committed in the present or some former existence, will become faqirs, and set out on pilgrimage, even at an advanced age; while many devout Hindus all their lives cherish the intention of some day undertaking the great penance, and when ordinary claims are fulfilled and opportunity occurs in later life, they carry out the pious resolve. At the same time, there are many who become Yogis at an early age and follow the calling through life. The Yogis or Yoginis having abandoned caste, and even given up their former name and identity, it is impossible to know who or what they are. People of all classes are included in their ranks, from the high-placed official or Rajput of noble family down to the lowest of the people. Many are no doubt sincere in their profession, but popular opinion sets a poor value on the class as a whole; and the abandonment of name, duty, and responsibility by so many must inevitably lead to abuses and the admixture of not a few "black sheep," who have but little religion or self-respect, and are fed and tolerated only because their curse is dreaded by the average Hindu more than anything else. Some years ago there was an ascetic living by a lonely temple a mile or two from Almora—a weird spot overshadowed by huge pipal trees—who was a Brahman graduate of Calcutta University, and had been a magistrate in Bengal. He spent his time in meditation and prayer, and was much reverenced by the people of the town, who would go out to consult him on difficult matters and take spiritual counsel. When asked why he had adopted such a mode of life, he would answer that he aimed at becoming one with the Universal Spirit. He was, in fact, a follower of the Yoga theosophy, and was practising the lesson of "detachment" in that solitary place.

"Tapoban" means "forest of recluses or ascetics." An Almora Brahman tells me that the place of that name in Garhwal is still frequented by devotees who desire to carry out the old Hindu regulations for observing the four periods of a Brahman's life—Brahmachari, Grihasth, Banprasth, and Sanyasi, or the stages of student, householder, forest recluse, and wandering devotee absolved from all social trammels. At the time of my informant's visit to the place there were about two hundred residents for religious purposes, as well as numbers of pilgrims sojourning there on their way to and from the great tirthas. The recluses were fed by several wealthy and charitable persons, who had established lodges or places for food supply in the neighbourhood.

The Vaishnava ascetics are called Bairagis, and those who follow Siva are called Sanyasis. Especially in Southern India, there is great rivalry, and even animosity, between the sects, which does not prevail in Northern India to the same extent, at any rate among ordinary people, though the special devotees of the sects used sometimes to come into collision, and when collected in great numbers, as at Hardwar during the great bathing festival, there were occasionally sanguinary combats. It is said that on one occasion eighteen thousand Bairagis were left dead on the field. We sometimes read of these great troops of ascetics joining themselves to an army in time of war, and deciding the conflict by their reckless bravery. The Sanyasis and Gosains (who are devotees of Siva) do not as a rule wear sectarial marks, but shave the hair of the head and face, and often wear a "jata" or wig of reddish coiled and matted hair, giving them a wild and unearthly appearance. They cover the body with wood ashes, as a sign of their abandonment of the world (and perhaps to preserve the warmth of the body). They carry a deer or leopard skin as dress, and in their hands are a pair of tongs for making their fires, a vessel formed of the shell or rind of a gourd to receive gifts of food, and a water-jug of peculiar shape, with a handle over the top of it.

An ascetic whom I met walking about in Almora a short time ago was an astonishing person. He wore a huge jata or wig of the most imposing style, and a short yellow robe, encircled by a belt with several bells attached to it. In the belt was a long and formidable-looking iron implement. His face and limbs were plentifully besprinkled with ashes, and in his hands were large brazen cymbals, which he clashed together noisily, bellowing the while in a most mournful fashion some mystic syllables which sounded like "Aum, Bhaum!" repeated many times.

He was the "dandiest" of the class whom I had ever seen, and probably his get-up was designed to attract attention.

A remarkable sect of devotees found in these hills are the Kanphata Yogis. The name means "ear-split," and they are so called because on initiation the lobe of the ears is widely pierced and a large pendant of rhinoceros horn, agate, or gold is passed through it. One of the two figures in the illustration here given will be seen to wear the large earrings. Crooke (*Tribes and Castes of the N. W. P.*) says there are over three thousand of these Yogis in Kumaon, and over three hundred in Garhwal; but Atkinson states that the rites peculiar to the sect are more common in Garhwal than in Kumaon. These statements may perhaps be reconciled, as Garhwal is largely frequented by pilgrims and wandering faqirs, and possibly many of the sect may have there preferred to conceal their adhesion to it at the time of the census. The garments of the Kanphatas are ochre coloured. They act as priests in the temples dedicated to Bhairava, a wild mountain deity who in modern times has been identified with Siva. They are said to follow the left-handed ritual, and to direct their worship chiefly to the "sakti" or female energy of the god. In popular religion a distinction is recognised between the followers of the right-handed and left-handed worship both of Vishnu and Siva. The former are more orthodox, and their rites are not disfigured by immorality. They offer the usual five oblations of milk, curds, ghee, honey, and sugar. The left-handed sects, on the contrary, are guided by the "tantras," or magical treatises of later invention, which seem to have been produced in

Bengal. Instead of the orthodox offerings, they make use of the elements of the five Makara, or words beginning with M, namely, matsya (fish), mansa (flesh), madhya (wine), maithuna (women), and mudra (mystical gesticulation). Their ceremonies are practised in secret, and are indescribable here. Wilson in his *Essays* defines their character with sufficient plainness. In Bengal especially these vile practices are said to have unfortunately spread to a lamentable extent. In the hills, the Kanphatas mainly are associated with such rites. They profess that there is no need to restrain the passions in order to obtain absorption in the deity. The god or goddess, indeed, seems to be regarded as the patron of vice. They have several large establishments in the province. There is little doubt that the kind of religion thus typified belonged to the non-Aryan aborigines, and made its way into Hinduism at a later period, taking hold of both Buddhism and Brahmanism in the early centuries of our era. The worship of Bhairava and Nagraja in the Himalayas is of the real orgiastic type that has led to the savage representations of Siva and Kali. Human offerings appear to have at one time been common, tradition pointing to several places in Kumaon as ancient seats of such sacrifice. In Tallades, for example a goddess was wont to be propitiated with human victims, and she is still declared by the priests to be one with the Kali worshipped at Calcutta with bloody rites. It is well known that right up to modern times various backward tribes of aborigines in India have been in the habit of occasionally offering human sacrifices, as is sufficiently attested by the criminal records of the country.

The Kanphatas belong to the class of devotees called Dandis, who are chiefly attracted to the worship of Siva as Bhairava, whose initiation ceremony always consists in drawing blood as an offering to the god. In some sects this is done by making an incised wound in the knee. In the case of the Kanphatas the *ear* is selected for this purpose, probably because the piercing of the ear and wearing of the earring is a more permanent and conspicuous mark of devotion to the service of the deity. These devotees do not burn their dead, but bury them in a kind of coffin and in an upright posture; or else, if the Yogi is the disciple of a poor man without landed property, they throw the corpse into a river. It has been surmised that they are really the same as the Kapalikas, who were so called because they used to drink out of human skulls (kapala). The Chinese pilgrim Hwen Thsang in the seventh century mentions them, and says that they used to wear about them a death's head, which they used as a drinking-vessel. The curious small double-headed drum, narrow in the middle, used by Buddhist mendicants in Tibet (I have one of these in my possession), and also used, I am told, by some Hindu ascetics, is said to represent the original form of two skulls joined base to base. Wilson translates from the Sankara Vijaya the following description of the Kapalika ascetic: "His body is smeared with ashes from a funeral pile; around his neck hangs a string of human skulls; his forehead is streaked with a black line; his hair is woven into the matted braid; his loins are clothed with the tiger skin; a hollow skull is in his left hand (for a cup), and in his right he carries a bell, which he rings incessantly,

Kumaon Yogis

exclaiming aloud, 'Ho, Sambhu Bhairava—Ho, lord of Kali.'"

In the interesting photograph here presented there are members of two classes of ascetics. The man on the right is a Kanphata, as is shown by the huge earrings. The elder man is a Jangama or Lingayat, a sect which always wears the emblem of Siva on some part of the dress or person. In this case it is seen on the head, forming part of the turban. They wear necklaces and carry rosaries of the rudraksha seed, and have garments of ochre colour. They are in some parts of Northern India occasionally met leading about a bull, the favoured beast of Siva, adorned with cowrie shells and other trappings. The conductor rings a bell and collects alms.

CHAPTER VIII

THE GREATER GODS

POPULAR religion in the Himalayas may be conveniently divided into two main types—the worship of the greater gods of modern Hinduism, and that of the local deities. In this respect there is a general likeness to the whole of North India, with the exception that the local godlings are perhaps more in evidence here than in other parts of the country.

The Hindu religion is certainly a very complex and mentally confusing subject, yet it is hard to understand why there should be such complete misconception with regard to it as one finds often even among cultivated people. I was once assured by a literary man of some repute, in England, that all the people of India were Buddhists, and my modest objection to the statement was overridden with some asperity. It may not be wasted effort, therefore, to offer a few general remarks on the religious history of India, with a view to rendering clearer the subsequent description of our own particular corner of it.

The religions of India present a vast, unrestrained, and naïve development of fancies, theories, and aboriginal customs. No line of thought that has ever been struck out in Europe is totally unrepresented in India; and in any modern Indian city, as has been well remarked, one may meet with types of spiritual theory broadly corresponding to those we find dividing men's minds in the West. Yet through the greater part of this maze of cults and beliefs and speculations we can trace lines of growth and connection. It is indeed "a mighty maze, yet not without a plan." The special researches of Oriental scholars have placed within our reach a wealth of material from which it is possible to generalise.

The modern religion of Hindus, in its various aspects, is widely different, in external form at any rate, from the ancient faiths to which it owes its origin. Writers often forget or ignore this obvious fact, largely because the history of religion in Europe presents such a contrast to that of India. Christians have their Bible, the sacred canon, of restricted range and well-defined character, while the so-called sacred literature of Hinduism is well-nigh boundless in extent, and of the most varied and heterogeneous character. The European student is apt to suppose that the Hindu is necessarily acquainted with the history of his religion and knows something of its literature in general, yet even this is in most cases a wrong assumption. The individual Hindu dwells in some creek or backwater of the great river of Hinduism, and usually has no wide outlook over its expanse. Even learned pandits are usually confined in their sympathies and interests to one school or sect. The Hindu is no more necessarily acquainted with the sacred writings in detail than the modern Christian with the works of the Fathers and mediæval Schoolmen. The whole Sanskrit literature, sacred and secular, has been made in a sense canonical, and indeed is full of religious ideas, but there is nothing corresponding to our Bible in the hands of the people and generally recognised as the standard of faith. The Vedas have often been called the Bible of Hinduism, being regarded in a vague way as the divinely inspired foundation of religious truth, and the treasury from which speculation must draw its materials, and to which it must appeal for confirmation; yet practically the Vedas, in their great threefold division of Hymns, Brahmanas, and Upanishads, are unknown to all but a few. Portions of the hymns, in the collections called the Yajur and Sama Vedas, are used by ritual priests, but most of these men are but scantily, or not at all, acquainted with the meaning of the Sanskrit. It is a rather surprising fact that the Vedas are very little read by Indian Sanskrit scholars. Their language is archaic, and few are found who can grapple with the linguistic difficulties. In the town where the writer lives, though it is a renowned centre of Sanskrit learning, there is but one man who can read the Vedas in the original with proficiency. The Vedas are, in the sarcastic sense of the word, classics —often spoken of, nominally reverenced, but practically shelved. A Hindu writer of eminence, Babu Bankim Chander Chatterjea, says: "To the Indian student the Vedas are dead; he pays to them the same veneration which he pays to his dead ancestors; but he does not think that he has with them any further concern. They do not represent the living religion of India, and the only interest that can be felt in them by any human being is merely the historical interest."

The only real appeal made to them in modern times has been that attempted by the new reformed sects, the Arya Samaj and Brahmo Samaj, which have tried to evolve a consistent theistic religion out of them. To this we must add the recent revival of interest in the Vedantist philosophy or theosophy, due in the first instance to European scholars, and dating, as a popular Indian movement, from the visit of Swami Vivekananda to the Chicago Parliament of Religious, when it was rather prematurely reported that the West in its multitudes had taken to sitting at the feet of Indian religious teachers. The Vedantist movement has spread during the last few years among a certain proportion of the educated classes, more especially in Bengal and Madras. It is a mistake, however, to regard it as embodying Hindu religion. It is a philosophical creed, not a popular cult. India has its national worships and beliefs, closely bound up with the whole life of the people, and it is no more correct to regard Vedantism as its popular religion than to think of Hegelianism or Utilitarianism as the creed of European Christians. The religion of a nation must always centre round personalities, gods or heroes, and Vedantism is the most abstract of theories, the very negation of personality.

The gods worshipped by the Aryan invaders of India were mythological representations of the forces of nature: as, Indra, the rain; Agni, typifying both light and fire; Rudra, the storm that brings the rain; the Maruts, or wind gods; Ushas, the dawn. There seems to be a constant tendency in pagan religions to gradual supplanting of one god by another, or one set of deities by another set. In the Vedas we find traces of an earlier worship of elemental personifications, such as Mitra, the sun; Varuna, the widespreading heaven; and even earlier than him, Dyaus, the bright expanse of space. Dyaus has already been forgotten, and Varuna and Mitra are passing into obscurity in the Vedic period. Similarly, as time went on, the gods of the Hindus were no longer the Aryan deities mentioned in the Vedic hymns, but gods taken from the tribes amongst whom the Aryans had settled, and with whom they had become more or less amalgamated.

It was once the fashion to regard the Vedic religion as the great example of a primitive aboriginal nature-worship—the poetry of the unsophisticated early world. Such a view is no longer possible. Everywhere it is found that the primitive religious stage is one in which animism, fetichism, and "sympathetic magic" are the prevailing features. Only later, and mainly by deliberate priestly direction, does the religion attain to the idea of personal deities possessed of large or universal powers. There are abundant traces in the Vedas of such a stage having been passed through, and the collection of charms and incantations preserved in the Atharva Veda (many of which are probably more antique and representative than the hymns of the Rig Veda) proves the survival of earlier ideas into the later period.[1]

It is indeed difficult to say exactly what was the type of religion brought into India by the Aryans. The

[1] For a clear statement of the modern scientific view of Vedic religion, see Oldenberg's *Ancient India* in the "Religion of Science" Series; or, for a more detailed treatment, the same writer's *The Religion of the Veda* (1894).

Vedas represent the carefully sifted material preserved by the Brahmans. Popular religion and priestly literature are widely different things, though often the latest stages of a religion depend entirely on the literature. So much, however, can be inferred with certainty, that at first there was no precise definition of castes or classes. Caste was rather a matter of occupation than of descent, though probably there were leading families and warlike chiefs who assumed a natural leadership. Religious functions were undertaken mainly by the head of the family or clan. These consisted in sacrifices and simple offerings. Gradually a set of ministrants acquainted with the religious hymns and the ritual formed themselves into a separate class, and more and more elaborated the sacrificial system. These were the Brahmans, who tended to rate their services very highly, and showed a great deal of priestly pride. Rich presents were made to them by Rajputs, or warrior chiefs, who wished to gain divine favour by costly sacrifices. But the Brahmans were not unopposed in their pretensions. For centuries, if we may judge from the early Buddhist Pali records recently translated, they were not in a very powerful position, nor did they by any means succeed in impressing their authority on Hindus generally. There were rival religious movements, represented in later times by Jains and Buddhists. The Rajputs generally were inclined to resent the Brahmanical claims. In opposition to the wealth and dignity of the Brahmans, schools of ascetics arose, whose self-denial put them to shame. The sanguinary sacrificial system, with its costly elaboration and heavy burdens, roused strong opposition. Heterodox sects arose, mainly under the leadership of non-Brahmans. The Brahmans in course of time strengthened their position by adopting the tactics of the opposition,—becoming themselves ascetics and embracing the philosophical schools in their system,—but not till the great Buddhist schism had rent the nation into two main camps for nearly a thousand years.

Buddhism grew out of the general system of religion prevailing in North India among the "Aryan" population in the sixth century B.C. The caste system was then in full force; the Brahmans had become all-powerful in many quarters, imposing their hard and fast regulations on the whole social life of the people. Some of them gained fame as hermits and ascetics, while others were the bards or the spiritual advisers of kings, who were mostly of the Kshatriya class. At first the doctrinal differences were not so great as they afterwards appeared between Brahmans and Buddhists. They both started from a common point, the system of Kapila, usually called the Sankhya school. But the essential ground of divergence was the question of authority. Buddha and his followers assailed the supremacy of the Brahman; they refused to regard spiritual truth as his exclusive property or privilege; they set to work to teach the common people what they believed to be the saving principles of religion, without reference to priestly privilege, miracle, or mystery, and without recognising distinctions of birth or caste. Thus they cut away the ground of the whole system of sacrifice and the exclusive claims of the Brahmans. Animal sacrifice was entirely neglected by them. They dispensed with the worship of the Brahmanical gods, though not disputing their existence. Early Buddhism, as we see from the character of Asoka's edicts and the general tone of its early literature, was an earnest moral reformation. As time went on, however, the wild aboriginal elements of the population asserted themselves and united their savage cults and Tantric ritual with the purer Buddhism, until, about 700 A.D., there was little to choose between the Brahmanical and Buddhist cults. The Brahmans, however, had meanwhile adopted, and made themselves the priests of, a new set of deities, whose names are not met with in the Vedas, though endeavours have ever since been made to find references to them there, and numerous descriptive epithets found in the Vedas are now traditionally applied to the newer gods. In the name of this Hindu pantheon, and with the co-operation of many princes and chiefs, who probably were not averse to getting their share of the rich plunder of the Buddhist monasteries, which, like the English abbeys, had gradually acquired vast landed property, the Brahmans succeeded in suppressing and expelling the Buddhists throughout India, about 900 A.D. The Buddhists themselves had become corrupt and feeble, and seem to have had little strength of resistance. The special work of suppression undertaken by Sankara Acharya in the Himalayas has been already mentioned.

The gods of modern India are those we meet with in the literature of post-Buddhist times, namely, the five great deities still worshipped by orthodox Hindus—Vishnu, Siva, Devi, the Sun, and Ganesa. The Epics, the Ramayana, and Mahabharata no doubt carry us back to very ancient traditions of the Aryan race in India, but they have been greatly modified by subsequent Brahmanical manipulation. Lassen supposes, from internal evidence, that in the original Ramayana, Rama was not more than a hero-king, and that the deification of Krishna is also a later introduction in the Mahabharata. Rama and Krishna may now be called the popular gods of Hinduism, but their worship is of comparatively modern origin. Wilson remarks that in the Sankara Vijaya—a work describing the Hindu religion, written by Ananda Giri, a disciple of Sankara, not earlier than the tenth century A.D.—there is no allusion to the worship of Krishna, nor are Rama and Sita once mentioned as receiving any special adoration. Both are now regarded as incarnations of Vishnu, who has appeared on earth nine times for its deliverance from the powers of evil, and will appear once more as the Kalki incarnation. It is believed that he will be known in that avatar by possessing white blood in his veins; and in former years the ignorant villagers believed that vaccination officers were persons sent by the Government to find out the Kalki incarnation and put him to death.

If a Brahman be asked what are the gods worshipped by the Hindus, he will give the names of the five deities above mentioned, and declare that all receive adoration alike, except that one or other is often selected for special cult as the Ishta Devata, or "chosen god." This statement is true of Brahmans generally, but Hinduism is no such simple affair. There have been many reformatory movements, usually started by persons of humble rank, such as those of Ramananda and Kabir. These sects have usually attached themselves to the Vaishnava side of religion, and have repudiated the supremacy of the Brahman, many of them indeed making such rejection of his claims one of the principal articles of their creed. Dissenting sects are widely spread in some parts of India; and quite lately the followers of Kabir in Cawnpore and its neighbourhood have greatly increased in numbers and influence. The romance and spiritual interest of Indian religion largely centre round movements of this kind, and, if it were not too remote from our subject, it would be a pleasing task to describe some of these strange and sometimes beautiful developments of true religious sentiment among the obscure Vaishnava sects.

There are also the representatives of aboriginal cults, such as those of Bhairava and the Pasupati form of Siva in the Himalaya, and the innumerable worshippers of Kali or Durga in her various forms, who are called Saktas, or devotees of the Sakti or female energy of the god. These range themselves mostly, though not exclusively, under the denomination of Saivas (Siva worshippers). To these sects belong several large bodies of ascetics, who also decidedly reject the authority of the Brahmans. The special worshippers of the Sun and of Ganesa, the elephant-headed son of Siva and god of prosperity, are few in numbers and may practically be neglected. Ganesa is addressed by most classes at the beginning of a work and at other special times, for good luck. Shopkeepers at the head of their accounts put a trifling sum (about a farthing) to the credit of this god. Some devotees of Ganesa are said to mumble prayers to him with their mouths full. The Sun has a few temples in his honour in Kumaon, and is invoked, as everyone knows, in the famous Gayatri, the morning prayer of the Brahmans, addressed to the Sun under the ancient name of Savitri:

TAT SAVITUR VARENYAM BHARGO DEVASYA DHIMOHI
DHIYO YO NAH PRACHODAYAT,

"May we attain to (or let us meditate on) that excellent glory of the divine Savitri; so may he stimulate our minds (or prayers)." Wilson says that this was in its original use a simple invocation of the Sun to shed a benignant influence upon the customary offices of worship. It is a quotation from the Rig Veda.

It is commonly said that Brahma, the Creator, whose name is not mentioned in the Veda, is no longer worshipped in India. This is true, with some exceptions. His worship is still observed at Pushkara, near Ajmir, and generally he may be said to be worshipped along with other deities. The idea of a Trinity or Triad, consisting of Brahma, Vishnu, and Siva, is an invention of later times. There is no support for it in the Veda; and when it is sought there, theologians are obliged to substitute for Brahma the names of Visvakarma, Prajapati, or Hiranyagarbha, who in various passages are represented as exercising creative power.

On the whole, therefore, the popular religion of India may be said to centre round the persons of Vishnu, Siva, and the Saktis, or female energies of these gods, especially the consort of the latter, under the various names of Devi, Kali, Durga, Bhavani, Nanda, etc. Nanda is a very favourite object of worship in Kumaon. She has many temples dedicated to her in the province, where animal sacrifice is performed at stated seasons. In the summer of 1903 a severe outbreak of cholera occurred in Almora and its neighbourhood, and its cessation was popularly supposed to be due to the grace of the goddess Nanda—mainly, I suppose, from the idea that she had demanded victims and was at length satisfied. There were great offerings of buffaloes and goats at the temple of Nanda Devi on Sunday, 30th August. The villagers of Khatiyari, close to Almora, sacrificed a buffalo, the body of which I saw, decapitated, being dragged with ropes through the bazaar by a crowd of people beating drums and shouting frantically. Women of the lower class from neighbouring quarters, dressed in their best clothes, were running with vessels to secure their portions of the blood and flesh. The people of the Dumtola quarter, inhabited by artisans of the Dom caste, sacrificed a hundred sheep, every family in which a death had occurred making an offering. The wife of Siva in most of her forms is peculiarly fond of blood-offerings, and there is no doubt that in former times human sacrifices were offered to her.

Along with the mingled conflict and fusion of religious ideas that went on in India during the early centuries of the Christian era, there was combined a great activity of pagan cults belonging to the tribes surrounding and mixed with the Indo-Aryan settlers. The Vedic gods were to a large extent forgotten, or only brought to mind in so far as the Brahmans consistently sought to identify non-Aryan gods with the deities of the Veda, and to bring the new cult into line with the older system. This seems to be the explanation of a great deal of the confusing detail of Hindu mythology. It is well known that the policy of the Brahmans from earliest times has been to incorporate the beliefs of any new tribe with which they came in contact into their own system, insisting only that the local godling should be regarded as a form of one of their deities, and that the supremacy of the Brahman should be recognised. Wheeler, in his *History of India*, observes: "The missionary operations of the Brahmans are worthy of special study. They have been carried on from time immemorial, and the process is still going on amongst hill-tribes and other remote populations. A Brahman makes his appearance in a so-called aboriginal village, and establishes his influence by an affectation of superior sanctity, aided by the fame of his spells, incantations, mystic rites, and astrological predictions. He declares the village idol to be a form of one or other of the great gods or goddesses of the Brahmanical pantheon, and he professes to teach the true forms of worship. He divides the villagers into castes, and introduces caste laws. In this manner the populations of India have been brought under the spiritual domination of the Brahmans, and the caste system has been introduced into secluded regions in which it was previously unknown." The bearing of this is obvious on the controversy which took place some twenty or more years ago between Sir Alfred Lyall and the late Professor Max Müller as to the claim of Hinduism to be a missionary or proselytising religion.

The consistent policy of the Brahmans, and their peculiar and well-marked character, have led some to ascribe to them a special origin. I believe the theory has been propounded that they joined themselves to the Aryans from Babylonia or Chaldea when that people was dwelling in the neighbourhood of Ariana, and were originally a kind of Chaldean astrologers and priests. The thought has even occurred to one that the leading ancient priesthoods of which we have records in classical times, such as the Egyptian, the Greek, and the Druids of the Celtic races, were all originally Chaldeans issuing out of the immensely ancient civilisation of Babylonia, and carrying out a regular scheme of sophistication or regulation of tribal cults wherever they went. The keen Semitic faces of many of the Brahmans of North India might be pointed to in support of this contention. One would not at present, without much further evidence, be prepared to adopt such a conjecture; and the more prosaic explanation of the origin of the Brahmans given above seems more likely to be correct. Priestcraft is peculiar to no race or religion, and its developments are naturally much the same in every land.

In addition to this tendency to identify non-Aryan gods with the Vedic ones, it is to be remembered that there were rival cults whose claims had to be reconciled. Thus in the Epic and Puranic literature we find the endless fluctuating genealogies and the assertion of the claims of rival deities, especially Vishnu and Siva, first one of them being held to be supreme, then the other, and one alternately the creator and lord of the other. The Puranas furnish a striking illustration of this strange jumble. They, if anything, are to be regarded as the Bible of the Hindus, for the religious reading of a Hindu is usually limited to one or other of these voluminous compositions (of which eighteen chief Puranas are reckoned); yet surely nothing can be more confusing and illogical than the usual character of the narrative in these works. They have probably been worked over and over by recensors and copyists, in the interests of rival sects, until in the case of most of them it is quite impossible to determine what is the original matter. The Puranas are Brahmanical fictions, largely a literature in the air, expressing what the authors wished to be believed or had some interest in representing to be, rather than faithfully reflecting any actual religious events or ideas. Doubtless they reflect a good deal of the beliefs of the people, but their main object was to keep up the supremacy of the Brahmans as the exponents and hierarchs of national religion. It is wonderful how the Brahmans have succeeded in their persistent effort to gain supremacy. Their success is in a sense deserved, for it is the victory of awakened intellectuality and of superior vitality due to regulated living. It is wonderful how thoroughly, by means of their literature and their proselytising policy, they have managed to maintain their leadership and get their social codes and creeds recognised as the law and custom of the land in modern as in ancient India, while other equally national memories and institutions have sunk into oblivion. It is wonderful, finally, how they have succeeded in imposing their view of things Indian on the learned world in general, so that, to read a great part of the European literature on Indian subjects, one would imagine that the history of the Hindu religion comprised only the Veda, the code of Manu, and the philosophical systems; the truth being, as we now understand, that these are of subordinate importance in reference to the real religious history of India and its present condition.

Out of the welter of conflicting creeds and races that struggled for supremacy in India, while Buddhism, having exhausted its energies, was sinking into spiritual death (as regards its career on the Indian continent), during the period that corresponds to the Dark Ages in Europe, there emerge two great divinities, with rival systems attached to their names. The prior of these, and the one more closely identified both with the primitive cults and with Vedic practices, is *Siva worship.* As a god of terror and demonism, Siva is peculiarly the deity of mountain districts and aboriginal tribes, and the study of Himalayan religion proves that he represents a multitude of local godlings, all endowed with similar attributes. The Turanian races appear to have been deeply impressed with the mysteries of life and birth, and to have represented those ideas by phallic symbols. Brahma himself is held by some to have been originally a deity of this kind. The emblems of Siva worship are still the most common religious symbols in many parts of India, especially the Himalaya, and throughout the Saivite sects.

It has indeed been surmised that the so-called phallic symbols really represent an original worship of *mountains*, and that the Turanians on their progress southward must have sojourned among and passed near the great Himalayan peaks, carrying with them, even to the far south of India, the memory of those most striking natural features, and figuring them as the home of their gods. Impressive objects that obsess the imagination seem often to have given rise to aboriginal cults. It may be remarked in passing that the influence of *mountains* on early religious ideas is a subject that has yet to be inquired into. The late Professor Robertson Smith appears to have entertained some speculations of the kind with reference to Hebrew origins, but, so far as I am aware, the matter has never been thoroughly investigated. With regard to Siva worship and the phallic emblems, the evidence for any such theory is very incomplete. Parvati, the "mountain-born," and daughter of Himavat, is the consort of Siva, and there seems to have been an early and unexplained connection between the Saivites of Southern India and the Himalaya. The southernmost point of the Indian peninsula is called Kumari, one of the titles of Siva's wife. Sankara Acharya seems to have been more closely associated with Siva worship than with any other form of Hinduism (though theoretically a pantheist, or even theist), and he came to the Himalaya and re-established the centre of Siva worship at Kedar, placing men of his own country as ministering priests there, and in the Himalaya generally.

As the god of destruction and death, Siva appears to have been largely adopted by the Brahmans to represent their philosophical ideas. We must remember that the fiction of a pure Aryan descent for the Brahmans, as well as many other Hindu castes and tribes, covers an extensive early amalgamation with the non-Aryan peoples, so that the peculiar religious notions of later Hinduism cannot be said to be altogether foreign to the Hindus, who inherited them from their mixed ancestry. Siva worship, originally a propitiation of demonic powers, and related to sorcery and devil-dancing, has become in later times the chosen vehicle of the highest abstract principles. Destruction is the necessary step towards recomposition and regeneration; death and birth in the natural world are eternal correlatives, both mysteries beyond human comprehension, yet lying at the basis of all existence. Siva, therefore, is never worshipped as an idol in the human form: he remains a mystic symbol, under a form that appears gross and impure to the uninitiated, though suggestive only of abstract truth to the Brahman. Bloody sacrifice being a mark of nearly all aboriginal cults, even human sacrifice of many, the practice of offering animals, or substitutes for them, prevails to a large extent in Siva worship, and approximates it to the Vedic system, of which animal sacrifice was the very soul. With Siva also are identified the favourite Brahman doctrines of the identity of the human and divine soul, and absorption into the divine essence—the Vedantic creed. It is to be noted also that Saivism was much mixed up with Buddhism and the Tantric doctrines, which took their rise in Bengal and Assam. In addition to sacrifice, which is more commonly offered to the Sakti or female energy of Siva under various names, notably those of Durga and Kali, the Saivite worship is very simple. "Water is poured on the linga, flowers and other trifling offerings are made." There are no occasions of congregational worship. The description of Saivite worship given by H. H. Wilson may be quoted here. The tinklings of the bell alluded to therein are constantly to be heard as one passes these shrines. "A Hindu temple comprises an outer court, usually a quadrangle, sometimes surrounded by a piazza; and a central edifice, constituting the shrine. This, which in Upper India is generally of small dimensions, is divided into two parts,—the 'sabha' or vestibule, and the 'garbagriha' or adytum, in which the image (or emblem) is placed. The course of worship is the circumambulating of the temple, keeping the right hand to it, as often as the devotee pleases; the worshipper then enters the vestibule, and if a bell is suspended there, as is commonly the case, strikes two or three times upon it. He then advances to the threshold of the shrine, presents his offering, which the officiating Brahman receives, mutters inaudibly a short prayer, accompanied with prostration, or simply with the act of lifting the hands to the forehead, and departs. There is nothing like a religious service; and the rapid manner in which the whole is performed, the quick succession of worshippers, the gloomy aspect of the shrine, and the scattering about of water, oil, and faded flowers, inspire anything but feelings of reverence and devotion."

With regard to the Himalayan connection with Siva, it has been conjectured that Kedar was the original name of Siva, as the word has no real derivation in Sanskrit. It has been supposed also that "the symbol of the linga may have arisen from the pointed peaks around his original home." It may be added that the common idea of Siva as being a great ascetic engaged in tremendous austerities, by which he excels in power and merit all the other deities, has been ascribed to the phenomena of mountain storms and the perpetual rolling of thunder among the great snow-peaks, which may be taken to represent his repetition of prayers and charms in the vast solitudes of his mountain home.

Siva has been identified by the Brahmans with the Vedic Rudra, who seems to be a form of Agni, the god of fire and lightning. Rudra is represented as having fierce and terrible attributes as a god of destructive powers. The name Siva is an epithet meaning auspicious or gracious, and is applied euphemistically in the Vedic hymns to Rudra. The latter was originally a personification of the thunder, represented as helping Indra in his conflict with the Vritras, or hostile elemental forces that were opposed to the coming of the rain-shower. Rudra was a kind of forest-beater who roared in the heavens to frighten away the Vritras. In course of time he became the god of thunder, the howling, terrible god of storms, father of the Maruts or Rudras. Armed with a bow and arrows (the thunderbolts), he is called the slayer of men. Yet he has his beneficent side, inasmuch as the thunderstorm clears the air and softens the parched earth; therefore he is said to bring health and prosperity to men, and is possessed of healing powers. [In Mr. Batchelor's recent book on the *Folklore of the Ainu in Japan,* I find the ascription of healing power to the god of mountains.]

It is obvious that many of the attributes of the storm-god have been transferred to Siva. Some have thought that the location of Siva's dwelling in the Himalaya simply typifies the fact that the storm sweeps down from the mountains, which appear to be its home, while (as was said above) the muttering and continuous roll of the thunder reverberating among the mountains represents the invocations and ascetic exercises in which the god engages, and by which he obtains ever-increasing might and merit. He is represented as having a third eye in the centre of his forehead, with a glance of which he strikes and reduces to ashes those with whom he is offended, and this is supposed to refer to the destructive force of lightning; while the dread violence of duststorms and cyclones, tearing up trees and overthrowing the strongest buildings, sufficiently explains his attributes as the god of destruction. He is the god of reproduction, again, because the effect of the rainstorm is to soften the parched earth and clothe it with verdure; and he has healing powers, because the tempest clears the air and imparts a feeling of energy to mortals.

It is quite possible that the Rudra of the hymns was himself a local deity adopted by the Aryans at a later period than some of the other gods. His functions would only seem important when the Aryans had settled down to an agricultural life.

There is an interesting passage in the Satapatha Brahmana (i. 7. 3. 8), belonging, of course approximately, to the Vedic age, in which not only Rudra but some of the common appellations of Siva are mentioned: "If sacrificial food is offered to any deity, Agni, the maker of good offering, is afterwards invariably offered a share of it; because the gods always give him a share after themselves. The offering then is certainly made to Agni, for indeed Agni is that god; his are these names: Sarva, as the Eastern people call him; Bhava, as the Babihas call him; Pasunampati, Rudra, Agni. The name Agni is doubtless the most auspicious."

Eggeling regards this passage as specially interesting, "as showing, on the one hand, the tendency towards identifying and blending originally distinct and apparently local Vedic gods, especially Rudra, with the person of Agni, the representative of the divine power on earth in the later Vedic Triad; and, on the other hand, the origin of the conception of Siva in the pantheistic system of the post-Vedic period."

By "the later Vedic Triad" we suppose Agni, Vayu, and Surya are meant. The modern Triad, as everyone knows, is that of Brahma, Vishnu, and Siva. The last of these has undoubtedly replaced Agni, as is definitely suggested by the foregoing extract from the Satapatha Brahmana. Weber remarks that the "destructive power of fire in connection with the raging of the driving storm lies clearly enough at the foundation of the epic form of Siva." The same writer tells us that in the Brahmanas the names Siva and Sankara occur only as appellative epithets of Rudra, and never as proper names to denote him (*Hist. of Indian Lit.*, p. 303). We find, however, in the Kaushitaki Brahmana a reference to Isana and Mahadeva, though the passage is regarded by some as a later interpolation.

The curious fact that the Buddhists in Nepal were accustomed to worship Pasupati is recorded in local traditions (see Wright's *Nepal*, p. 178). It is said that Sankara Acharya, when engaged in his reforming work in Nepal, "turned out the Bauddhamargi-Grihastha Brahmans" (Buddhist householders, as distinct from monks), "who hitherto worshipped Pasupati, and appointed in their stead Brahmans from the Deccan."

The question naturally arises, What led Sankara to devote so much of his attention and reforming zeal to the Himalaya? He was himself a native of Travancore in the far south of the peninsula. Though primarily a follower and expounder of the Vedanta philosophy, he was, it seems, a devoted worshipper of Siva, whose incarnation he was afterwards believed to have been. He established great monasteries, where his followers might learn to practise his doctrines, in Mysore, Joshimath in Garhwal, at Dwarka, and at Puri, and is said to have died at Kedar in the Himalaya at the early age of thirty-two. Though he himself evidently preferred the worship of Siva among national cults, his doctrine really transcended the popular religion. As H. H. Wilson says: "His leading tenet is the recognition of Brahma Parabrahma as the sole cause and supreme ruler of the universe, and distinct from Siva, Vishnu, Brahma, or any individual member of the pantheon." At the same time, he recognised that men who had not attained to this highest conception of truth might with advantage worship individual gods, and he even re-established the worship of Siva and Vishnu, and allowed these lower religions to be taught by his disciples. He recognised as orthodox the following creeds, which still continue to be regarded in the same light in India:—the Saiva, the Vaishnava, the Saura (worshippers of Surya, the sun), the Sakta (followers of Devi, the female energy), the Ganapatya (worshippers of Ganesa), the Kapalika or Bhairava (another form of Siva worship).

It is remarkable that Siva worship should have taken such a strong hold in the far south of India as to cause the cape at its extremity to be called Kumari (Comorin), one of the names of the wife of Siva. We can only suppose that Siva in some early form was an important deity of the Turanian races who at some time or other invaded India from the north, and that his worship was spread among them extensively throughout the Indian continent. At first the Indo-Aryans would not be brought into very close contact with this form of worship, but as they penetrated into the Himalaya and into the Deccan and other parts of India, they would meet with it more, and consequently we have the gradual rise of Siva—at first under other names, as noted in the Brahmanas—to a prominent place in their mythology, as he became more thoroughly adopted by the Brahmans. This is, of course, no more than a hypothesis, but it appears to explain the facts better than any other theory. It is confirmed by the fact that there was a marked and early amalgamation between Buddhism and Siva worship, at any rate, in the Himalayan region.

In the Mahabharata, Krishna describes Siva as "Rudra with the braided hair and matted locks, shaven, frequenting cemeteries, the performer of awful rites, the devotee, the very terrible." He is thus described by his father-in-law, Daksha: "He roams about in dreadful cemeteries, attended by hosts of goblins and spirits, like a madman, naked, with dishevelled hair, laughing, weeping, bathed in the ashes of funeral piles, wearing a garland of skulls and ornaments of human bones, insane, beloved by the insane, the lord of beings whose nature is essentially darkness." In another passage he is described as "bearing the symbol adored by devotees, ashes, a staff, a tuft of hair, an antelope's skin, and a digit of the moon, his body shining like an evening cloud."

This notice of Siva and attempt to explain his origin and relation to earlier Vedic religion may suitably be closed with two illuminative extracts from Atkinson's *Himalayan Districts* (vol. ii. pp. 721 and 738). "Weber regards Siva as doubly derived from Agni and Rudra,—the howling storm and crackling flame,—both striking and terrible objects. Flame, the cause of wind, and wind, the cause of flame, unitedly formed the great terrible being. Hence the epithets assigned to him are separable into two classes. Those which make him the 'dweller on the mountains,' 'having dishevelled hair,' cruel, fierce, healer, auspicious, are derived from his character as lord of storms; and those such as 'blue-necked' (nilakantha), like wreathed smoke, golden-armed (hiranya-bahu), and thousand-eyed, like sparks, belong to him as lord of fire. In the older writings there is no trace of his names Isa or Mahadeva, or of his form as the linga or phallus."

The second extract deals with the connecting ties between Siva worship and Buddhism and modern Brahmanism: "We know that amongst the Buddhists the germs of the later Tantric beliefs and the advanced Sakti doctrines are to be found in the developed Sutras of the Mahayana school. These remained in abeyance for several centuries, but none the less achieved their object when revived by the successors of their founder (Nagarjuna). The same source gave the idea of Mahadeva to the Brahmanists; and thus the two great branches of mediæval religion sought by union with pre-Brahmanical beliefs to widen and establish on a broader basis their respective cults. The masses, through the popular deities, were brought into some semblance of obedience to priestly authority, and interest led the priests to retain the allegiance of the people by introducing order amongst the local gods, improving and extending their ritual and assimilating it to the highly complicated and ornate ceremonial of the Aryans. Once on the downward path along which all efforts to please the popular palate lead, the lower phases of demonism supplied both Buddhist and Brahmanist with the doctrines of advanced Saktism, magical rites and formulæ, and all the corrupted usages which mark the Tantras of both sects in their later developments. Learning was considered of no account, and the verses of the Vedas, becoming unintelligible to the celebrants, served only as wonder-working spells by which the gods were compelled to attend to the wishes of their worshippers."

The other great deity who divides the allegiance of India with Siva is Vishnu. He is incidentally mentioned in the Veda, where he appears as a sun-god, who traverses the heavens in three strides, representing his rise, meridian, and setting. It is difficult to say when and how the special worship of Vishnu arose. There seems to have been much contention between the followers of Vishnu and Siva after the time of Sankara, who had recognised both as orthodox forms of Hinduism. Wilson says: "Early in the eleventh century Ramanuja, a follower of Vishnu, undertook to depose Siva and set up his own divinity, not only in the belief of the people, but in the more substantial benefits of temples and endowments." The Vaishnavas spread rapidly in Northern India, under the followers of Ramanand, as disciples of Ramanuja. The popular cults of Krishna and Rama became associated with Vishnu worship, as incarnations of the god. In Western India the family of Vallabha set up as hereditary priests of the infant god Krishna, and the Krishna worship at Jagannath in Orissa originated in a similar way. The modern developments of religion belonging to the Bhakti or "Faith" department of Hinduism are mostly connected with Vishnu worship, and profess with rapturous fervour that simple devotion to the *names* of Rama, Krishna, or his wife Radha, without any further trouble, are sufficient to secure salvation. Some of the more spiritual sects, such as that of Kabir, also speak of the Divine Being under the name of Rama. The incarnations of Rama and Krishna represent the tendency to hero-worship and the longing for human sympathy. Vishnu under these forms has come to typify all that is favourable and happy in human life. He is the preserver, the protector of man against the powers of evil, the defender of the good old ways, the deliverer who from time to time has come down in varying form to free the suffering earth from the tyranny of monsters and wicked demons. The avatars or "descents" have been nine in number. In them some portion of the god's essence has been incarnated, either in some wonderful animal or superhuman form, or else as an heroic figure more or less historical, but finally regarded as a manifestation of the deity himself.

These avatars of Vishnu are: (1) The Fish (matsya). (2) The Tortoise (kurma), which he is said to have assumed in Kumaon (Kurmachal). (3) The Boar (varaha). (4) The Man-lion (nara-singha). (5) The Dwarf (vamana). (6) Parsu-Rama, a Brahman, champion of the Brahmans against the Kshatriyas. (7) Rama-Chandra, the hero of the Ramayana, who destroyed Ravana. (8) Krishna, who came to destroy the tyrant Kansa. (9) Buddha. By representing the last-named as an incarnation of Vishnu, no doubt an attempt was made to reconcile the Brahmanic and Buddhist religions, just as in modern times it has been proposed to regard Christ as a form of the same deity. A tenth and last descent of Vishnu is to take place at the close of the present or "kali" age, called the kalki or kalkin avatar. He is, according to some predictions, to appear in the heavens, only when the world has become utterly corrupt, seated on a white horse, for the punishment of the wicked, the rewarding of the righteous, and the restoration of the Satya Yuga, or age of Truth.

The earlier incarnations might almost be taken as symbolising man's gradual ascent through lower forms of animal ancestry, or at any rate of development from savagery. The later stages present the bright heroic figures of Rama and Krishna, most human of men in their earthly aspect, living a life of adventure, with keen affections like our own—life-stories that the Hindu mind loves to dwell on. Orthodox Vaishnavism differentiates the divine and human soul, and so allows of intelligent worship on the part of man and a reasonable theistic creed. It declares the world to be real, and in this respect its standpoint is more like the Veda than that of its rival. It generally supports caste and its distinctions and the Brahmanical supremacy; while Saivism, "borrowing largely from local cults, taking into its pale the aboriginal tribes and their village deities, is inclined to be careless in matters of caste and ceremonial, and neglectful of the priestly class." (The fact is that, according to the regular standards of life and doctrine, Brahmans are supposed to be spiritually above ministering to idols, and to look down with contempt on any of their number who officiate in such a capacity. Ministering priests are very often not of the Brahman caste.) Yet the theosophising spirit has dealt with these human personalities of Rama and Krishna also, and, as in the Mahabharata, has dressed them out in vague pantheistic trappings, though leaving aside the dark and mysterious elements that belong to the character of Siva. Animal sacrifices are entirely absent from Vaishnava worship, and meat-eating is generally abhorrent to its followers, at any rate in Northern India. (I observe that Abbé Dubois makes a quite opposite statement regarding the Vaishnavas of South India.)

Vishnu is the god of the contented middle classes, of those to whom life is dear and enjoyable; and in Krishna worship there has always been a tendency to exalt the pleasurable, and even to give a religious sanction to profligacy, which has been sadly illustrated in the case of the Vallabhacharis of Bombay, and similar instances. The idyllic shepherd life of Krishna with the Gopis of Brindaban expresses an ideal of light-hearted mirth and enjoyment that in the faulty constitution of human nature is only too ready to run into licence.

A Brahman of Almora, whose sympathies seem to be on the Vaishnava side, though he of course, like Brahmans generally in North India, as a Smarta, or follower of the orthodox traditions, acknowledges the legitimacy of Saivite worship, has supplied me in conversation with some information as to the cult of the *Di Majores* and the practices of Brahmans in this part of the country. His account may very possibly be found to differ in some particulars from other similar descriptions, but they have the merit of being locally correct, which is as much as can be demanded in India.

The Vaishnava temples are called Thakurdwara, or "gate of the lord." There are four of these in the town of Almora, and they are common throughout the province. They are separately named after either

Vishnu, the Sun, Badrinath, Krishna, or Nara Singha. Not only is there the usual worship and offering as described above, but a kind of popular service takes place at times in these temples, called Katha, when the smritis or shastras (sacred scriptures, including the Puranas) are read and expounded. A learned pandit is employed for this purpose and paid by subscription. In some temples such religious services or lectures take place only during the rainy season, when people have more leisure, from three to six in the afternoon. In others they are held all the year round. On festival days there is worship at the different temples, when the priests read portions of the Yajur Veda as prayers and invocations, and these are not explained.

All caste Hindus wear the "janeo" or sacred thread, which is put on with set ceremonial observances during boyhood, at eight or nine years of age. Before that period a child is not supposed to possess caste, and even the eating of forbidden food or association with casteless people is a matter of small consequence. After the janeo is assumed, caste rules must be strictly observed, and, as an Indian writer tells us, "a man of a lower caste might be dying, but a man of a higher one will never let him take water out of his cup, for fear of its being defiled." The ceremonies attending the first wearing of the thread resemble those of marriage. The higher castes who have the privilege of wearing it are called Dwija, "twice born." The boy then must always bathe before eating, and perform his religious duties. The thread passes over the right shoulder and comes down to the waist on the left side. Brahmans, Kshatriyas (the farmers), and Vaishyas (the shopkeeping class) wear a double thread of six strands.

Shudras and Khassiyas (the cultivators in Kumaon) wear only a single thread of three strands, as prescribed by the Hindu shastras. But nowadays, under foreign dominion, when there is no fear of Hindu rulers, other lower tribes and classes have adopted the janeo. In fact, in Kumaon the Doms alone refrain from wearing it.

Certain sectarial or religious marks are in common use. All are required to wear them on the forehead on festival days. The red mark, called "pitawa," in the middle of the forehead is auspicious, and must be worn on all occasions of marriage, feasting, or fasting. This red mark is common to all. The white or yellow marks differ. Thus ordinary people wear a white "chandan" mark on the brow shaped in a figure with the lines diverging upwards. The Vairagi or Vaishnava ascetic wears one shaped like a W, or a broader figure of the same kind. Other chandans consist of a waved line along the forehead, two parallel lines of the same kind, or a crescent. All of these are combined with the red dot or pitawa. These marks are affixed by the family priest, who visits the home on every festival day. The Saiva devotees are not in the habit of using any special marks. They usually shave off the hair of the face and head. Some put on a great wig of coiled hair (jata), which gives them a strange and terrible appearance. They cover their bodies with wood-ashes, carry tongs for their fires, a "tumba" or vessel made out of gourd for food, and a "kamandal" or water-vessel of peculiar shape, like a jug with two tiers or bodies and a handle over the top. They have also about them a skin of tiger, leopard, or deer, called the "mrigachala." Ordinary Saivas (not ascetics or Sanyasis) put a dot of "sendur" (red lead) on the forehead. The red marks,

Ascetics returning from the Great Pilgrimage

before referred to as commonly used on auspicious occasions, are made from the root called turmeric (haldi), boiled and ground. The white marks are made with chandan (sandalwood). A grain of rice is stuck in the centre of the forehead.

My informant tells me there is a distinct movement at the present time among the higher castes to give up the taking of animal life. Even the Kayasths (writer class) of the plains of India are giving up the eating of meat. Saivas also, when taking goats to the temple of Kali for sacrifice, are content to give a slight cut or scratch to the neck of the animal with the sacrificial steel, just enough to draw a drop of blood. In the hills, the Brahmans and Baniyas are giving up meat, but the sacrifices of animals still go on in Saivite temples and those dedicated to village deities, as their flesh is eaten by other classes.[1]

The *purohita* or *family* priest is usually an office hereditary in a family. A rich household may have one to themselves, though this would be rare. The purohita lives in his own house, and he and his sons, if he has any, visit a certain number of homes to perform religious ceremonies. They receive no regular fixed salary. On the occasion of a marriage they receive large sums, fifty or a hundred rupees at least. When the boys of a family have the sacred thread put on, the priest receives a good present. The sraddha ceremonies are also paid for. At minor festivals each family visited

[1] This modern movement, on the physical side, seems as self-destructive as the popular return to Puranic superstitions on the spiritual side. The two together may be called "India's Suicide." In another sense this abstention from flesh may be considered the final triumph of Buddhist principles in the land which has formally rejected Buddhism.

by the purohita will give him a small sum. Perquisites at sraddhas given to the purohita for the performance of the ceremonies are cloth, money, rice, etc. In winter he receives a "razai" or quilted rug, a blanket, and such things. The gifts naturally depend somewhat on his personal popularity.

Temple priests are supported by offerings, and the endowment of the temple, where such exists. A curious endowment in Almora is that of the temple of Bhita Ganesa, or "Ganesa in the wall," whose shrine is a mere hole in the rock, with an image, just below the cart-road. It has some land belonging to it, bringing in an income of some five rupees monthly. The family priest or purohita is always a Brahman (for the higher castes), and is distinct from and more respectable than the priest in an idol temple.

The hill-people nowadays retain no trace of sectarian animosity. They will worship indifferently in one temple or another. Indeed, in many temples there are images of several gods. I am told, however, by another Hindu, whether correctly or not I cannot say, that many of the Almora Brahmans regard as their tutelar deity or Ishta Devata a form of Durga named Singhavahini, the "goddess seated on a lion." When any work is completed, or deliverance obtained from any calamity, she is worshipped. Thus, when an outbreak of cholera ceases, or when a student passes his examination, she would receive due attention. I have a small copper medallion of this goddess, such as is fixed in the home sanctuary.

Before leaving the subject of sectarial marks and emblems I should refer to the use of *rosaries.* These are used both by ordinary worshippers and by devotees, but especially by the latter. The vegetarian Vaishnavas wear a rosary or necklace of tulsi berries, a small black seed. Vaishnavas in general wear the "rudraksha," composed of larger berries, which are valued because each berry or seed of the rudraksha tree has five faces or sides. Anything fivefold is regarded as specially sacred, probably because of the number of the orthodox deities of modern India. This "mala" contains eighty-two seeds, for the eighty-two names of Vishnu, one of which is repeated, with appropriate mantra or verse, by the learned for every berry passed through the fingers. A rosary of very large black rudraksha berries is used by the Saivite ascetics. These seeds are rather expensive, and are said to be brought from Nepal, which country seems now to be the chief producer of religious apparatus of various kinds. Nearly all the implements of the kind that I have managed to collect came originally from that quarter. Among them is an "arti" made of brass, consisting of *five* small lamps or oil receptacles attached together, in each of which a small wick is placed. In a larger central receptacle camphor is burnt. This is used for *waving* before an idol, or auspiciously over a great man. Another vessel is the "tarpan," a round, bright copper dish, used for various religious purposes, such as giving water to the dying, making the "pindas" or offerings of dough cakes presented to the manes of the departed, and for "arpan" or offerings to the gods in general. Still another is the "argha," an oval copper vessel for making libations to the gods, and pouring water on images or symbols. I have an inscribed copper plate, an antique object also from Nepal, used for worshipping the planet Mars (Mangal). Such worship is always performed on Tuesday, which the Hindus call by the same name Mangal (Dies Martis, Mardi). The plate has on it a "yantra," a magical diagram containing twenty-one triangles, each of which bears one of the names of Mars. For each name a series of twelve slokas or charms (mantra) is to be repeated. These incantations are recited, and offerings are made to the planet Mars every Tuesday, by those desiring children or money. The offerings must always be of *red* colour (to correspond to the hue of the planet), and sweet, mixed with honey, sugar, or treacle, as the deity is supposed to like such things. If cloth is presented it must be red, and the edible offerings must have a reddish tinge, such as the cakes of gurh or solid molasses.

We have now met with the three terms "tantra," "mantra," and "yantra." A *tantra* is properly an incantation, consisting often of meaningless words or mere sounds supposed to have magical virtue or invocatory power, and employed in charming away disease or calamity, for acquiring magical influence, blasting one's enemies, etc. A *mantra* is simply a verse or text, usually in Sanskrit and derived from the sacred books, used in worship or regarded as a secret charm or preservative. A *yantra* is a magical figure, such as the pentagram, etc. The relation of all this to magic as formerly practised in Europe is obvious.

I cannot attempt here to describe all the images and idols, of various size and materials, that are kept and worshipped by Hindus in temples or in the family oratory. Small ones are usually of brass—tiny representations of the infant Krishna (a child on all fours), the bird-god Garuda, etc.

In addition to the family priest, every Brahman and other high-caste Hindu must have a "guru" or spiritual preceptor, who teaches him, at the time of initiation, the mantra or secret form of words which every pious Hindu repeats many times in his morning devotions. This is whispered into the boy's ear when he puts on the janeo or sacred thread for the first time. The guru is either a Brahman priest or else some friend of the family, of good character and attainments. In former times he instructed his pupil during the years of his Brahmachari or period of studentship, and the scholar was required to render the most unbounded reverence and obedience to his guru. At present, however, beyond formally teaching the mantra, he appears to have little further relation to his disciple, like the godfather in English society; though in some instances he may be asked for spiritual advice.

The mantra or "gayatri" repeated in daily worship is different for the several castes. Thus there is a gayatri for the Brahmans, one for the Kshatriyas, and another for the Vaisyas. The Sudras have none. (These ancient terms and distinctions are carefully kept up, as regards all religious matters, in modern India.) These gayatris are Sanskrit quotations from the Yajur Veda. The Brahman gayatri has already been quoted, and is found in the Rig Veda (iii. 62. 10). Its repetition is required twice a day at the Sandhya or daily prayers—once in the morning after bathing, and in the evening. Before the repetition of this prayer or invocation no food can be eaten. Some very devout Hindus, like Daniel, add a third hour of prayer, at noon. These are called the "trikala" (three times), or "trisandhya" (three services). The Brahmanical thread is wrapped round the hands during the repetition of the gayatri, and the number of times of repetition is marked on the fingers, the hand being usually kept covered from observation. Mr. Atkinson speaks of the use of the "gaumukhi" or "cow's mouth," a kind of bag in which the hands are placed for religious gesticulation during prayer, and states that he learned all the movements from a Brahman while at Almora; but I have not been able to find any evidence of its use in recent years, and, as regards Kumaon, it is probably only a part of the complicated ritual prescribed in some religious books, though it may be in actual use in some other parts of India. My pandit tells me that one hundred and eight times is the least number of repetitions that can properly be observed. The number seems large, and I very much doubt if the ordinary Hindu goes to such a length in his devotions, "vain repetitions" as they emphatically are.

The guru is still nominally regarded as the spiritual father, and treated with great respect. After his death the "chela" or disciple must mourn for him for three days, offer sacrifice in his name and pray for his soul, giving presents to Brahmans and beggars.

A few words may be said here about the worship of the Sakti, or female energy of the gods. Each of the great deities is supposed to possess a female counterpart or consort, who embodies his power of granting prayers and effecting favours for his worshippers. The later forms of Buddhism have recognised the same idea with reference to their Bodhisatvas, each of whom is provided with a spouse. With this notion seems to be mixed up an ancient and aboriginal worship of the sexual principle; and this it is that gives life and realism to the infamous Tantric doctrines and rites of the left-handed sects, professing to secure the liberation of the soul from earthly bonds. It has been remarked that "the germs of Saktism and Tantric practices appear to have been the common inheritance of all the pre-Aryan tribes"; and Brian Hodgson says: "I suppose that the Tantrik admixture must have existed in the prior superstitions of the sons of Tur forming the pristine sole population of all these countries, because those superstitions, as still extant amongst the *disjecta membra* of that population where-ever found, exhibit a prevailing Tantrik character—a mixture of ferocity, lust, and mummery—and bear everywhere from Siberia to Ceylon a resemblance that amounts to identity."

I will conclude this chapter with a quotation from the *Himalayan Districts*, showing the number of temples of the respective deities now existing in the province:

"There are 250 Saiva temples in Kumaon and 350 in Garhwal, and but 35 Vaishnava temples in Kumaon and 61 in Garhwal. To the latter class, however, may be added 65 temples to Nagraja, the serpent-king, in Garhwal, which are by common report affiliated to the Vaishnava sects, but in which Siva also has a place, under the form of Bhairava. Of the Saiva temples, 130 in Garhwal and 64 in Kumaon are dedicated to the Sakti or female form alone, but of the Vaishnava temples in both districts only eight. The Sakti form of both Siva and Vishnu, however, occurs also in the temples dedicated to Nagraja and Bhairava, or rather these deities and their Saktis are popularly held to be forms of Vishnu and Siva and their Saktis. Of the

Saiva Sakti temples, 42 in Garhwal and 18 in Kumaon are dedicated to Kali; whilst the Sakti forms of the Bhairava temples are also known as emanations of Kali. Nanda comes next in popularity, and then Chandiga and Durga (all are names of Siva's wife). The remaining temples are dedicated to the worship of Surya (the sun), Ganesa, and the minor deities and deified mortals and the pre-Brahmanical village gods. The outcome of this examination is, therefore, that Siva and Vishnu and their female forms are the principal objects of worship, but with them, either as their emanations or as separate divine entities, the representatives of the poly-demonistic cults of the older tribes are objects of worship both in temples and in domestic ceremonies."

CHAPTER IX

GHOSTS AND GODLINGS

IT has already been pointed out that the Puranic religion, the worship of the greater gods of Hinduism, though universally spread by Brahmanic influence, is more or less of a foreign imposition upon a vast undergrowth of aboriginal cults, animistic worship, and propitiation of spirits and demons, prevailing among the masses of the population. Our study of the popular religion of Kumaon, as distinct from the orthodox faith, amply confirms this view. We have seen also that the Puranic religion itself grew up from similar elements.[1] Certain names, ideas, and legends of a popular origin came to have a peculiar sanction and vogue, being adopted by the Brahmans, and were woven into a system which has become fixed and stereotyped. I purpose in this chapter to give a large amount of detail regarding the animistic and demonist beliefs of the lower classes in Kumaon, because it is only by gathering together such a mass of particulars

[1] "Krishna and Rama are totally unconnected with the Vedas, and are purely popular inventions produced on Indian soil to glorify the lunar and solar races respectively, and are probably nothing more than advanced demonism on which the ever-willing priests have engrafted as much as they could of Vedic ceremonial and ritual" (*Himalayan Districts*, ii. 720).

that any definite idea of the nature of this popular religion can be formed. Some very remarkable features will become apparent from the description, features of which one may remain ignorant even after spending a lifetime among the people. My chief sources of information have been personal inquiry, MS. notes kindly shown me by Pandit Ganga Datt Uprety of Almora, and the work *Himalayan Districts* so often referred to.

Speaking generally, we may assert that the official standards of Hinduism do not really represent the actual religious practices of the people, of the great mass of Hindus. In this respect a far safer guide than the literature, is the ritual to be observed among the people. Indeed, a great part of the real religion of India has never been reduced to writing or in any complete way described. Concrete instances are the best proof. In the last Census Report, just published, the Census Commissioner, Mr. Risley, under the chapter on "Religion," describes Hinduism as "Animism modified by philosophy," and refers to the common practice of worshipping the distinctive articles of a man's craft at a certain season of the year, known as the Sri Panchami. At that time the peasantry of the Panjab have a ceremony in which they worship their ploughs, the soldier worships his arms, the oil-maker his mill, etc. So ingrained is the superstition connected with this idea that the peasants employed at Simla to carry about despatch-boxes and attend on the various Government offices, on the annual migration of Government to Calcutta for the cold season, have taken to paying adoration to their despatch-boxes and the stationery associated with their calling. The reader will easily forgive me for introducing Mr. Risley's amusing account, especially as it admirably illustrates the phase of Indian religious life we are describing:

"Two years ago I asked one of the orderlies what worship he had done on this particular occasion, and he was good enough to give me a minute description of the ritual observed. The ceremony took place on the flat roof of the huge pile of buildings which is occupied by the Secretariats of the Government of India. The worshippers, some thirty in number, engaged as their priest a Panjabi Brahman who was employed in the same capacity as themselves. They took one of the large packing-cases which are used to convey office records from Simla to Calcutta, and draped its rough woodwork with plantain leaves and branches of the sacred pipal tree. On this foundation they set up an office despatch-box, which served as a sort of altar. In the centre of the altar was placed as the principal fetish a common English glass inkpot with a screw top, and round this were arranged the various sorts of stationery in common use: penholders and pen-nibs, pencils red, blue, and black, penknives, ink-erasers, foolscap and letter paper, envelopes, postage stamps, blotting-paper, sealing-wax, in short all the clerkly paraphernalia by which the Government of India carries on its work. The whole was festooned with attendant coils of red tape. To the fetish thus installed each one of the worshippers presented, with reverential obeisance, grains of rice, turmeric, spices, pepper, and other fruits of the earth, together with the more substantial offering of nine copper-pice or farthings—the perquisite of the officiating priest. The Brahman then recited various cabalistic formulæ, supposed to be texts from the Vedas, of which neither he nor the worshippers understood a single word. When the ceremony was over, the worshippers attacked a vast mass of sweetmeats which had been purchased by a subscription of a rupee a head. The Brahman ate as much as he could, and they finished the rest. I asked my informant, who is a small landholder in one of the hill states, what he meant by worshipping an imported inkpot when he ought to have worshipped a country-made plough. He admitted the anomaly, but justified it by observing that after all he drew pay from the Department, that the inkpot was the emblem of the Government, and that he had left his plough in the hills. These are the lower aspects of Hinduism, survivals of magical observances which show no signs of falling into disuse."[1]

The "animism" represented in such types of worship as the above is purely a propitiation of powers supposed to reside in *things*, with the idea of escaping calamity or in some way securing good fortune. To the mind in this state, everything appears mysteriously endowed with capacities of doing good or ill to the individual. It is the egotistic view of a semi-savage mind looking out apprehensively on the world of phenomena, understanding nothing, but hoping or fearing for itself. As a form of "religion," it is absolutely without value or moral effect; and such, we are assured by the most competent observers, is by far the larger part of Indian popular religion.

The type of worship prevalent in Kumaon partakes more of the character of *demonism* than of animism. It is startling to find that the idea of *possession* seems

[1] The operatives in the jute mills near Calcutta are said to bow down to the Glasgow-made engines which drive their looms.

to be its very life and soul. It is believed that there exists a multitude of gods or spirits, some of them being old kings or members of the royal families of Kumaon in former days; others, grotesque goblins, like those of our European fairy-stories; others, ghosts of deceased persons who have died a violent death, committed some great crime, or differed in some way from the ordinary run of people—ghosts of women who have died in childbirth, of men whose funeral ceremonies have been neglected, and so on. These are nearly all malevolent by nature, and all calamities and diseases are attributed to one or other of them. When a man imagines he is under the evil influence of some god or spirit, he goes to a professional wizard, named a "gantua" (or "calculator"), who professes to find out what demon is tormenting him. By appropriate means he brings himself into relation with the deity, becomes "possessed" by him, and then as his mouthpiece orders what offerings or penances are required by the god. Here we have an ingenious system of priestcraft, the possibilities of which it is easy to perceive. Sometimes quite a number of people, by dancing for a long time on certain ceremonial occasions, succeed in hypnotising themselves, and believe themselves to be possessed by one or even several deities. There can be no doubt that this kind of demon worship typifies a vast amount of old-world superstition, and may be found to throw light on some hitherto unexplained beliefs.

The people of Kumaon reckon two classes of gods—those of royal descent and those of demoniacal origin. The former are supposed to be possessed of more reasoning power than the latter, to be indeed almost omniscient; while the demons are often of only half-human intelligence, and may easily be deceived by false show or promises. The royal deities are generally well-disposed, or may be made so by employing proper means of persuasion, and are asked for boons. The demons, on the other hand, are spiteful and evil-minded. No good is to be expected from them, but when they prove troublesome they must be propitiated. I take the following details from Pandit G. D. Uprety's MS. notes:—

In Kumaon when a person is suffering from any calamity he seeks out the deity or ghost to be propitiated, by going to a gantua. The relatives of a man attacked by serious disease, or who has been robbed of property, or whose cattle have been stolen or lost, or who are anxious about the safety of a member of their family at a distance, and so on, go early, fasting, taking a handful of rice (called pearls!), with a pice or farthing, to the sorcerer, and present them to him. He keeps the pice as his fee, and, taking the grains of rice in the palms of his hands, moves them up and down, uttering incantations and the names of the local gods and ghosts, professing to calculate by the movement of the grains of rice. He then declares who is the cause of the trouble, and gives advice as to the worship of the deity whom he names, and to whom the disorder or misfortune is ascribed.

When the name of the god under whose baleful influence the afflicted person has fallen has been thus ascertained, resort is next made to the "dungaria," a devotee or "dancer" of the particular deity. The name is derived from "dungari," which means a hilltop, as these rustic rites are often performed in such "high places of the field," or perhaps because the dungaria usually resides in such places. In case of sickness very frequently he is invited to the house; and on his coming and taking his seat there, incense is offered to him, and he is begged to make himself at home and overlook any faults inadvertently committed by the afflicted person or by any other member of the family. Then a little tobacco is given him to smoke in a "katori," or earthen vessel used for the purpose. After smoking it the man appears to show signs of intoxication or narcotic influence, and then suddenly jumps up with a wild yell. This is supposed to be the moment when he is "possessed" by the deity. Incense is again offered to him as the incarnation of the god, and he is humbly entreated to cure the sick person. At this stage the man sometimes remains mute, and deaf to all entreaties. Again and again he is besought with clasped hands and many prostrations. After a while the god deigns to attend, and the inspired man utters some stammering and mystic words. Then he unfolds the cause of the disease or calamity, and enjoins certain gifts, offerings, or services for the satisfaction of the offended deity.

Besides such occasional worship, there are concerted *dancings* held in honour of the gods, or to obtain deliverance from their wrath. Any person who is suffering from a special misfortune, believed to be due to the displeasure of a spirit or demon, collects his family and friends and gets them to dance, either in his own house or at the temple of the god, which is often merely an erection of a few stones. This dancing goes on from one to twenty-two days, or even, in some cases, is repeated daily for six months. Large fires, called "dhuni," are kindled round the place at night. After dancing, the deity is worshipped. In most villages there is a temple to the local god or spirit. No idol is placed in it, but on all ordinary Hindu festival days offerings are made there, though the real and original purpose of the erection seems to be this curious dancing, with the object of being inspired by the demon. The dancing ceremonies and other rites usually take place during the moonlit halves of the months of Asoj (October), Mangsu (December), and Chait (March). The villagers contribute for the purpose of these rites, which are believed to secure the welfare of the community.

The occasional ceremonies referred to above, on behalf of individuals who desire to gain the favour of the god, are usually performed on Tuesday or Saturday. The offerings consist of he-buffaloes, goats, cocks, pigs, lizards, and pumpkins for sacrifice. The last-named article has a sinister interest, as being probably a substitute for the ancient human sacrifices. Other offerings are sweet cakes fried in ghi or oil, sweetmeats of ghi, treacle, and flour, rice-pudding, milk, curds, fruit and flowers. A portion of the offerings is taken as a perquisite by the house-priest or temple-priest, and the rest is eaten up by the persons making the offering, and their relatives and friends. The god is believed to make certain people, subject to his influence, dance at the request of the priest and people, and to inspire them to give oracles, and predictions regarding the granting or refusing of their prayers by the deity. These rites are held in high estimation, and are fervently believed in by women of all castes, by the rustics generally, and especially the Doms. These are the people who believe in and practise the ceremonies above described. As a general rule, the Brahmans, traders, and townspeople take no part in such cults, and would disclaim all knowledge of them. It is highly probable that the system of worship referred to represents the ancestral religion of the aborigines, the Doms.

The priests who officiate at such shrines, as may readily be imagined, are not high-caste Brahmans. They may be Khassiyas, that is, ordinary villagers, or ascetics of some sect. The Doms appoint persons from among their own class to act as priests. A son-in-law or brother-in-law performs religious rites for a man and his family. (As already mentioned, a man who pretends to be possessed by any spirit or "bhut" is called a "dungaria.")

The deities of village temples (often a few stones piled together, though sometimes of more elaborate construction), besides being worshipped in the ordinary ways, are often appealed to for redress of grievances, and as avengers of an enemy's unjust deeds. One who has been forcibly or fraudulently deprived of property, money, or wife, or otherwise injured, and is unable to go to law, or can get no remedy by law, will go early in the morning, fasting, with a handful of rice and throw it before the god, with an earnest plea for redress and vengeance on his foe. Such complaints to the god are called "ghat." The people believe that if the complaint is true, the god will cause the suppliant's enemy to suffer, or if it is false, the complainant will himself suffer. Often enough the offender does get some illness or suffers some loss or disgrace, in which case he will send for the injured party, after having inquired the cause of his calamity from a gantua; and when he is reconciled to his enemy by making up the loss or injury and by worshipping the deity, he is freed from the anger of the god, gets well, and prospers.

It is remarkable to what an extent the idea of *incarnation*, or rather *personation*, enters into the popular religion of the country. The spirit of a god or demon is supposed to enter the bodies of favoured worshippers, who are then to all intents and purposes incarnations of the deity, capable of uttering his mind and endowed with his supernatural knowledge. It is something more than *inspiration*.

The royal gods, or Katyuri gods, so called from their descent from the old Katyuri royal family, are opposed to a more plebeian party of spirits called by the name of Haru, and will not associate with them, though in general the two main classes of deities, the royal and demoniacal, can be got to unite in the same dancing ceremony. The Haru faction of gods have a place near temples, named "dhuni" or fireplace, where dancing is done. The Katyur or royal deities have a place called Khali for the same purpose. The devotees of the former dance after applying to their bodies the ashes of the dhuni, or altar for kindling fire. They dance with a bamboo or great cudgel in their hands. The Katyur gods are fastidious, and will not allow anyone to bring into their dancing companies tobacco, a dog, a pumpkin, a black blanket, or a turban. He-buffaloes, pigs, cocks, he-goats, and cocoanuts are offered to them. The devotees who personate the god are called "deo," (divine), and are tinged with "pitya" or red powder as a mark of their high rank and functions.

The popular belief is that each of the principal local gods is accompanied by a band of ghostly attendants, namely, sixty-four "jogans" or goblins and fifty-two heroes, who remain at his command. These subordinate genii are also incarnated and worshipped along with the chief gods. The common people believe that unless periodically worshipped and personated, the deities become angry, and in their wrath allow their evil sprites and ministers to prey on men in the form of epidemic diseases and suchlike calamities. When worshipped and propitiated in due form, however, they are ready to confer blessings and preserve the people. During the prevalence of epidemics these rites are of course more largely practised.

The Pandit adds: "Such beliefs and practices are generally confined to the women of all classes and the more illiterate males. Mainly through the entreaties of their women-folk, and in order to humour them, the better educated and more enlightened men are led to observe them." The natural conclusion from which seems to be that the spread of education will eventually cause the decay of superstition, but that it must be extended to the female half of the population.

Ghosts, it appears, are rarely worshipped or personated singly, but generally in connection with other deities, whose staff or retinue they form. The deities of royal descent are said to have the faculty of knowing the wishes and propensities of men's minds, whereas the ghosts and devils have no such power, but can perceive only what is openly done or said. They are also said to be more troublesome and destructive when they are out of the control of the royal gods. Meditation and heartfelt worship are useless as addressed to the ghosts and demons, so they are usually worshipped with pomp and outward show. They are propitiated along with the royal spirits so as to avoid their spite and malevolence, but the latter are worshipped seriously with the hope of obtaining worldly prosperity, and are regarded in the light of patron saints.

When ghosts are worshipped, it must be done in a particular way. The ghost is propitiated with an offering of half-cooked "khichhari" (rice and pulse), prepared hastily, the idea being that while being thus worshipped it might take possession of the soul of the worshipper. The rite must be performed in a great hurry at night, in a jungle or place where four roads meet.

A peculiar class of deities are the fairies, known by the names of Ancheri, Kechari, Pari, or Chauchari. These are supposed to be young females, of great beauty and sumptuously clothed, belonging to the court of Indra, to which they are attached as dancing-girls. Their habitat is the firmament, and they are very fond of bathing and disporting themselves in water, and gathering flowers on the top of lofty mountains or by the side of crystal springs and lakes in remote forests. They correspond to the Apsaras, or heavenly nymphs, of whom we read so often in classical Sanskrit stories, whose principal occupation seems to have been that of tempting ascetics to break their vows, lest they should rival the gods in merit and consequent power. On certain days they descend in great numbers to sport on the earth, returning again to Indra's paradise. They are said to fly or float along the sky without visible support or the help of wings. Young men and young women fall victims to their evil glances, and become ill and die, unless their friends find out the cause of their sickness and offer worship to the fairies, together with dancing at night. The fairies inspire young women to dance on these occasions as their incarnations. The offerings presented to them are a goat, which is sacrificed; rice-milk, "halwa" made of ghi, flour, and sugar; and female apparel and ornaments. The garments and jewels are given in miniature, for the sake of economy. Fairies are not regarded as goddesses, but as spirits, troublesome and destructive to those who are possessed by them. The snowy ranges are their proper haunts on earth, and they are mainly worshipped in the villages skirting the snows, though other high mountains and remote places are often visited by them. Even in the daytime, in the neighbourhood of places deemed to be haunted by them, young men or women are not allowed to go alone. Fanciful stories are told of their falling in love with mortal youths, and doing wonders for them. Some of the legends about Gandharvas and other mythical Himalayan races current in Indian literature are probably due to superstitions of this kind reported vaguely by visitants from the plains.

As an illustration of the belief in possession by demons, requiring violent methods of exorcism, the following description may serve as a picture of what has often enough occurred in Himalayan villages. I have brought together, in no spirit of exaggeration, several details of these peculiar superstitions.

One day a villager who was credited with powers of casting out evil spirits was sent for, to treat two members of a family, a father and son, in a certain village. They were both suffering from a severe form of malarial fever, and occasionally became delirious. It was declared that they were possessed by demons.

The father, it was said, had been passing a funeral ghat or place for burning dead bodies down by a river late one evening, when the demon Masan, who makes his abode in such spots, and appears of a black colour and headless form, came out and chased him to his village, since when the poor fellow had never been like himself. Not long after, the man's son, when going through a dark glen of the forest, under a high beetling crag, heard a strange noise, which sounded sometimes like the cry of a goatherd pasturing his flock, and sometimes like the grunt of a wild boar. He looked about him, but could see nothing. A few moments later, when he came on the path, he was met by a wandering Yogi of wild and terrible aspect, who began to address him volubly, though his words were quite unintelligible. For hours and hours the strange mendicant, like the Ancient Mariner in Coleridge's poem, kept him there, mowing and gibbering, and always putting forth a skinny hand to detain him when he essayed to depart, until at last the young man, in wild terror, tore himself away and fled homewards, pursued all the way by the Yogi, whose demoniacal shrieks and laughter goaded him into a kind of madness, from which he had never since recovered. This was understood to be a form of possession by the demon-god Khabish, though in reality due to the lightheadedness resulting from fever, from which the lad was already suffering, acting on the material of superstitious stories with which he had been familiar from infancy. The mode adopted for ridding the unfortunate men of the evil spirits who had taken possession of them was sufficiently drastic. All the neighbours gathered at their house, and the protecting spirit of the dwelling was invoked to come and take possession of the exorciser. Then all the people began to dance with noisy vociferations. Wilder and wilder grew the movements of the dancers; louder and louder rose the shouting, until at length the exorciser worked himself into a state of frenzy, and taking a club, seized hold of the elder man, who was sitting up in a corner of the yard looking on with unmeaning stare, and began to belabour him lustily with the cudgel. The poor old man screamed, the people shouted, the children wept with terror, and the indescribable din and beating went on for an hour or more. The end of it was that the old man perished under the treatment, while the other, being young and of strong constitution, survived, and after a few days recovered. The people of the village were quite satisfied, since in both cases it was clear that the demon had been thoroughly got rid of, and the elder man had only died from "karma rog," or disease due to his fate.

Devil-dancers, after working themselves up to a great pitch of excitement, sometimes pose as oracles possessed by the deity; and the people, seated gravely before him, propound questions, which he answers by divine inspiration. All this does not differ materially from the ancient oracles of Greece, or even from the goings-on of our spiritualists and "mediums" in the West, though it may be rather startling to find them parodied, or rather forestalled, by superstitious practices of so primitive a type.

The people of a village called Anariyakot, not far from Almora, are credited with the power of exorcising evil spirits. They obtained this reputation in the following way, according to the local legend. Down by the river Sual, to the east of Almora, there is a burning ghat, where the corpses from the town are usually cremated. At this ill-omened spot demons would rise up on dark moonless nights and beat their drums with horrid din, and dance, waylaying the hapless villager going late to his home in one of the hamlets across the river. Some of these goblins were headless, some without legs or arms, some with bleeding eyes jutting out of their heads, some with eyes sunken like two holes, some with bleeding hair, some with huge faces and projecting teeth, some walking on the ground and bearing their king, who was in a still more appalling form, in a litter, others flying and dancing around him, but all (and this point is much insisted on) with their feet turned backwards. There was once a man of this village, named Anariya, who was a person of extraordinary courage. When the grisly procession met him repairing to his village by night, he rushed forward in his desperation and seized the leader of the demons, and in spite of all their threats and fearful gibbering kept hold of him until at last the king of the ghosts was forced to submit and ask what he wanted. Then there came into the valiant rustic's head the idea of demanding from the demon king the greatest boon that he could imagine, namely, that all the rich manure-heaps in the village of Khatiyari, on the other side of Almora, should be transferred to the fields of his own village, and that all the millet crops near his village should be weeded without any exertion on the part of the owners. The ghost king had to consent, and was then liberated. Next morning when the hero awoke, he looked out of his cottage door and found to his wonder and delight that the village was full of heaps of fine manure; but when he went to examine the millet fields, he saw that the plants had all been pulled up along with the weeds. Great was his wrath; and having lost all fear of ghosts since his last night's encounter, he set out with a big cudgel that same midnight to waylay the king of demons. Again the weird procession met him by the river, and again he seized the king riding in his "dandi," and holding him tightly by the neck flourished his shillelagh, and in a loud and fierce voice reproached him for the damage done to the crops. The ghosts, quite humbled, pleaded that they did not know how to weed fields, and that their mistake had been quite unintentional. Thereupon the villager, with many hard words for their stupidity, explained the proper mode of weeding, and before he released their king made them promise to impart to him and his descendants the power of exorcising any of them from the body of any person of whom they had taken possession, and that all of them would be at his service in future. He then went home, and in the morning found all the fields properly weeded. Ever since that time the members of his family have been famous exorcisers in all the country round, and their services are in requisition whenever any poor peasant has to be delivered from possession by a demon. The ghosts nowadays never appear to anyone in that village, so terrified were they by the brave Anariya.

The earliest connected account of the province of Kumaon is found in Traill's *Settlement Report*, 1820. Traill[1] found the population divided into two classes, human beings and ghosts. "The ghost tribe," he says,

[1] As quoted in Sir W. W. Hunter's *Life of Brian Hodgson*, pp. 53–54.

"is divided into many varieties. The first and most formidable is the bhut, or ghosts of persons who have died a violent death, by murder, drowning, or public execution, and to whose *manes* due funereal honours have not been paid. These require to be appeased by sacrifices and offerings. Masan or imps are the ghosts of young children, the bodies of whom are buried and not burnt, and who prowl about the villages in the shape of bears and other wild animals. Tola or will-o'-the-wisps are ghosts of bachelors, that is, males who die at mature age unmarried, dwellers in solitary places and condemned by other ghosts. The Airi or ghosts of persons killed in hunting, wandered about the forests in which their death occurred, and might be heard from time to time hallooing to their spectral dogs. The Acheri or hill-fairies were the ghosts of young female children, who flitted about the tops of mountains, producing wondrous optical illusions among the distant ranges, and descending at dusk to play in the valleys. The Deos or demons formed a numerous and malignant class, indeed scarce a village but had its peculiar deo."

The particulars given by Traill do not quite agree with the later accounts furnished by Atkinson and G. D. Uprety, but are interesting as proving the great prevalence of such superstitions in Kumaon. The last-mentioned observer writes regarding the present generation of Kumaonis: "It is common to hear people professing to have seen spectres and ghosts or evil spirits at night assuming male or female forms, disappearing, and then appearing in some other form, it may be in the shape of animals, and with their appropriate voices. Occasionally they are reported to have appeared in hideous gigantic figures, then turning into a misty pillar and vanishing. These are seen by one or more persons, and always at night, preferably when people are alone. They play these tricks to frighten people. If a person is really frightened they take hold of his soul, but cannot harm anyone who does not fear them. The personation of the deities (as described above) drives away ghosts from people who have been possessed by them. They are said not to dare to appear to a devout person or one who is clean in mind and body. Dirty and wicked people fall into their clutches. They are generally malevolent. Money received from them at night turns into pieces of bone the next day. They often try to imitate the conduct of human beings, but fail in the end. They understand human language, but cannot speak it clearly. They are pleased when they cause the death of a human being through their devices. People therefore guard against them, and have recourse to the personation and worship of the deities as a safeguard against their influence."

Bhuts in general are defined by G. D. Uprety as ghosts or demons who are supposed to haunt, unseen, funeral ghats, glens, rivers, and lonely places, especially at night, and to take possession of boys, girls, and women, and make them ill. They are driven out by enchantments, or by persons inspired by other deities. Persons supposed to be under their influence offer cocks, pigs, and khichhari, and the bhuts are worshipped at night.

A special kind of bhut is the Ghar-bhut or family ghost, who is confined to a single household, and is the spirit of one who has died a violent death and has not been atoned for by his or her kinsmen. Unless due worship and propitiation is offered them, they haunt members of the family, who suppose their afflictions or accidents to be due to them.

Masan is said to exist in places where dead bodies are burnt, generally at the confluence of two rivers. He is the chief or head of the other ghosts who haunt such places, and rules over them as a giant king of genii. The belief is that wicked people, or those who die by accidents, such as falling from a tree or precipice, by drowning, snake-bite, or wild beasts, women who die in childbirth, suicides, and all who die a violent or wilful death, or those whose funeral rites have been neglected, after death become ghosts for a time. When the term of a thousand such ghosts expires, that is, when they have expiated their sins by a ghostly existence for a period, the souls of all the thousand are concentrated and transformed into one body, and the being thus formed is called Masan. His features are said to be very huge and hideous. He is of black hue, with feet turned to the back. Anyone who sees him by mishap dies at once. Any person taken possession of by him falls ill. When this is the case, drummers and cymbal-players are sent for to excite some man who professes to be possessed by Masan to dance. While under the inspiration of the demon, incense is offered to him, and he is worshipped. Then he pronounces an oracle, and demands certain offerings and service to Masan. These are duly rendered, but not always with good results. Some villages have established shrines for him within their boundaries.

In *Himalayan Districts* we find some interesting

particulars about the local gods worshipped in Kumaon. The legend of Satyanath, a Yogi whose memory has long been retained in Garhwal, and who was a favourite deity of some of its early kings and chiefs, is often told.

The lower classes worship a peculiar deity called Ghantakarna, or the bell-eared, who is adored under the form of a water-jar, and is supposed to cure skin diseases. His image stands at the entrance to many temples of the greater gods. The local deities are thus recognised in many places as attached to the great system of Hinduism, though but as doorkeepers in the houses of the *Di Majores.* Bholanath is worshipped by all classes at Almora, even by Brahmans, who explain him to be a form of Siva. The elevation of a human being to divine rank in comparatively recent times, and his identification with the great god, is a striking illustration of the way in which Hinduism has grown up and adapted itself everywhere to local circumstances. It is related that Udai or Udyot Chand, raja of Almora from 1678 to 1698, had two wives, each of whom bore him a son. The elder of the two sons followed evil courses and was expelled from the kingdom. He wandered into Nepal, and subsequently, after his younger brother, Gyan Chand, had succeeded to the throne, found his way back to Almora, where he remained unknown, and for some time carried on a liaison with the wife of a Brahman, or, according to another account, of a Baniya. The king, getting to know of his presence, gave orders that he should be assassinated, and this was done by a man of the Bariya or gardener caste. Both the prince and his mistress were slain near the temple of Sitala Devi. After his death he became a bhut or goblin, commonly named

Bholanath (which is an epithet of Siva). The woman became a female sprite, known as Barhini (that is, Brahmani), and the unborn child also became a bhut. These three demons are wont to trouble the Almora people, especially those of the gardener caste, who attribute all their mishaps to their influence. There are no fewer than eight temples dedicated to them in the town. Bholanath is sometimes worshipped in the home, where a small trident is placed in a corner of a dwelling to represent him. (The trident is the common emblem of Siva.) Local tradition relates that after the British occupation the temples of this god were allowed to fall into disrepair, whereupon Bholanath showered such quantities of stones on the British settlement that the English officials immediately set on foot inquiries, and learning that it was due to the anger of this god, they had his temples put in good order and the worship revived!

A very similar and equally unedifying legend relates to Ganganath, one of the favourite gods of the Doms. A temple in his honour is to be seen in their quarter, the Domtola of Almora. Ganganath was the son of a raja of Doti, and became a religious mendicant. In consequence of a wicked intrigue, he was murdered in the village of Adoli by the injured husband, a Brahman of Almora. He and the woman and child all became bhuts. He is said to vex and afflict especially the young and beautiful, unless they propitiate him with gifts. He sometimes takes possession of one of his devotees, and through him promises almost anything to anyone who will offer to him a kid, cakes, sweetmeats, beads, a bag, and a pair of Yogi's earrings; and to his mistress, Bhana, a skirt, sheet, and nose-ring; and to the child, a coat and anklets. The dungaria or devil-dancer thus gets a fairly good "haul" from the worshipper of Bholanath.

The Doms regard as the chief of their gods Nirankara (the name meaning simply the "formless" or "bodiless"), and are said to have worshipped him from time immemorial. He is treated as a "royal" deity, though no story of human origin is told concerning him. He becomes incarnate in both men and women. He dislikes animal sacrifices, but is pleased with adoration and worship, or at most a simple offering of rice-pudding. He is believed to possess immense power of driving away demons and conferring boons on his worshippers. This is one of the most interesting of the aboriginal deities, and quite possibly is a relic of some far-off, forgotten religious reform among the peasantry of Kumaon, who had turned for a time from idols to the "Unknown God."

Most of the gods of royal descent appear to have come from the neighbouring region of Doti, where a branch of the Katyur dynasty was settled for many centuries. Other gods are said to have hailed from Tibet, the plains, the Deccan, or even China. There is a touch of pastoral simplicity about the cult of Chaumu (as described by G. D. Uprety). He presides over cattle, and has a stone put up to him in a rustic shrine, or mere niche of a wall, or under a rock. Lamps are lighted and sweetmeats offered to him on all Hindu festivals in nearly every village. The milk of every cow and buffalo which calves is offered to him before it is used. The custom is that when a cow or buffalo calves, it is milked to ease the animal, but the milk is not taken or used by anyone for eleven days, during which time the animal is thought to be unholy. The milk of the twelfth day is first offered to the deity and then used. This god is the protector of cattle from wild beasts and accidents, and there is no dancing or "incarnation" in connection with his worship.

A strange deity, whose temples are found on mountain summits and in desolate places, is the sylvan god Airi.[1] He is believed to have a third eye on the top of his head. If anyone sees that eye, or is seen by it, he instantly dies. He is worshipped by the inhabitants of villages situated amid forests. He is accompanied on his nightly rambles by a troop of goblins in various shapes, and by a pack of hounds with bells attached to their necks. Many profess to have heard the baying of these ghostly dogs and the ringing of their bells in the night-time. Airi is carried on a jhampan or litter by his bearers, Sau and Bhau. This god seems to have been the ghost king met by Anariya in the story related above. He is fond of spitting about wherever he goes, and if his spittle falls on anybody, a wound is made by the venom, and the part affected has to be rubbed with the bough of a certain tree to the accompaniment of charms. Should any bold spirit survive the sight of Airi, or escape being torn to pieces by his dogs after meeting him, the god reveals hidden treasures to him, sometimes gold, but just as often merely old bones. In his temples are found tridents representing the god, and sometimes an idol surrounded by figures of his bearers, Sau and Bhau, and others of his attendants. Bonfires are lighted during the moonlight nights of Chait near the temple, and the

[1] Explained somewhat differently by Traill in the passage quoted on p. 218.

A Brook by the Way

villagers dance themselves into a state of intense excitement, believing themselves to be possessed by the god. Some brand themselves with heated iron spoons, or even fling themselves into the fire. If they escape unhurt they are regarded as really possessed; those who get burnt are mere pretenders. The truly possessed are called "dungaria," and are Airi's slaves or "horses." They put on a turban dyed with red ochre, and take alms from the villagers. Their persons are supposed to be holy as long as the festival lasts, and none must touch them or the temple of Airi. Kids are sacrificed to the god, and a piece of cloth dyed in the blood is set up near the shrine as a sacred banner. Milk, sweetmeats, and such offerings are provided by subscription, and eaten by the worshippers. Water is poured over the images and stones in the temple (the usual rite in Siva worship), and, says Mr. Atkinson, the following prayer is used: "Hallowed god: be pleased with me, forgive my trespasses, and accept this kid that is offered thee. I am devoid of understanding; thou art a knower of hearts." A spell or a mantra is whispered into the ear of the goat that is about to be sacrificed, to the following effect: "Thou art not a horse, nor an elephant, nor a lion. Thou art only the son of a goat, and I sacrifice thee: so God also destroys the weak." If the victim shakes itself when water is sprinkled on it, the god has accepted the offering, and the goat's head is cut off with a heavy curved knife or "kukri." If he does not shiver, or if he bleats, it is taken as a sign that he is not accepted, and he escapes.

The malignant sprite Runiya is propitiated in the northern part of Kumaon. He is said to roam at night from village to village on steeds formed of huge boulders of stone, whose rumbling and clattering noise is heard in the darkness and stillness. He is of amorous propensities, and women who attract his attention pine away, and soon join him in the spirit-land.

The last two kings of Katyur, Brahm and Dham, who were famous for their cruelty and tyranny (see Chapter V.), are worshipped at Katyur and Pali every third year. Having been slain by Vikram Chand in a great battle, their bodies were thrown into the western Ramganga river, and they became bhuts.

Nearly all the foregoing deities are malevolent demons, but there are a few who are represented as being of milder and even of benevolent character. Haru was formerly a raja of Champawat in Kumaon, his full name being Harishchand. In his old age he devoted himself to religion and visited many holy places. On his return to Champawat he formed an ascetic fraternity, which was joined by his brother and many of his servants and retainers. By his austerities he became unable to move from the place where he sat, but he acquired such power that whatever he willed was accomplished—the sick were healed, the poor were made rich, and the wicked became virtuous. He is worshipped to the present day as a good spirit, and a considerable fair is held in his honour every third year in his temple at Than in Katyur.

Kalbisht or Kalua is a deified Khassiya or ordinary peasant of Kumaon. He was a neat-herd living at a village near Binsar, about two hundred years ago. He had some enemies, who persuaded his brother-in-law, Himmat, to drive a peg into the hoof of one of his buffaloes, intending that Kalua should be killed in trying to extract it. The plot failed, and thereupon Himmat attacked him from behind with an axe. Kalua received a fatal wound, but he had strength left to turn on his assailant in the forest and tear him limb from limb. He became a benevolent spirit, and several temples are erected to him. His name is used as a charm against wild beasts. The descendants of his enemies especially propitiate him when they suffer from illness or when their crops are injuriously affected.

Kshetrpal, the "protector of fields," also called Bhumiya, the "land god," is generally worshipped. Most villages have a small temple only a few feet square sacred to him, and at the time of sowing in a field a little grain is sprinkled as an offering to him at the corner of the field nearest to his temple. He is expected to protect the growing crops from hail, mildew, and wild creatures. He receives the first-fruits at harvest-time, and is besought to protect the garnered grain from rats and insects.

The most popular of all the gods worshipped by the humbler orders in Kumaon is Goril. The story connected with his name has a kind of wild dreamlike charm not often associated with these rude legends. I will give it as related by Mr. Atkinson.

Once upon a time, many centuries ago, a Katyuri raja of Champawat went to hunt in the forests near the Kali river. Unfortunate in the chase, he came, weary and disappointed, to the village of Dubachaur, and saw there two buffaloes fighting together in a field. The raja in vain tried to separate them, and being very thirsty sent one of his servants to fetch some water, but none could be found. A second servant volunteered to search the neighbouring hills, and whilst wandering about heard the noise of two waterfalls, and going towards them soon found himself in a little garden attached to a hermitage. The waterfalls were within the garden. Pushing his way towards them, he found himself obliged to pass through the hermitage, and there he saw a beautiful woman so immersed in contemplation on the deity as to be altogether lost to all external influences. Seeing her in this condition, the servant resolved to break the spell, and in a loud tone asked who she was. She slowly opened her eyes, and, as if recovering from a trance, begged him not to cast his shadow over her and so disturb her meditation. He then told her who he was and why he had come to the hermitage, and received permission to draw some water for the raja. He then approached the water-jar bottom foremost to the waterfall, and the water and spray rebounded on the maiden, who at once arose, saying that it was no wonder that everything was done upside down by the followers of a raja who was unable even to separate two fighting buffaloes. The servant, astonished at these words, begged her to accompany him to his master and attempt the feat herself. The maiden consenting, and gliding onwards as if in a dream, reached the place where the buffaloes were still contending; then, meditating on the deity, she advanced and seized each by the horns and separated them. The raja was amazed, and demanded of her what manner of woman she was. She told him that she was Kali, the niece of a raja with whom she was engaged in great austerities for the purpose of propitiating the deity, until she was disturbed by his servant.

The raja, thereon, resolved to marry the maiden, and visited her uncle, whom he found to be an old leper suffering terribly from that loathsome disease. So strong, however, was his love for Kali that the raja remained for several days performing menial services for the old man, who was so pleased that he gave permission to the raja to marry his niece. She had devoted herself to a life of celibacy, but at her uncle's command she married the raja and lived very happily with him. In due time Kali became pregnant; and the raja being obliged to absent himself from home, charged her by her magical power to ring a bell, which he attached to his girdle, should a male child be born in his absence, and he would at once return on receiving the signal. The other wives of the raja were envious of Kali, and determined to thwart her in every way. One of them mischievously rang the bell, though Kali had not yet been delivered. The raja at once returned, and, very angry at having been deceived, set off on his travels again. In the meantime Kali gave birth to a beautiful son; but the other Ranis placed a bandage over her eyes, and removing the child showed her a pumpkin (others make it a stone), which they said she had given birth to. The boy was then placed in an iron cage and buried in a pit lined with salt; but lo! the salt turned into sugar, and the child ate thereof and flourished. Nothing daunted by this visible sign of protecting influence, the Ranis took both cage and boy and flung them into the river, when again the cage floated down the current and came to land near a fisherman's hut. The fisherman was childless, and, deeming the boy a gift from the gods, took him home and brought him up as his own child. The boy grew up to man's estate, and one day asked his reputed father for a wooden horse, on which he rode to the ghat where the wicked Ranis used to go for water. He broke all their water-jars, saying that he was in a hurry to make his horse drink. They all laughed at the idea; but he retorted that if it were possible for a woman to give birth to a pumpkin, it was possible for a wooden horse to drink water. The story reached the ears of the raja, who sent for the boy, and in presence of the entire court the boy recounted the wrongs done to his mother by the Ranis, and the deception that they had practised on the raja. The child was at once recognised as the son of the raja, and the Ranis paid the penalty of death by being boiled alive in cauldrons of oil. In course of time the young prince succeeded his father; and as everyone believed him possessed by a portion of the deity, from the knowledge of the past shown by him in his discomfiture of the Ranis, he was an object of worship even during his lifetime, and since his death is recognised all over Kumaon. The river down which the iron cage floated is the Gori Ganga, hence his name Goril.

A curious story is told to explain the neglect of the cult of Goril in Garhwal. One day Sudarshan Shah, son of the raja of Garhwal at the beginning of the nineteenth century, heard the sound of drumming and dancing in one of his courtyards. On inquiring the cause he was told that Goril had taken possession of one of his female slaves. In wrath he took a thick bamboo cane, and so laid about him that the votaries of Goril declared that the deity had departed. Possession by Goril was then formally prohibited; and now, if any Garhwali thinks himself possessed, he has only to call on the name of Sudarshan Shah and the demon departs. The same king is said to have rid Garhwal of "bhoksas" or sorcerers by calling them all together with their magical books on pretence of consulting them. When all were assembled he had them suddenly bound hand and foot and thrown into the river along with their books.

Enough has now been said to illustrate the demonolatry prevalent in the province, and it would be profitless to multiply details further. The worship of the village gods is the real religion of the Kumaon peasantry—that is, the immense majority of the population—and it is a religion of fear, which regards the divine powers as nearly all malevolent and requiring to be pacified by offerings. These gods are believed to be most exacting in their demands, and always ready to punish those who commit any kind of "pap" or offence against their ritual and peculiar requirements. Some are believed to do all the harm and evil they can, and to be willing, if they had the power, to overwhelm the whole universe in ruin.

Monier Williams, writing about this class of Hindu cults, declares: "I verily believe that the religion of the mass of Hindus is simply demonolatry. Men and women of all classes, except perhaps those educated by ourselves, are perpetually penetrated with the idea that from the cradle to the grave they are being pursued and persecuted not only by destructive demons, but by simply mischievous images and spiritual goblins."

If we combine this view with Mr. Risley's opinion stated at the beginning of the present chapter, we shall have something like the complete truth about the popular religion of India.

A word in conclusion about snake worship. This seems to have been almost universal throughout both Kumaon and Garhwal. The Nagas or snake worshippers were once widely spread in the Himalayas. They are represented in Buddhist sculptures as beings half-man half-serpent in form (see Rhys Davids' *Buddhist India*). A great number of temples now reckoned as sacred to Siva or Vishnu were originally dedicated to snake or "nag" worship. These "nags" are of various colours, black, white, blue, etc., and are named chiefly according to their colour. They are popularly said to have come from China in time immemorial. They are worshipped in the daytime, according to G. D. Uprety, and dancing is practised at night by those whom they inspire. Their cult is chiefly followed in parganas Gangoli and Danpur. In the domestic worship of serpents, says Atkinson, figures of snakes are drawn on the ground in the light half of the month Sravan (August–September), and offerings are made and lamps waved before them. Sometimes a wandering Yogi brings a live serpent with him, to which offerings are made, and milk is placed near holes in which snakes are known to live.

CHAPTER X

A CHAPTER ON CUSTOMS

THOUGH prohibited by Government in recent years, much to the regret of the younger part of the population, for centuries a curious custom prevailed in Kumaon called the Badi, which was resorted to when there were apprehensions of a bad harvest. The villagers of a valley or countryside used to unite in celebrating this quaint ceremony, with the help of a Badi or "wind-flyer," one of whom resided in most subdivisions of the province. It was supposed that drought, barrenness of land or of cattle, destruction due to rats and other vermin, and all such untoward accidents of agricultural life, were caused by the displeasure of some local god; and in order to appease him, the Badi was called in to perform his perilous task. First of all, the neighbouring villagers visited all the temples near and made offerings; then a prodigious amount of singing and dancing was indulged in, probably with the object of attracting the attention of the god or demon, whoever he might be, who was threatening the place with his wrath. The Badi then set to work on making a huge rope, nearly two inches thick, of strong Bhabar grass. As his life was to depend on the strength of this cable, he always made it with his own hands and in the most careful way, testing every few feet of it with the aid of the crowd of people who usually gathered day by day to watch his operations. The cable having at last reached a vast length, sometimes as much as three thousand feet, it was carefully measured by the head-man of the village or villages concerned, the acrobat being rewarded at the rate of a rupee for every hundred feet of rope. Then it was made fast to a stake at some distance from the foot of a steep mountain or cliff, and a number of men carried it up the face of the opposite ascent and tied it to a rock or strong pine-tree, after passing it through a running block of wood. The rope was made as tight as possible by the united exertions of the crowd. The Badi had then to slide down the rope to the bottom. He was placed on a wooden saddle which had a deep groove underneath to keep it on the cable, and to each of the Badi's legs were tied heavy bags of sand to preserve his balance. After the sacrifice of a kid and various other ceremonies, not forgetting the very necessary precaution of plentifully greasing the saddle to prevent it taking fire, the Badi was seated, and started off on his aërial flight amid wild acclamation. The rope being stretched at a sharp angle, he would shoot down it at a tremendous speed, which was somewhat stayed by the bend in the heavy rope near its lower extremity, so that he would reach the end of his course at a moderate rate and tumble off, on a soft place prepared for his reception, apparently none the worse for his dangerous descent. The wooden seat used to give out dark volumes of smoke during its passage, and would have burst into flame but for the oil with which it had been drenched. The transit if successfully achieved was accepted as a good omen by the villagers. Should the Badi fall, however, he almost certainly lost his life; and in ancient days, if he reached the ground alive he was despatched with a sword, and his head was cut off as an offering to the offended deity. The performance being ended, the cable was cut up into lengths, under the headman's superintendence, and the people would take home pieces to hang on the eaves of their houses for luck. The Badi was fêted for the rest of the day, and portions of his hair were begged, to keep as charms. The cause of prosperity to others, it was believed that he could never secure fertility to his own land. He had forfeited the good fortune that he conveyed to others, and no grain sown by his hand would ever grow. The first account of this curious custom to be met with is in the eleventh volume of the *Asiatic Researches*, where the two explorers who visited Kumaon in 1808 to search for the sources of the Ganges were privileged to witness its performance.

Another strange custom once widely prevalent in the Himalayas, and still practised annually at a few places in Kumaon, especially at melas or fairs, is the Bagwali or stone-throwing festival. It is said to have been introduced originally from Nepal, where one of the kings named Gunkam drew up a strict code of rules for the sport. I have recently read of its being practised among the Coreans, and it seems to be common all over Central and Northern Asia. In Nepal it formerly resembled actual warfare: the men of rival villages or districts used to fight fiercely, and the prisoners taken on either side were offered as sacrifices to the bloodthirsty goddess Kali! In Kumaon, however, it assumed a milder form, and parties on either side defended a passage over a river, or similar place.

A relic of the custom is still to be witnessed at Devidhura, about twenty-five miles east of Almora. A stone-throwing contest takes place between the inhabitants of some rival villages.[1] The two factions range themselves along opposite sides of the public road, each man being provided with a leathern shield to protect himself. Wounds are simply treated by applying the leaves of nettles, which grow there in abundance. The contest is supposed to be in honour of Kali, a goddess who is always pleased with the shedding of blood as an offering. Some native Government official, usually the Tehsildar of Almora, is present to see that the strife does not degenerate into a regular mêlée, and if it goes on longer than an hour he puts a stop to it.

Birth, marriage, and death are phenomena of such universal occurrence that in themselves they can scarcely be reckoned among "curious customs"; but in connection with all three of them there are many rites and popular observances that are interesting enough to deserve mention in this chapter. The following is an abridged account of the ritual proper to be observed after the birth of a child in one of the higher castes of Kumaon. I cannot say whether the whole ceremony is carried out in individual cases, or whether it may not be altered sometimes at the option of the priest or the parents, but it is prescribed in a religious work, the *Manual of the Ten Rites*, which is highly esteemed in this part of India. A good deal depends, of course, on

[1] This is said to have some connection with the famous old quarrel between the Maras and Phartiyals, which divided Kumaon for so many centuries.

the means of the persons for whose benefit the rites are performed. A rich man can get the whole ceremony observed in the fullest manner, while the poor man must be content with maimed rites. On the sixth day after the birth of a son the father must rise early and bathe, in his clothes, and then tie to his wrist a small bag containing a few coins, with turmeric, betel, and white mustard-seed, a necessary preparation for the performance of domestic ritual in the hills. The bag with its contents is afterwards made over to the officiating Brahman. The father then worships Ganesa, the elephant-headed son of Siva and the god of protection and good fortune, and prays for blessings on the son and mother. Later in the day the neighbours and friends of the family are assembled in the courtyard of the house or other suitable place, and the Brahman who has been asked to conduct the ceremonies places in a bright vessel provided for him a mixture of ghi and honey, and taking the infant in his arms anoints its tongue with the composition. Then the father has to present a coin to the priest, and the latter dips it in a mixture of ghi and charcoal and applies it to the forehead and throat of the father and son in turn, and afterwards, with a Sanskrit prayer or invocation, places flowers on their heads. Then the father takes the child in his lap and touches its breast, shoulders, head, and back, while the Brahman reads suitable mantras from the sacred books, used as charms and prayers for the health and soundness of those parts of the body. Finally, the priest takes a little brush formed of the sacred Dub grass, and, dipping it in the water of the sacrificial platter, sprinkles the assembled people, and marks the forehead of all the men present with red sanders. He also presents each with a flower as a token of the god's protection and favour. It may be remarked that these acts, which are of unknown antiquity, are not without some suggestion of the rites observed on similar occasions in the Roman Church.

The chief ceremonies or sacraments observed by Brahmans and other higher castes are the following:—

1. Birth ceremony (Jatkarma).
2. Sixth-day ceremony (Khasti Mahotsava, great joy of the sixth).
3. Naming, on the eleventh day (Namkarna).
4. Ear-piercing, in the fifth or sixth year (Karnaveda).
5. The Brahmanical thread ceremony or janeo, about the ninth year (Churakarna), combined with the head-shaving rite, which was originally distinct from it and marked one of the four periods of a Hindu's life.
6. Marriage (Vivah).
7. Death ceremony (Agni Sanskar or cremation).

On the eleventh day the Namkarna or name-giving ceremony takes place, when a very unsavoury mixture is made up (according to the orthodox prescription) of the various products of a slate-coloured cow, a black cow, a copper-coloured cow, a white cow, and a piebald cow. It is formed into little balls, part of which are used as a "homa" or burnt-offering, and the rest is scattered about the house and cow-byre and over the mother as a purification. Coins are thrown into the fire as a sacrifice, and afterwards appropriated by the priest. The name is written on a small piece of cloth and whispered into the ear of the child, with the prayer, "Thy name is so-and-so; mayst thou have long life, health, and prosperity." A figure of the sun is made in the courtyard and worshipped. The boy is allowed to see the sun for the first time on this day. For girls there appears to be no such ceremony.

Names in India are not given in the European manner. There are, properly speaking, no family names, the castes rather than the family being regarded. This answers to the general submergence of the individual in Hindu society, and the exaltation of caste rather than personal distinction. Brahmans in Kumaon have various caste names denoting subdivisions of their order, such as Panth, Pande, Joshi, Tiwari, Upreti; and personal names, usually two in number, are prefixed to this, as Ghana Nand Tiwari, Badri Datta Joshi. Datta, which is frequently the second member of a Brahman's name, means "gift of," and the latter appellation signifies "the gift of Badri." Baniyas, or members of the Vaishya caste, are usually called Sah or Shah (royal), and the personal names are prefixed in the same way, Lal being often the second part of the name, as Sham Lal Sah. The farming class generally regard themselves as Rajputs, and take the title, belonging to the martial Kshatriyas, of Sinha, meaning "lion," usually with only one name prefixed. The Doms and those belonging to the lowest classes generally are known by a single personal name, and sometimes add the name proper to their occupation, as Barhai, carpenter; Lohar, blacksmith.

The Hindu social system loves to have all things decent and orderly, and to see everyone in his right place: his rank, status, and the respect due to him carefully assigned. Thus we have the curious gradation of titles and appropriate salutations between class and class. I give below a fairly complete list of the titles and greetings current in Kumaon (kindly supplied by Pandit G. D. Uprety).

Brahmans are addressed as	. .	Pandit (learned).
Kshatriyas ,,	. .	Raja (of royal rank).
Vaishya or Baniya ,,	. .	Sah (king) or Lala.
Shudras (cultivators) ,,	. .	Padhan (headman).
Doms ,,	. .	Bairshuwa.
Drummers ,,	. .	Anji or Das (servant).
Tailors ,,	. .	Khalifa (prince) or Dholi.
Goldsmiths ,,	. .	Padhan or Chaudhri (overseer of the market).
Barbers ,,	. .	Thakur (prince or chief).
Mohammedans ,,	. .	Miyan.

A village woman is usually addressed as Padhani, "wife of a padhan or headman." An old or respectable villager in the outlying districts I have heard spoken to as Burju (= Budha ji, old sir). Europeans are commonly addressed as Sahib, ladies as Mem-Sahiba (Mrs.) or Miss-Sahiba. More respectful terms are Huzur (presence) or Garib-Parwar (supporter of the poor). Mohammedans and Persian-knowing men will say "Janab-i-ali" (excellency) to a European.

Brahmans when they meet each other salute with "Namaskar" (salutation). When Brahmans meet Kshatriyas, or persons of royal rank and descent, they say "Jaya dyo" (victory to you)! When they meet Rajputs and Khassiyas they say "Rama, Rama." All the above will answer "Pailayo" (I touch your feet) to a Brahman who greets them with "Swasti," "Ashirbad," or "Kalyan" (blessing, or success). A Dom will say "Meri syo" (may I serve you) to all upper or Bith castes, who will reply "Ji rao" (live on)! An elder Dom, however, will say to a younger one "Ji jas" (live grandly)! A common salutation is Salam (peace), used by and to Mohammedans and Christians, and Bandagi (service).

Wives and husbands must never address each other by their personal names. The wife who becomes a mother is known as the mother of so-and-so, and is so referred to in the third person. Similarly, the husband is the father of so-and-so. A father, guru, or other respected elder, must not be addressed by name.

Girls of the Brahman caste, instead of being called by the name assigned to them by their father or guardian, are called (in formal language) after their respective husbands, with words of feminine signification added, Sundari or Manjari (meaning "fair one"). For example, the wife of Siva Datta will be termed Siva Sundari, and the second or any subsequent one will be Siva Manjari. The wives of rajas or Kshatriyas bear the epithet Devi (goddess). The Baniya women suffix Mati (mate or spouse), as Durga Mati. Among Shudras or Khassiyas the wife is called after the name of her father's caste, as the daughter of a Bisht is called Bishtani.

It is impossible here to enter into a detailed account of the many ceremonies belonging to the life of a Hindu, and to the worship of the various deities. Reference has been made in Chapter VIII. to the daily worship or Sandhya. The rites connected with *marriage* are very elaborate, and the meaning of many of its details have exhaled or become obscure in the course of ages. The caste system has very complex rules for intermarriage, which, with their Gotras, exogamy, and endogamy, constitute a kind of special science in themselves. It may be said in

16

general that the Brahmanical polity takes a relatively high view of the marriage state; and indeed, with regard to all matters of personal status and decorum, it reaches what must be considered a lofty standard, in view of the general state of Asiatic society. There is, of course, little recognition of the equality of the sexes, and in European eyes this must always appear a serious defect; but considering the age in which these social rules were framed, they must be held to deserve high praise. I quote here with pleasure the remarks of Abbé Dubois in his *Hindu Manners, Customs, and Ceremonies,* especially as the Abbé is not usually distinguished by too favourable an opinion of the people amongst whom he spent so many years of intimate communion. "The Hindus," he says, "spend their wedding-days in religious observances, of which the greater number are well calculated to leave a lasting impression on the minds of those attending them. The innocent and artless games with which they amuse themselves afford them none the less pleasure because they are innocent. In the domestic festivities of the Brahmans, decency, modesty, purity, and reserve are always conspicuous. This is the more remarkable," he adds, "as they obey a religion whose dogmas are for the most part saturated with immorality."

At the same time we must acknowledge, as educated Hindus themselves are often ready to do, that in some respects Hindu family life is very defective. The want of companionship between husband and wife, the crowding of so many branches of the same family into one household by the joint-family system, the absence of a home atmosphere, and the tyranny exercised by the elder females over the younger ones, often giving rise to keen suffering; the condition of widows, often mere children, condemned through life to renunciation and servitude through no fault or desire of their own, and other features that have been dealt with by writers better acquainted with the subject than the author, all combine to condemn a great part of Hindu domestic arrangements. The cure must be found in the growth of education and moral training of the right kind, especially among the women, who at present, through their ignorance, are the most obstinate defenders of all the old customs and superstitions.

A general outline of the Hindu view of marriage, as regarded by grave Brahmans, is contained in the following note by G. D. Uprety. It shows a high sense of the solemnity and sacredness of the marriage relation. "The binding part of the marriage ceremony is when the father, elder brother, or other proper guardian gives away the girl with her dowry as a religious alms to the bridegroom, for this world and the next, and the bridegroom receives her as such. The pair make mutual vows in the presence of the deities, the sacrificial fire, the sun and moon, the wind, the firmament, the earth, water, the mind, day, night, morning, evening, the priests and Brahmans, as witnesses of their vows of faithfulness in both worlds. Henceforward they are considered as one, in life and death, in joy and sorrow; and any sin committed by either will be visited on both. It is distinctly the Hindu idea that husband and wife make up the complete human being, and apart are incomplete."

The chief and indeed only way in which Hindu

marriages in the hills come to the notice of Europeans is by seeing and hearing the Barat or marriage procession. The bridegroom, often of course a mere child, crowned with a kind of tiara, is seated in a "dandi" or litter carried shoulder high, with a gorgeous umbrella held over his head, and is accompanied to the house of the bride by a great number of male relatives and friends. One or more persons from every family connected with the bridegroom must attend. If the houses are only a short distance apart, it appears to be the custom to describe a détour and perambulate the place, to the loud accompaniment of drums, conches, horns, and the firing of guns. Rich people have a display of fireworks at night and entertain in grand style. The marriage present is also generally carried in procession, at any rate among poor people, consisting of cooking vessels, bed and bedding, etc.

Very early marriage of daughters, as everyone knows, is considered absolutely obligatory among Hindus, and should it be delayed beyond the age of puberty, it involves indelible disgrace on the girl and her family. Every girl must be married, either actually or figuratively. Thus a dumb or blind daughter (or son), or one otherwise unfitted for the marriage state, goes through a rite of marriage with an earthen jar filled with water, or a pipal tree. Divorce is not permitted. No woman must ever be married a second time; hence among the Brahmans and Vaishyas widow remarriage is forbidden, though among the Khassiyas of the province the custom of the levirate prevails. The Khassiyas have a rustic saying that when the wall of an upper field or terrace yields, it must fall into the lower one, so the wife of an elder brother *may*, though not necessarily, enter the home of a younger brother on the decease of the former, but only for the purpose of raising up children in the brother's name, if such do not already exist. Such a connection is considered quite improper by the higher castes, and no marriage ceremony takes place in such cases. Polygamy is not usual, but is allowed to some extent. Thus a cultivator may have pieces of land in two or three different villages, and such a man will sometimes have a wife at each place, to cultivate the ground for him—the chief work of the Kumaon country-women. If a man's first two wives die, and he marries a third, he is first wedded symbolically to the ank or ark plant, then afterwards to the woman. The reason for this is that the third of any series is always considered unlucky, and his actual marriage to the woman is thus made the fourth. The same practice is said to prevail among the Naidus of South India.

I am told that if a man contracts a *seventh* marriage, the ceremony must be solemnised on the roof of his house! probably with some similar idea of averting ill omens.

Before leaving this subject it may be mentioned as an interesting fact that, in the complete Brahmanical ceremony as observed in Kumaon, at one stage in the rites "parched rice is sprinkled from a sieve on the pair as they move slowly round the altar." It would be interesting to know if there is any connection here with the European custom of rice-throwing.

Among Hindus a widow never wears any jewels or fine clothes, nor does she eat animal food. Her hair is cut off. She is expected to lead a sad and ascetic life, to "go mourning all her days." Only in tribes or communities of low social organisation is widow re-marriage at all permitted.

Let us now turn to *funeral rites.* The dead bodies of all Hindu castes, including Doms and Bairagis (Vaishnava ascetics) are burned at the confluence of two streams or on a river-bank, or else on a mountain-top. In the former case the ashes, and if the people are poor, too often a great part of the corpse itself, are thrown into the river. If the cremation has taken place on the top of a mountain, the remains are left there. If the deceased was well-to-do, a few pieces of bone are picked up and sent, or taken, to be thrown into the Ganges, and thus obtain Paradise for the spirit of the departed. The corpses of Yogis (Saivite mendicants) are either thrown entire into the Ganges or other large river, or buried in a suitable spot. If they have disciples or children (in case of their having adopted an ascetic life at a mature age), they build a masonry grave over the dead, called Samadhi; but the bodies of the poorer sort are buried without any such memorial. For twelve days after death funeral ceremonies are performed and offerings made, with the curious idea of supplying a body to the disembodied spirit, and to allay the purgatorial sufferings through which it has to pass. During each of the twelve days the soul has to traverse a separate hell, the name of which is specified, and in each day some portion of the new "spiritual body" is formed by means of the "pinda," or offerings of balls of dough.

In the hour of death the last services for the dying are performed by a Brahman. In the case of a wealthy man, it is expected that certain gifts will be bestowed on the officiating priest, as an offering for sin, including a cow, which is dedicated to help the spirit after death in its passage across the Vaitarani river, and through the awful entrance to the realms of Yama (the Indian Pluto). "His feet and hands are bathed in water taken from the Ganges or some other sacred stream, whilst the frontal mark is renewed and garlands of the sacred tulsi plant are thrown around his neck. The ground is plastered with cow-dung, and the dying man is laid on it, with his head to the north-east; and if still able to understand, verses in praise of Vishnu (the Preserver) are now to be recited in a low, clear voice suited to the solemn occasion. The priestly instinct is even now alive, and the family astrologer appears on the scene to claim another cow, that the dying man may pass more easily and at an auspicious moment."

The body is adorned with saffron-coloured garments (the sacred or religious colour) and garlands, and wrapped in a shroud. It is placed on the ground with its head to the east, while the near relatives are shaved, in token of mourning. Then the body is carried to the burning-place. In our hills it is usually slung with straps and ropes to a long pole carried on the shoulders, and one sometimes meets on a road the swiftly borne burthen, and for a while the sad refrain sounds on the ear, "Rama, Rama, satya Rama" (Rama, Rama is true). The body is laid on a pyre, and on it are placed sandalwood, cedar, or other fragrant woods, mixed with ghi (which makes it burn more readily, and as a product of the cow is itself a sacred substance). The son or nearest male relative applies fire to the pile, while the mantra is recited: "Om! mayest thou arrive at the blissful abodes; thou, with thy deeds ill done, whether purposely or unknowingly, hast become an inhabitant of another world; thy body, encompassed with its load of desire, weighted with its deeds of right and wrong, has been completely resolved into its five elements." On the next day several offerings are made to the priest, with appropriate mantras, upon an altar extemporised near the burial-ground, for the benefit of the departed spirit, which is supposed to be somewhere near the spot, in a disembodied and not happy condition. Kusa grass is laid on the altar, as a seat for the spirit. One of the mantras recited has been thus rendered: "Thou hast been burned in the fire of the pyre, and hast become separate from thy brethren. Bathe in this water and drink this milk, thou that dwellest in the ether without stay or support, troubled by storms and malignant spirits; bathe and drink there, and having done so, be happy."

The full ritual is very complicated, and is only performed for the wealthy. The various materials, some of them costly, such as gold, sandalwood, etc., prescribed in the complete ceremony must render it beyond the means of the very poor, though doubtless, as in Europe, a man likes to be well treated at the last, and the survivors do their best to give him a respectable funeral. Similar ceremonies are performed on behalf of those who have died in a distant place, or whose bodies are not recoverable. A puppet of kusa grass is made in the name of the deceased and burned with the same rites as the actual body, and Sraddhas are observed at the appointed seasons. The funeral rites of the Hindus exhibit a strange mingling of the sublime and the puerile, of lofty ideality and grovelling superstition. The Sraddhas are ceremonies observed for the benefit of the dead at periodical seasons, and are similar to the rites performed immediately after death. Pindas are offered by the son or nearest male relative. These rites take place on the day of the anniversary of the death, and for about ten days at the end of the rainy season, in October, for the benefit of three generations of the worshipper's ancestors, male and female.

It may be mentioned, as a detail of the daily life of the higher castes in Kumaon, that two meals in the day are eaten, one in the morning about 9 or 10 a.m., consisting usually of rice and dal or pulse, and the second in the evening at 9 or 10 p.m., consisting of chapatis or griddle cakes and vegetable curry. Meat is not ordinarily eaten by Hindus, and great numbers never touch it. Its place is taken to a large extent by free use of ghi or clarified butter. The food is cooked with great care in a portion of the house or premises specially devoted to the purpose, except of course on a journey, when a man usually prepares his own food in the best way he can. Both in cooking food and in eating, a caste Hindu must put off his clothes, except the loin cloth. The higher castes may not eat without bathing and performing the Sandhya ceremony, though children, young women, and invalids may be indulged with an early meal. It has also become a custom with many in modern days to take a drink of *tea* early in the morning. This is conveniently assumed not to be food. My informant states that Brahmans never eat any stale food. The women and girls of a family eat after the men have finished, and after they have done waiting on their lords. The reader unacquainted with India should also understand that tables and chairs are articles unknown in the ordinary Indian house, and meals are taken seated on the ground. Chairs and even elevated bedsteads are regarded as articles of luxury, though their use is becoming every day more common, especially among the educated classes.

The most important of the many festivals of the Hindus in this part of India is the Holi, which falls in the month of March or end of February. It is the spring festival, connected with ideas of the renewal of life and joy and merriment, when friends visit and wish one another joy, as at Christmas time in Europe. Nominally it celebrates the slaying of a female demon in ancient times, about whom several varying legends are told. She was got rid of by the children singing all kinds of songs and making merry round a bonfire, and this custom is kept up on the appointed day, though the festival is not now confined to the children. People of all ages and ranks for three days perambulate the roads, or go from village to village in the country districts, singing ditties, said to be of improper character, in honour of Kanhaiya (Krishna) and his "gopis" or cowherdesses; playing rough jokes, abusing each other, and throwing over one another's clothes a red powder called "gulal," made from the flowers of the rhododendron tree. White cotton clothes are worn, in token of the commencement of warmer weather, and to suit the throwing of the red dye, which can be easily washed out of cotton cloth. The Khassiyas seem to connect the festival with their more special cults, by setting up the triangular standard of Bhairava (their form of Siva) and making offerings to his Sakti. Day and night a kind of saturnalia and feast of unreason goes on, the general character of which is by no means commendable. Wilson, in his famous essay on the *Religious Feasts of the Hindus*, has a discussion of the origin of the Holi, and points out some interesting parallels to similar observances of the Romans and ancient Germans, and the modern carnival. In earliest times in India it appears to have been connected with Kamadeva, the god of love, and was a spring celebration in his honour. This appears from some extant practices of the Tamil races, and the connection is further evident in the celebration of Krishna, who in his youthful form is a kind of Cupid. The English custom of April Fool's Day has also some resemblance to features of the Indian Holi festival.

Nanda is a favourite goddess in Kumaon, and her birthday, the Nandashtami, in the month of Bhado (August–September), is an occasion of great rejoicing. There is a large fair and concourse of people at Almora, when a young buffalo is sacrificed in the precincts of the goddess's temple. The first blow is struck with a kukri, or short, broad, and heavy sword, by the descendant of the Almora rajas, and then the animal is despatched. In some villages, it is said, a buffalo is kept for two days; fed and adorned with garlands, and worshipped. Finally it is let loose, and the villagers pelt it with stones and hack it to death with knives. Such sacrifices remind us of the old paganism of the West, and carry us back to the day when Paul and Barnabas entered Lystra and healed the lame man, and "the priest of Jupiter brought oxen and garlands unto the gates, and would have done sacrifice with the people"; or, with Keats, our thoughts return to classic Greece—

> Who are these coming to the sacrifice?
> To what green altars, O mysterious priest,
> Leadest thou that heifer lowing at the skies,
> And all her silken flanks with garlands drest?
> What little town by river or seashore,
> Or mountain-built with peaceful citadel,
> Is emptied of its folk this pious morn?

Only that the sacrifice of a heifer or an ox would fill the Hindu mind with horror at the present day. Buffaloes and goats take the place of Vedic beef, even among the least orthodox tribes and castes.

The festivals of Dasehra and Diwali, as observed in Kumaon, do not differ in any important respects from the same as practised in the plains of India. The Diwali is the feast of lamps, held in November in honour of Lakshmi, the wife of Vishnu and goddess of luck and prosperity. On a certain evening the exterior of all the houses is illuminated with innumerable little lamps, consisting of a tiny earthenware vessel in which a wick floats on some mustard oil. The general effect of the town, when thus lighted, is very charming. The great occupation and amusement of the people during the fair is gambling, which used to go on for a longer period, but is now usually restricted to three days. It is believed that no one can expect good fortune during the year unless he gambles a little at the Diwali. The festival is also a time to look out for thieves about one's premises. Professional "cracksmen" have a notion that they should try their luck on the last night of the Diwali, and if they can succeed in carrying off even a trifle, they believe that the succeeding year will be a good one for their craft. The gambling is often very wild, and people are not infrequently beggared during the three days of the festival. Mr. J. E. Goudge in his recent Settlement Report (1904) refers to the remarkable prevalence of gambling in Kumaon, and says it is a proof that the people are exceptionally well-off, and thus the enhancement of the land revenue is a blessing in disguise to them, inasmuch as it curtails the opportunity for this destructive vice.

The Dasehra, in October, commemorates the victory of Rama over Ravana, the monstrous ten-headed king of Lanka or Ceylon, as described in the Ramayana. During the days of the festival a theatrical entertainment, provided by public subscription, is generally held in the open air near the Badrishwar temple in Almora, when the main incidents of the Indian epic are represented by native actors to large and admiring audiences, filling all the adjacent ground.

When the British assumed the government of Kumaon in 1815 they found a rude system of justice in force, somewhat resembling what we have read of as prevailing among our Anglo-Saxon ancestors. One of the early commissioners of the province, George William Traill, in his interesting Report (1820)—which by the way is a kind of classic of its kind, and has been much quoted by antiquarians and students of religion—gives the following details of the *ordeals* formerly employed in Kumaon. "Three forms of ordeals were in common use: First, the Gola Dip, which consists in receiving in the palms of the hands and carrying to a certain distance a red-hot bar of iron; second, the Karai Dip, in which the hand is plunged into a vessel of boiling oil, in which case the test of truth is the absence of marks of burning on the hand; third, Taraju Ka Dip, in which the person undergoing the ordeal was weighed at night against stones, which were then carefully deposited under lock and key and the seal of the superintending officer. On the following morning, after a variety of ceremonies, the appellant was again weighed, and the substantiation of his cause depended on his proving heavier than on the preceding evening.

"The Tir Ka Dip, in which the person remained with his head submerged in water while another ran the distance of a bowshot and back, was sometimes resorted to. The Gurkha governors introduced another mode of trial by water, in which two boys, both unable to swim, were thrown into a pond, and the longest liver gained the cause. Formerly, poison was in very particular cases resorted to as the criterion of innocence; a daily dose of a particular root was administered, and the party, if he survived, was absolved. A further mode of appeal to the interposition of the deity was by placing the sum of money, or a bit of earth from the land in dispute, in a temple before the idol. Either one of the parties volunteering such test, then, with imprecations on himself if false, took up the article in question. Supposing no death to occur within six months in his immediate family, he gained his cause; on the contrary, he was cast in the event of being visited with any great calamity or if afflicted with some sickness during that period."

CHAPTER XI

THE VILLAGE WISEACRE

THE Oriental is generally "full of wise saws and modern instances." He usually treasures up in his memory a large collection of verses and popular sayings, which he produces on occasion with much zest, and expounds at great and even inconvenient length. Many native visitors, if acquainted with Sanskrit or Persian, will at the slightest provocation pour out a long string of sonorous lines, and then begin a laborious translation and commentary in the approved manner, finishing up with an application to the matter in hand. This takes up a good deal of time, but it makes the good man happy, and one must learn to be more prodigal of time in the East than in the busy West. The humbler Indian, whose learning does not extend to repeating Sanskrit *slokas*, will venture on a familiar proverb in the vernacular, and show the same pleasure in explaining and applying it. To a large extent such sayings, and the stories from the sacred epics which are used to illustrate them, constitute the wisdom and learning of the people, and there is no source of information that casts more light on their ways of thinking and homely customs than the study of Indian proverbial lore.

The folklore and proverbs of this remote part of India have a pleasant flavour of originality. They have grown up, to a large extent, independent of outside influences, and many of them are plainly of entirely local growth, referring to peculiar features of mountain life and embodying local names and customs. A retired native official, Pandit Ganga Datt Uprety, has spent some of his years of leisure since resigning his "Deputy-Collectorship" in gathering a large number of popular sayings and stories, which he published some years ago under the title of *Proverbs and Folklore of Kumaon and Garhwal.* I had the pleasure of helping the Pandit in the preparation of his book, and of writing an introduction for it. The author has given each proverb in its native shape—that is, in Kumaoni, a patois of Hindi—and has translated it into English, with such application as was needed to make its application clear, and in many instances has added stories such as are commonly related by village wiseacres and rustic philosophers in illustrating a particular proverb. They have the merit of being genuine popular sayings, derived not from books but from the living speech of the people. Many of them are in verse, or have curious rhymes and jingles which it is quite impossible to render in a translation, and so they lose much of their point and picturesque quality by being turned into another language. At the same time, in any form, they afford interesting glimpses into the life and mind of the people, and I propose to bring together and arrange a few of the more characteristic ones in their English form, occasionally altering a little to bring out the meaning.

A common saying in all parts of North India is that

"man is a corn-grub," dependent for his life on food, in its special form of the staple grain eaten by the people. In Kumaon the villagers say, "Rice is the headman, millet (madua) is the king, and wheat the slave." This means that their annual crops are disposed of in various ways. The paddy (rice) is sold, and the proceeds of it go to the headman (padhan) of the village in payment of ground-rent or revenue; the wheat is used for satisfying chaprasis, Government peons or messengers, whose visits to the villages are much dreaded, there being, indeed, a proverb that the peasant dreads the face of a chaprasi more than that of a tiger; while the madua or millet is the only support of the family, and their common daily food, made into chapatis or thin flat cakes baked on a round iron plate always carried by the travelling Kumaoni. Madua grows with large heavy ears containing a small blackish grain. A characteristic of this grain is embodied in the following, "Madua is a good fellow (literally a king), for he becomes fresh when heated," alluding to the custom of the village folk of making cakes of the madua meal when they are going on a journey. Before eating them, the cakes are warmed up, which makes them taste as fresh as when newly baked.

In all countries the inhabitants of certain places gain a peculiar reputation. The English reader will remember the characteristics ascribed to "Yorkshire tykes," or "Lancashire lads," or more locally to the wise men of Gotham, and the like. An evidence of the truth that human nature is much the same all the world over is seen in the prevalence of such caustic judgments in every community. In this part of India, for example, there has always been a kind of traditional rivalry between the two neighbouring districts of Kumaon and Garhwal, which together make up the province. The people of the latter district, when dissatisfied with the decision of some native official, usually a Kumaoni, whom they suspect of partiality towards their neighbours in the eastern half of the province, have a saying, "Looking towards Kumaon and turning the back on Garhwal." The Kumaon people, in their turn, are inclined to ridicule the tendency shown by the Garhwalis towards pride of birth. Just as in Scotland it is commonly said that every man claims to be a gentleman connected with some ancient house, so in Garhwal many profess to be descended from rajas. This trait is alluded to in the saying, "Damari ko sahu, tipari ko rau," that is, one who has a damari, a copper coin worth about one-eighth of a farthing, is called a man of wealth, and one who owns the top of a hill is called "rau" or raja. In former times, before the conquest of Garhwal by Kanak Pal about the seventh century, the whole district was portioned out between petty rulers called Thakuri rajas, each of whom would seize a mountain peak, build his fortress on it, and tyrannise over a few surrounding villages, much like the robber nobles of mediæval Europe. The proverb is used tauntingly to describe the anarchy and poverty of ancient Garhwal. The people of Garhwal retaliate by accusing their neighbours of clannishness and a keen commercial spirit: "Kumaoni, cares for himself, lets others go hang." The Garhwali, when compelled by business or necessity to live in Kumaon, feels himself an exile, and misses the "fleshpots of Egypt," the creature comforts that can only be obtained at home. He

A Baniya or Shopkeeper in Kumaon

says, "There may be fine scenery in Kumaon, but give me Garhwal for food and drink."

The Baniya, or shopkeeper, and the peasant are two contrasted characters to whom we find frequent allusions. The former is represented as cunning and plausible, while the latter is rough and uncouth, yet in the end quite able to hold his own. Thus we have, "The Baniya is a sly fellow, but the villager is slyer." This is to be understood as referring more to the cunning of the Kumaoni peasant. The following, however, clearly refers to the Baniya's subtlety: "Come in, sir, and eat some gurh" (solid extract of the sugar-cane). "Write it down, write it down." The Baniya invites a simple fellow to come and taste his wares, but at the same time orders his shop assistant to enter the item against him in the account book. Again, "If a man is 'cuter than a Baniya he must be mad." The villagers like to relieve the seriousness of their dealings with the shopkeepers by a little pleasantry. We are told that they turn the common title or distinctive caste name of the Baniya, which is Sah, into Sau, meaning a hundred, because he has a hundred cunning tricks.

The villagers of Gangoli, a pargana or parish of Kumaon, have acquired a peculiar reputation for apparent simplicity and real "downiness," which we find perpetuated in two sayings: "The flour-seller of Gangoli. Cheat him well, cheat him well." A man of Gangoli once brought some flour, the produce of his fields, to Almora to sell. The Baniya who was to buy it received a hint from a friend of his standing by, in the words just quoted; but this suggestion was overheard by the villager, who, having completed the bargain and received payment, replied, as he went off, "The poor simpleton of Gangoli—five parts of chalk and one of flour," which was the actual composition of the article that he had palmed off on the Baniya. The villagers are rather hardly dealt with in the following: "A Khassiya, when addressed politely, turns surly." "No people so generous as the hillmen, but they give nothing without a stick." They have to be threatened before they will do anything. "A Khassiya's wrath is like the thirst of a buffalo;" that is, when in rage he will spare no one, just as the buffalo drinks up all the water of a pool when he once begins. "A hillman's 'No' is worth a hundred rupees;" if he once refuses to do anything, no amount of persuasion will turn him from his dogged purpose. "The Khassiya is so simple that he will demand a long coat in exchange for a cap." "The Khassiya will never prove a friend, nor the croton-plant holy." "You can only manage a villager by professing to agree with him."

Very numerous are the allusions to the class of Doms, the aboriginal tribe who do the menial work for the higher castes, and have a separate quarter of their own in or near the villages of their more respectable neighbours. They are invariably spoken of in terms of contempt and dislike. The vituperation of "low people" is unfortunately very characteristic of the Hindus, and apparently regarded as proper and meritorious. Their literature and conversation abound with expressions of scorn towards humbler communities, and the exclusiveness of the caste system has always put out of the question any attempt to improve the condition of their inferiors in the social scale or to teach them better things. It has also to be said that the

Hindu in giving advice is apt to act on the principle of admonishing by pointing to bad examples as warnings. A few only of these hard sayings will be quoted here as specimens. "The marriage of a Dom simply pains the eyes;" that is, the Biths or partricians take no part in any ceremony or festival of the Doms, and their merry-making is felt to be rather offensive than otherwise. "The Dom, too lazy to plough or manure, but at dinner-time is envious," used as an admonition to idle people. The Doms eat the morsels and leavings of food given them by people of higher caste. This is referred to in the following: "The Dom's vessel says, When shall I go to the dwelling of the Biths?" This is applied to the desire of low people to be connected with the higher castes. The Pandit adds, "Even an injury done by a Bith to a Dom is welcomed by him so long as it also disgraces the Bith caste." A story is told of a Dom who was once spoken to by a king. On going home he sat quite silent for a long while. His family addressed him several times, but he returned no answer. Thinking him to be out of his wits or possessed by a demon, his wife earnestly entreated him to speak to her, whereupon he took a stick and began beating her, saying, "O curst foolish one! how can I speak with you, a poor woman, with the mouth that has spoken to a king?" So the saying is current, "Pride in the head of a Dom." "The singing of a Dom with a goitre on his neck is no singing at all," is an allusion to a common complaint in some parts of the hills, and is a saying used by one who finds that his work is not appreciated by his superior. "No one thinks of a Bith being poor, or notices the death of a Dom." Contempt could not go much further than the following: "Brother Bruin was killed and the Dom's house was burnt down—both good things," originating from a story of a bear who once entered the house of a Dom after honey in the hive, and accidentally set fire to the hut by stirring up the embers. So, in the judgment of the Biths, two birds were killed with one stone. [The hive in the house is a peculiar custom of the hill people. They take stones out of the outside wall, leaving an aperture in which bees are led to settle and make their honey; and then, by withdrawing the inner block of stone in the wall, the comb can easily be abstracted when ready for use.]

The Khassiyas, Baniyas, and Doms have had their turn. The chief remaining class, the Brahmans, are not allowed to escape some humorous *badinage*. Their minute subdivisions, and fastidiousness in matters of caste are ridiculed in the saying, "Eight Brahmans of the Patiya village, but nine hearths." Patiya is a place about seven miles north from Almora, below the Bageswar road. It is said that eight Brahmans, kinsmen of that village, together with a Khassiya coolie, set off on a journey. At the first stopping-place, each of the Brahmans began to arrange a separate cooking-place for himself, none of them being willing to eat the food prepared by another. It must be explained, for the benefit of the British reader, that Hindus on a journey at the close of the day undress and set to work to cook their food at a little hearth oven, which they construct of stones or earth, and that the greatest importance attaches to the act of eating and drinking with other people. No caste Hindu will demean himself or endanger his Hinduship by eating with a person of inferior caste, or a non-Hindu. Indeed, dragging with wild horses would not induce the poorest "twice-born" Indian subject to dine with the Viceroy, for thus he would lose all that he counts valuable—his status, as a member of Hindu society, in his proper caste. To return to our story: the Khassiya coolie, though having no objection himself to eat food prepared by Brahmans, became disgusted on seeing their disunion, and began to suspect that they were all of doubtful caste; so he resolved to prepare his own "chula" or stove also, thus making the ninth. This proverb is also said to be quoted by the Garhwalis against the people of Kumaon, who are much more scrupulous in such matters than themselves.

The period of Sraddhas or worship of ancestors is a joyful time for the Brahmans, as they then receive invitations to ceremonial feasts, and live on the fat of the land. "At the approach of the Sraddha fortnight, when the Kans grass (used religiously) begins to flower, the Brahmans leap with joy nine bamboos high." At the end of the rainy season, as explained in a former chapter, sixteen days are set apart for the worship of deceased ancestors for three generations back, and these are called the sixteen Sraddhas. The principal part of this ceremony nowadays consists in feasting Brahmans and kinsmen and giving alms. The more special feeding and propitiation of the ancestors' spirits which is enjoined in the scriptures appears to have been largely given up and commuted into this general feasting. It is supposed by the entertainer that the satisfaction and benefit of the forefathers will be in strict proportion to the number of Brahmans fed and the value of the offerings made to them. Another proverb with the same meaning is, "The Sraddha begins, the Brahmans rouse up; the Sraddha ended, the

Brahmans get thin," a satire on poor Brahmans who live chiefly on such invitations. "A Bhatta (or Brahman) uninvited, is like the land near the village of Nauti." A Brahman who thrusts himself into a feast without being invited receives no attention from the host, just as the land of Nauti in Garhwal, being too high to grow any crops, is left waste.

"What the Panth says, do it; what the Panth does, eschew it." The Panths are a powerful caste of Brahmans, and in old days could do much as they pleased, while poor folk dared neither follow their example nor disobey their orders. This is the local explanation of the proverb, though we might be inclined to suppose it to be a replica of our saying attributed to the priest, "Do as I say, but not as I do."

"The Khassiya feels cold after bathing, and a Brahman feels cold after dinner." The former, like Dr. Johnson, is not bigotedly fond of water, but on the rare occasions when he bathes, at some religious festival, he experiences an unaccustomed sensation; while the Brahman, who has to undress before eating, feels cold by the time the meal is ended. The Khassiya is said to show his usual cunning by calling out, when he falls by accident into a stream, "Har Ganga, Har Ganga," that is, he assumes that he is bathing for religious merit, and makes a virtue of necessity.

The Yogis, or wandering religious mendicants, of whom a considerable number are always to be met with in the province, on their way to or from the sacred shrines in the snowy range, also come in for their share of banter. They occasionally take up their abode for a considerable time in a neighbourhood, and become well known to the countryside, sometimes acquiring a reputation for sanctity; otherwise, their foibles are observed with keen criticism. "One who is called simply a Yogi in his own village will be called a Siddh (or saint) in another place," corresponds to the biblical, "A prophet is not without honour save in his own country." "A Yogi while he lives is always munch, munching, and when dead is always being buried." The poor mendicant eats as often as he receives alms, which usually take the form of food, and when dead his body is buried (not burned) by those of his disciples or near kinsmen who are at hand; but whenever an absent disciple or relative arrives at his tomb, it is the custom for him to add to it or adorn it in some way. This practice of burying ascetics seems to have come down from Buddhist times, when the veneration of relics and of holy persons took the place of the Brahmanical worship and sacrifice to the gods.

An instance of Indian humour is found in the following story, the point of which is embodied in the saying "Nothing is forbidden to the Sadhu" (one who has risen superior to caste rules, etc.). A man one day invited a famous Vaishnava ascetic, one of the sect which rigidly abstains from flesh-meat, to a grand feast. The hermit declined the invitation, as he said that mutton would be cooked there. The host admitted the fact, but assured him that the meat would be cooked quite separately from the other kinds of food. On receiving this assurance, the ascetic agreed to be present. The man then went home and had the meat cooked in a separate kitchen. When the dinner was ready, all the guests sat down in rows, the ascetic also taking his place among them. The various dishes were placed before them. The Vaishnava, being very anxious that he should not have occasion to ask for anything after the meat was brought on, insisted on being supplied with everything that he required at the beginning, lest his food should be polluted by the touch of the vessel in which the meat had been cooked. In due course the meat came on for distribution. While it was being served out, the ascetic, tempted by the savoury smell of the meat and broth, said, "I think the soup consists of nothing but Ganges water," to which all present said, "Certainly." Then said he, "I must have some of it; if it is only Ganges water there can be nothing wrong in taking it; but let the cook take care that none of the pieces of mutton come into my dish—otherwise I will leave the food and go away." They gave him some of the broth, which he found very delicious. He accordingly asked for some more; but by that time very little liquid was left in the vessel, and so the cook was obliged to empty it into the holy man's dish, putting a spoon to the mouth of the vessel so that all the remaining soup in it should flow out, but none of the bits of meat. Seeing this, the ascetic, completely casting away his vegetarian principles, called out, "All things are lawful to the Sadhu; why do you stop the pieces of meat? Let 'em come, let 'em come."

The caustic tone of the above story shows that a good many of the people of Kumaon take pleasure in baiting the religious orders and telling tales to their discredit, in exactly the same way as people do in some European countries. Indeed, there is said to be a considerable number of downright infidels in the province, who, dissatisfied with what Hinduism can offer them, profess to have no religious belief, and to be Epicureans of the frankest kind. They are fond of quoting the proverb, "Everyone sings his own song." They do not hesitate to declare that the doctrines of future punishment and reward are inventions for the purpose of frightening people into good behaviour. As men have never known anyone to appear after death, they decline to believe in a future life. The Pandit informs us: "There are many of these Nastiks or atheistic philosophers, who attribute everything to chance, in Kumaon and Garhwal. They observe no sacred days. They say a tree has many leaves, which all fall in autumn, but the same leaves will not grow next spring; so men are like leaves that flourish and decay, and their memory is lost."

In the folklore of most nations some notice is taken of the characteristics of animals, and such allusions are not the least interesting part of the popular wisdom of Kumaon, evincing a good deal of kindly observation of our dumb fellow-creatures. "The grain was eaten by partridges, but the Musabhya-kurhas (a kind of small bird) were entrapped." Villagers make stone traps for birds with grain spread under them, which the shy partridges pick up gingerly and fly off unhurt; but the little birds named, being of an unwary nature, enter the trap and bring the large stone or slate down on themselves by pecking at the stick supporting it. This is applied to those who make use of simple folks as "catspaws" to accomplish their ends.

The fat of the Lestiya (a very tiny bird) is in its "ghercha" (a small internal sac). This is applied to poor people, who hide away their little bit of money and spend it with great circumspection and unwillingness. "The wound inflicted by a 'takua' (thin iron bar heated in the fire) is enough for a hen to bear." These bars are attached to the hand of a spindle, and are used for making slight burns on the body—a favourite remedy for pain in the hills. The application is of course to a loss incurred by a poor man: a small loss is more than he can bear. "The voice of a Tuti (another small bird) in a house full of sounding drums," aptly describes the plight of one who finds himself too poor and insignificant to have his claims attended to by great people, or who is thrust aside by more bold and clamorous neighbours. "What is a Piddi (still another little bird), and how much soup can be made from it?" is used in ridicule when comparing small things with great. "Phechua's flight is only up to the roof." The phechua is a small winged creature which can only flutter a few yards, hence it is compared to the limited powers of a poor man. An amusing apologue is current regarding the active little singing-bird known as Pyurari. Once, while catching insects and worms, she found a small copper coin, and danced about with it in her mouth, singing, "What is the king's wealth compared to mine?" The story reached the king, who had the coin taken from her. Then the bird began to sing, "The king is wealthy by my wealth." The king, ashamed of the accusation, returned the coin to the little bird, whereupon she began to sing, "If he took my wealth, why could he not enjoy it?" The impudence of the tiny creature, hopping about and singing, is well expressed.

"The chirping of birds in the bushes," is applied to random and irresponsible criticisms, to which one should pay no heed. A snatch of song sung by the hill people runs as follows: "After Ma (January) the bees feed well; after Phagun (February) the cows; after Chait (March) the monkeys feast." In January there are no flowers, in February the grass is dried up, and in March fruit is scarce in the woods; but these hard times once over, the creatures referred to get along well enough. This is used to cheer up one's friends, equivalent to our saying, "There's a good time coming." "The mouth of the pot was open, but the cat ought to have had some sense of shame," refers to the misdeeds of some domestic pet who had yielded to temptation. It is used to imply that an honest man may be depended on to keep the straight path, in spite of opportunities of going wrong. Titira, meaning partridge, is proverbially used for a wide-awake person. To call a man a titira is the same as saying that one must rise very early in the morning to get the better of him. "The kakar barks," that is, the place is become a jungle, in which only the voice of the kakar or barking deer is heard—applied to an undertaking that has miserably failed. "The cuckoo utters his voice," is used in the same sense. In the Bhabar people go on working till about April; when they hear the cuckoo's voice in that month, denoting the approach of the hot season, they know it is time to pack up, and leave their fields at the foot of the hills (cultivated in winter only) to return to their villages in the highlands.

A crow is supposed to produce only one brood in its lifetime, so the expression "a crow-birth" is applied to a woman who has only one child. "A cat's eating grass," is used of a man doing something suspicious, or beginning to contract evil ways. Cats are observed sometimes going to eat a particular kind of grass, and this is regarded as unnatural.

A few examples of sayings connected with *place-names* in the province may be of some interest. These are probably the most original of all.

"Nine days for going two-and-a-half kos" (about five miles), is thus explained. There are temples at Kedar and Badari that once were connected by a road of five miles. These temples were then served by the same priest, but he grew weary of having to visit both places on the same day. So the gods caused a huge landslip which made the road impassable, and the two temples are now separated by a nine days' journey. This proverb is quoted by one who misses his way.

"Mahruri was made by gathering from here and there." This is the name of a small parish or pargana in Kumaon which formerly did not exist; but when the Gurkha government had to assign villages to feed pilgrims to Kedar and Badari, this new pargana was formed by cutting off portions from others. The saying is equal to "raising the wind," "by hook or by crook." "A skirt for Kanda." Kanda is a village in Garhwal, near Srinagar, where an annual fair or mela is held during the Diwali festival in October. Women always wear their gayest clothes at that fair, and often put on borrowed garments for the occasion. The saying is applied to one who makes a great show, though in reality he is very "hard up." Almost an exact parallel to our "castles in Spain" is "gold of Lanka," it being supposed that the ground in Lanka (Ceylon) is made of gold-dust; but to one who is not there, it is useless, being out of reach when needed, whereas "the vegetables in one's own garden and the fire in the flint and steel (still used in the hills) are always at hand." "Sunshine on a ridge, and a morsel in the mouth," applied to things that soon pass, or transient and unreal objects of desire. "The villages are scattered here and there, but the ways of the people are the same," is used to enjoin sympathy with others in matters that affect the common weal.

"Khatiyari for vegetables, and Gangoli for tigers." The former is a village close to Almora, which supplies the town with garden produce. Tigers are said to be as plentiful in Gangoli as vegetables in Khatiyari, so much so that they are said to be hardly dreaded by the people of the place. Once, hearing screams and yells, the neighbours in Gangoli ran to see what was the matter; but finding that only a tiger was the cause of the uproar, they regretted going, and said they thought it had been a chaprasi or court messenger from Almora.

"What will Badrinath give me if I go to his house, and what will he bring me if he comes to mine?" The shrine of Badrinath is considered by the Garhwal people as their peculiar property, to which they have no need of presenting offerings, like the pilgrims from other parts of India; rather they expect to gain something from it. The saying is applied to selfish and interested people. "Mal ki lai, kab kab khai," is a fair example of these proverbial jingles. It means, "How seldom do we eat the mustard of the plains!" Such mustard is to be had only occasionally, so people are exhorted to depend on their own efforts.

"The stony land of Bidoli gives grain, though fair to see is Gostu-ki-bare." These are the names of two villages in Garhwal, one of which appears unpromising, but is well cultivated, while the other deceives the eye by its beauty. All is not gold that glitters. The coolies, as they struggle up the steep roads of Kumaon with their heavy loads, quote the proverb, "Let me not be a man in the hills, nor a he-buffalo in the plains," as these have to do all the heavy carrying work. "Has eyes, yet falls down a cliff," suggests the precipitous paths leading to Kumaon villages, and points the finger of scorn at the rash and improvident. Of the same nature is the saying, "One who goes to Dhangu must come back carefully" (Janu Dhangu, aunu angu). The place referred to is a precipitous part of Garhwal, and the application is to a perilous task. Gaya Gaya gayai gaya, "one who goes to Gaya goes for ever," is still used to dissuade friends from a long journey or dangerous pilgrimage. The journey to Gaya, holiest of pilgrimages, used to take several months on foot, before the spread of railways turned pilgrimages into pleasure trips. "Without thinking of all the ascents and descents, everyone wants to go to the plains," is a similar warning.

Wild animals are still a source of danger in Kumaon, and every year some five hundred people are reported to owe their death to them. There is therefore some point in the saying, "One whose father was killed by a bear dreads even the black trunk of a tree." In the northern part of the province the black bear is very common, and devours a great part of the crops, so that in some valleys the men have often to watch all night in their fields. "The tiger carried off the people in the lower storey, and those in the upper storey awoke," implies that warning should be taken from the distresses of others. Many of the villages consist of a single row of stone cottages with two storeys, the lower one being called the Got, and usually reserved for keeping cattle. Tigers are common enough in the Bhabar, and occasionally wander up the river valleys into the very heart of the province. There is also a species of tiger peculiar to the Himalayas, very large and hairy.

"Why ask after the path to a village whither one does not need to go?" reminds one of the steep and winding tracks up and down the mountain-sides, where in turning an ugly corner one has sometimes to "hang on by one's teeth," or at any rate climb on hands and knees.

An interesting historical reference is found in the saying, "Khati ruling in the hills, and Hathi (elephant) in the plains." Before the Chand dynasty drew Kumaon together into a single kingdom, a powerful and oppressive Rajput tribe from the plains, named Khati, held sway for a time at Phaldakot in the hills; and at that time the ancient Hindu civilisation at the foot of the Himalaya being broken up by invasion of non-Aryan tribes, the wild elephant possessed the land. The proverb describes a state of anarchy. "A cow that has fallen down a bank is always said to have been a grand milker," expresses in homely fashion a trait of human nature which Tennyson has clothed in pomp of melodious words—

> The Past will always win
> A glory from its being far;
> And orb into the perfect star
> We saw not when we moved therein.

The tendency to grumble at one's lot, and to imagine that other people differently circumstanced are better off, is illustrated in the saying of the Kumaonis, "The east for disease, the west for sorrow, the north for penance, and the south for pleasure." This seems to be a saying expressing envy of those who live in the plains. It may mean that the eastern part of the province is unhealthy, as cholera and typhus often break out there in summer; the west has been the quarter from which successive invasions have come; in the north are the painful "tirthas" or places of pilgrimage, reached by snowy and difficult paths; while the plains in winter represent ease and enjoyment to the toiling highlander. The native form of this saying, with its chime of assonances, is calculated to fill the soul of an English rhymester with envy: "Purab rog; Pachcham sog; Uttar jog; Dakhin bhog."

"A moonlight night and irrigated land (are fine things)." The fields at the bottom of the valleys, watered by springs or from the tumbling brooks, are highly valued, as there the best kinds of rice can be grown. So also on a moonlight night the wayfarer can find the path with ease.

There is keen satire of both sexes in the proverb, "A vegetable seen by a man and a tiger seen by a woman are not to be credited." In villages the women cultivate the kitchen garden, as well as doing most other work, and the men know nothing about the vegetables, so that it is not much use asking them to attend to that department—any more than one can trust the exaggerated story of a frightened woman.

A rather pessimistic saying carries back our thoughts to the "good old times" of oppression that once prevailed under the native rulers: "Money saved is sure to be taken by the king, and the body pampered is sure to be seized by death."

Bhotiyas at Bageswar

"His property is in Rau, and he keeps watch in Salam," two villages ten miles apart. This saying is applied to those who neglect their business, or live away from it.

"No village beyond Mana, and no number above eighteen." Mana is the last inhabited spot on the Mana pass to Tibet, and there are only eighteen spots on dice. The proverb implies that there is no further expedient to be found, or no higher court of appeal.

Our familiar "rolling stone" finds its analogue in the saying "moving like a pestle," that is, like the beam of wood wielded by the women-folk of the family when they husk the grain in the "okhli" or stone mortar.

An allusion to the secret and sudden movements of the old kings, ever surrounded by plots and intrigues, is found in the following: "None knows when the king will move, or the cloud rain," reminding us of Solomon's proverb, "The heaven for height, and the earth for depth, and the heart of kings is unsearchable."

The Banj oak (*Quercus dilatata*), with its great twisted boughs, covers great tracts of high ground, but is evidently not considered a thing of beauty by the Kumaonis. "Neither mouth nor nose: a regular oak," is used to describe a very ugly person.

Charas is an intoxicating drug made from the hemp plant, which grows in great plenty everywhere in the rainy season. Though the effects of most preparations of hemp are not very injurious, leading only to light-headedness and exaltation of spirits for a time, charas seems to be an exception, probably because it is also mixed with opium; and men are sometimes seen who have been reduced to a state of insanity by its constant use. The two following sayings must be characteristic of confirmed devotees of the drug: "The boy who does not smoke charas—a girl is better than he;" "Any-one who speaks against charas, may his children perish!"

In an old volume of Indian travels, Honiberger's *Thirty-five Years in the East,* I find the following curious account of the preparation of charas: "The intoxicating drug called charas, used for smoking, is prepared as follows: the fresh and ripe hemp plant is held over a mild fire to soften it, and afterwards bruised in a mortar till it becomes a compact mass. Another very curious method of obtaining it is by persons wearing leather breeches passing through the hemp fields so that they come in contact with the hemp plant, by which a quantity of resinous substance attaches itself to the leather garments and other parts of the body, which they afterwards scrape off and collect. But the best way is to get the resinous parts by rubbing the plant in its growing state with the hands."

"The frost is hard till the sun rises," is a striking metaphor applied to oppression coming to an end on some appeal to justice.

A deep saying, reminding us of New Testament teaching, is, "A barha is made by being pierced in the middle." The "barha" is a cake of pulse-flour with a hole in the centre, and cooked in oil or ghi for festival days. The proverb teaches that a man becomes great by voluntarily sustaining loss for the good of others.

"The feet of the simple are in the path" (of blessing or profit), refers to the good fortune often accompany-ing a man not distinguished for wisdom. Bacon has given it as his opinion that the successful man must have "poco di matto," a little of the fool about him, in order to escape envy.

"God gives, even through the roof of one's house," declares that one will certainly receive what is fated. "Not a farthing to his name, yet wants to marry two brides," reflects on the conduct of an impecunious spendthrift, and refers to the custom in Garhwal and Kumaon requiring the bridegroom to pay a heavy sum to the bride's family on marriage. The condition of things as prevailing in other parts of India is thus completely reversed, the reason probably being that a wife is a valuable commodity to the hillman, as she does nearly all the field-work. A man with two wives is thus better off and can cultivate more land. The scant welcome accorded to daughters in India generally is due to the fact that they have to be provided with a handsome dowry, which impoverishes the household.

"A bear made of blanket," is a false alarm, a *canard*. Monkeys and deer are kept from the fields by a scarecrow formed with one of the ordinary black blankets worn by the people as a coat or covering in winter. A foolishly extravagant person is described as one who "Kills his buffalo for the sake of toras, and pulls down his house to get woras." The "tora" is a musical horn made from a buffalo's horn, and the "wora" is a boundary-stone or pillar separating fields.

"While the Topal was preparing the cannon (top), the Chandal seized the kingdom," is a Garhwali proverb enjoining readiness in time of danger. These are said to have been two petty rajas in Garhwal in early times.

A contented spirit utters itself in "Bread is bread, what matter though it be thick or thin." The folly of over-indulgence of children is expressed by "Loved overmuch, went to a deeper ditch."

That there are some things in which a man must depend on others' help is exemplified in the proverb, "No one can shave his own head." There are various ceremonial occasions when this act is prescribed, and a familiar sight in an Indian bazaar is the barber, seated in the open street on the ground, operating upon the head of a man sitting in front of him.

A sharp and fault-finding person is called in Kumaon "a digging hoe." "The advice of an old man is like the aunla fruit," bitter but medicinal.

The well-worn themes of Time and Death furnish some rather striking sayings. "Moonlight for a few days and then the dark fortnight," is analogous to "Work while it is called to-day."

"Men say that Time passes: Time says that men pass," is used as a reminder of the brevity and uncertainty of life.

"The mind of another is a foreign land," expresses the mystery of personality.

"Destroying the leaf from which one eats," is applied to an ungrateful person, and recalls the familiar sight of poor people taking their food on leaves sewn together in lieu of a dish.

"A quarrel between husband and wife is like a meal of rice and milk," that is, soon over; an idyllic touch reminding us of Tennyson's

> As through the land at eve we went
> And plucked the ripened ears,
> We fell out, my wife and I,
> We fell out, I know not why,
> And kissed again with tears.
> And blessings on the falling-out
> That all the more endears.

Only that Kumaonis probably are not in the habit of kissing. The Pandit tells us in another place that it is a custom among the village people, when a man is pleased with something his wife has done, to throw lightly a bit of stone or earth towards her. Hence the proverb, "When my husband is pleased, he heaves a great stone at me," implying that the blockhead threw a large missile with such force as to hurt his wife; and applied to one who, when relied on for help, does something awkward which injures the other.

Such are a few of the tales and proverbial sayings that are told around the burning logs, of a winter's night, in the little stone villages that cling nestlike to the sides of the steep mountains of Kumaon. I shall conclude this chapter with a story illustrating the rudimentary idea of *humour* among the people of Kumaon. Such tales usually refer to the *gaucheries* and amusing blunders of rustics and people wanting in sense. The Hindu, as a rule, has a large measure of self-possession and *aplomb*. Moreover, we cannot help making the confession that if a comparison were made between the rustic population of Britain and that of India, the latter would be found to have a great many more ideas and a far richer vocabulary than the former. This is no doubt largely due to the tropical or semi-tropical climate, which stimulates the feelings and imagination.

Lachua Kothari was a worthy man who had seven sons, all strong and well grown, but each more incurably stupid than the other. On one occasion they were sent to cut some beams of wood for roofing, but finding them rather heavy, they thought it a good plan to cut them into quite short lengths, and brought them home in that state, of course perfectly useless for the purpose. Another time, they were told to sew skirts for the women of the family. (The men do the tailoring work in Kumaon, as the women's hands are unfit for such occupation owing to their having to do the rough field-work.) A brilliant idea struck one of the brothers, that instead of taking measurements for the garments, it would be much easier to fix them on some pine-trees, and sew them at their leisure in that way. This was done; but in the end it was found that the skirts were firmly sewn round the trunks of the trees, from which they had to be cut off by their afflicted parent. Being ordered to dig some wells, they went and made great holes, which still remain, on the top of some hills, and were much surprised because no water flowed, after all their labour. The eldest son wished to be a shop-keeper. His father accordingly sent him to a distant town, and gave him sufficient money to set up a cloth-shop. After a while he wrote to his father telling him that he was getting on excellently and making great profits, as he was buying cloth at three yards for a rupee and selling it at the rate of four yards. All the brothers being at home one day, and walking out into the forest, they suddenly espied a tiger. Fear seized them all, and they began counting their company to find if anyone had been carried off by the beast. Each of them forgot to count himself, and with one consent they rushed off to their father to announce that one of their number had fallen a victim to a tiger. The father ran out on hearing the shouts and weeping, and receiving the dreadful news, fell down in a fit.

CHAPTER XII

THE ROOTS OF HINDUISM

IN every country there are certain religious ideas that are universally diffused and form the material of popular thought. Thus in Christian lands every man, however ignorant or degraded, and however vague and rude may be his few notions of life and destiny, will be found to have some conception of a Supreme Being, of heaven and hell, reward and punishment, and moral responsibility. The origin of these ideas is to be traced to the prevalent religion, which has been exerting its influence for so many centuries. In those lands, whoever has reflected at all has thought in terms of Christianity, and those terms are the only current coin of religion.

Similarly, in India there are certain ideas universally current, from the Himalaya to Ceylon, and one cannot converse long with the people or read their literature without encountering them. From the educated official or Brahman priest down to the unlettered peasant, all agree in these fundamental ideas. They strike one at first as being ideas of startling strangeness, depth, and subtlety, very far removed from our ordinary plane of thought. They are, in brief, the doctrines of transmigration, or metempsychosis, and

Karma. No description of the Hindus or any section of them could be complete without some reference to these underlying beliefs. So far as we know, they have always been accepted in India, and with the exception of a handful of sceptical thinkers, none has ever ventured to question them. No matter how great be the divergences between the philosophical systems of Brahmanism, here they are practically agreed. Buddha, the iconoclast and foe of priestcraft, never doubted them. One has talked with poor, almost naked, labourers by the wayside who uttered them as commonplaces of daily thought. They are the deepest marks that the Brahmanical system has left on the body of Hindu life. Deriving their source from the far-off days when the Brahmanas and the Upanishads were written, say about a thousand or eight hundred years before Christ, when men were thinking deeply on the great questions of creation, soul, and destiny, they have taken shape in a fixed and stereotyped form, and been gradually disseminated by Brahmanical influence throughout the length and breadth of India. The earliest and most influential name connected with such teachings is that of Kapila, the father of the Sankhya school of philosophy, who takes us back to a vast antiquity. It was from his system that Gautama the Buddha, and no doubt other Buddhas before him, drew their chief inspiration. The religious creed called Buddhism on its speculative side is mainly a working-out of the conclusions of his philosophy. So evident is this that the great Orientalist, Lassen, was led to propound the theory that Buddhism is no more than an allegory or objectifying of Sankhya philosophy under the names and forms of a fictitious biography.

He points to the Sakya clan, to which the Buddha belonged, as none other than Sankhya; to Kapilavastu, "dwelling of Kapila," the traditional birthplace of the Enlightened One. It is not inconceivable that an allegorical account may have gradually been accepted as a genuine story, and that bit by bit the details of place, time, and even individual traits and anecdotes may have grown up around it as a nucleus. Quite as strange things have occurred in India; and when credulity, a lack of all historical sense, and constant wars and revolutions and wholesale removal of populations have been at work, as in India again and again, it would be rash, with regard to Buddhism, to attempt to draw any hard-and-fast line between myth and history. The recent study of Pali literature, however, appears to have greatly strengthened the case for the real existence of Gautama.

The doctrines of transmigration and Karma seem to have a common origin in the notion of the antipathy of matter and spirit, of the casual or temporary wedding of the soul to matter and its striving to escape therefrom. Matter, whether, as in some of the Six Systems, conceived as a real principle, or, as in the Vedanta, regarded as mere illusion, is what the soul, to acquire Moksh or liberation, must get rid of. It has become connected with matter by some cosmic law, and the deeds of its past lives or material connections weigh upon it, and impose the necessity of working out the merit or demerit gained by good or evil actions. This is Karma—the absolute law that every action must bear its fruit, and that as long as action continues, or its consequences are not worked out, so long must individual life in some form or other continue: the fruit of good actions leading to higher states of existence, of bad actions plunging the soul into lower and lower forms of being. Only when the soul can get itself into a state of *indifference*, doing neither good nor ill, having the mind absolutely colourless, without desires of any kind—only then can perfect deliverance be obtained. (This is the characteristic Indian travesty of the virtue of unworldliness.) The doctrine explains the Yoga forms of asceticism, the attempt to abstract the soul from earthly desires and fix it on the contemplation of Pure Being. When that state is won, the weary round of individual existences will cease of itself, Karma will be exhausted, and the soul, freed from the burden of the past, will fall as a drop in the ocean of eternal being, unknowing, undisturbed. This is Nirvana of the Buddhists, the "going out" of the fires of individual will and desire, the everlasting rest. Only the few, the initiated, can reach this state, to know, as the Vedantist says, that the world is nothing, the soul is all; to realise at last the delusion of life, and know that there is but one Spirit existing, and "I am it." For common men there must be the struggle of desire, and the lengthening out of lives in endless vista, to work out the activity of the past. *Their* hope is in doing well and rising to a happier stage or a heaven of the gods. The gods themselves are but forms of evolving soul, greater and more powerful than men, through austerities or merit in some former world, but not essentially different. This is the teaching of Buddhism, and that of Brahmanism is the same.[1]

[1] It will be observed that I do not regard Buddhism as atheistic. It is a vexed question, and cannot be discussed here. The characterisa-

It is not difficult to see what are the practical consequences of such a creed, really, firmly, unquestioningly believed. The first and most lamentable is Fatalism. Whatever a man does or suffers is simply a consequence of something that went before, and of which the individual soul retains no recollection. There is therefore neither reward nor punishment in any real sense. It has been plausibly said that Karma is only the doctrine of heredity in another form; but heredity is no more than a tendency, and in its later, and we may suppose truer, form the doctrine of heredity is far less stringent than it appeared a while ago, and leaves the will really free. But Karma makes absolute the power of the "dead hand" of the past. The conclusion naturally is, What is the use of striving? What will be, must be. My fate will evolve itself with unswerving movement, and my very endeavour after higher things is only part of that fatal impulse; or, on the other hand, my evil courses are but the effect of a destiny, against which I may struggle in vain. Listlessness, hopelessness, are the fruit of such a belief, and must ever be.

The question may be raised, Are fatalism and desire for annihilation the result of climatic conditions? Did they originate with the darker Turanian population of India, and begin to influence the simpler-minded and more energetic Aryans when they had become mingled with them, and had felt the enervating effects of the Indian climate? If so, they are the natural outcome of tropical life and a relaxed tone of mind and body. But we can never consent to reduce spiritual

tion of Hindu philosophy is also very general, and does not enter into the varying doctrines of the Six Systems.

facts to physical equations. Palestine is nearly as hot as India, and probably quite as trying; so also is Egypt; yet think of the grandeur of the hopes that arose in both.

Beneath all the confusing variety of cults that we have tried to describe to some extent, we now come to the underlying unity of Hinduism. The religion varies infinitely in its outward forms, but the root-ideas are everywhere the same. This may suggest to our minds an important consideration. Possibly too much has been made, by modern religious thinkers, of the *fact* of religion, and of the principle that man is naturally religious, to the obscuring of the need of *truth.* Pagan cults and superstitious practices are of very little value. Their influence is often entirely evil. Like some of those here described, they may rest on mere fear of malevolence and wrong; they may involve no appreciable moral ideal; their worship of the god may be not because he is good, but because he is evil and spiteful. It may be an empty custom or tradition utterly devoid of meaning. It may be a gratification of lust and savage instinct, or a mere appeal to curiosity or to selfish feelings. To found upon all these facts, of such endless variety and differing value, any general idea that all religions are of God, as many writers seem to do, or to assume even that these practices are in any way good for those who observe them, is entirely wrong. Lucretius was doubtless justified in his day, and from his observation of the pagan cults around him, in his famous line—

Tantum Religio potuit suadere malorum.

It was divine philosophy rather than religion that was the guide and light of men in the age of Lucretius, and it is the teaching of what is usually styled philosophy that is the really important thing in India. The cults are everywhere, and everywhere different, but the theory of life is constant. It is the real mainspring of life; and because it is false, the life cannot be what it ought to be and what it is capable of becoming. The "practical" man will very likely smile at such assertions, but, after all, it is a fact that ideas rule the world. The true friends of India are those who would change its fundamental ideas. Those conceptions are very firmly rooted. Among all the reforms and suggestions of its educated men, there are few or none who as yet question these fundamental dogmas. Yet social reform has no chance while they flourish undisturbed. All ancient wrongs are right so long as those dogmas hold the field. Hinduism rests on a philosophy, and can be transformed only by a truer conception of God and man—that contained in the Christian religion. These are the healing waters that go to the roots of human life, cleansing, vivifying, and making all new. Christ is a far more perfect key to the dark problems that India loves to meditate than the subtleties of her ancient sages, and He alone can lay His hand on the downcast head of India, where she lies in the dust of self-despair, and say, "Arise, and I will give thee light."

The peculiar conditions of modern India and its dependence on the British Empire render the attitude of Government to its deeper problems one of the greatest interest and importance, and the Churches and the Christian worker cannot afford to neglect this aspect of the subject. For good or for ill (and vastly, we believe, for good) the destiny of the Indian population is bound up with its Imperial Government and the course adopted by its rulers to benefit and guide the people. The declaration of religious neutrality was doubtless a necessity of the situation, and its maintenance a matter beyond question. Yet there are important issues in which, one thinks, the Government should look with fearless candour at what are usually considered spiritual questions.[1] The great need of the hour is a system of moral instruction of the young in India, in view of the chaotic character of its religious influences, and the marked absence of clear guidance regarding the simple principles of ethics. An inquiry such as we have in part attempted, if carried out thoroughly, would, I am convinced, lead to the conclusion that Hinduism has no system of moral teaching, with definite sanctions or adequate basis, to impart to its followers, and that consequently there is the gravest and most pressing need of laying stress on moral guidance in the system of public education, both primary and secondary. Exactly how this is to be done may not be easy to determine, but an earnest effort should be made to devise some plan of ethical teaching which, while transgressing no pledges as to religious neutrality, may form the mind and character of the young, so as to make it at any rate possible for them to appreciate the best ideals of citizenship and social life. The Government schools and colleges are naturally debarred from teaching

[1] The deliberately expressed opinion of one of the greatest authorities, Lord Lawrence, may be quoted. In his minute on the Mutiny he wrote: "Christian things done in a Christian way can never be politically dangerous in India." While scrupulously abstaining from interference with the religions of the people, he held that Government should be more explicit than before in avowing its Christian character.

religion, but there is really no reason why they should not attempt much more than they do in forming character. Every educationalist is a moralist by his calling, and has a moral responsibility to his charges; and an educational officer who has no interest in the ethical training of the young is by that very deficiency rendered unfit for his public position and duties. The establishment of training colleges for teachers, of late years, has been a great step in advance; but care should be taken that the training given to teachers is of the right kind, conducted by the best and most suitable men, men of character as well as intellect. The difficulties of the situation are of course evident to the most superficial observer; but they will have to be grappled with, and the bogey of religious neutrality, in so far as it connotes moral indifference and inefficiency, will have to be laid to a considerable extent, if Britain is to carry out her self-appointed (rather, we would fain believe, God-appointed) task in India. Else in the end we shall have to make the confession that we as a nation have no rational objects in India beyond commercialism and exploitation. An imperial government, by its very imperialism and denial of *laisser-faire* notions, is bound to see to the moral well-being of its subjects, especially with regard to education. The Christian, and especially the Christian missionary, believes that only by adopting his faith can true moral sanity be secured, but he will co-operate with and wish God-speed to every effort to teach right principles of morals. He will see in such training the preparation of the "law" going before the proclamation of the "gospel," and the testimony of the prophet or declarer of the ethical will of God, laying the necessary foundation for the true appreciation of Christ, "preparing a highway for our God." By so doing he gives the greatest possible proof of the sincerity of his belief and his confidence that it will be justified in the end.

Returning for a moment to the subject of the "Hindu Revival," as it is called, especially in its relation to education, the words of one of India's most distinguished sons, who was Senior Wrangler a year or two ago at Cambridge, are worthy of notice. Mr. Paranjpai, now Principal of the Fergusson College at Bombay, is a Hindu, not a Christian. Writing in *East and West* about religious education in India, he expresses his disapproval of recent movements. He says: "We see a gifted foreign lady blowing loudly the trumpet of this kind of education, and trying a heroic experiment in Benares," but he does not think that the experiment will prove a success. "In this age," he writes, "when Western ideas are being grafted on Eastern minds, there is sure to be in some cases a disturbance of mental equilibrium. Those of our people who have imbibed Western ideas are sure to reject many of the moral standards of their forefathers. This is a perfectly natural result. If a child on growing older refuses to crawl and begins to walk, the remedy is not to tie its legs and thus prevent its walking, but to let it continue to walk. It may tumble down at times, but that is the only way in which it will learn to walk properly. It is not the right thing to confine our young men forcibly to the old way of thinking, but to let their intellects have free play. In so many ways do modern ideas overtake young minds that it is next to impossible to ward off their influence by a few minutes of religious instruction every day. The only effect that is possible is intellectual hypocrisy. We shall only have numerous prototypes of the child for whom the earth went round the sun while at school and the sun went round the earth when at home. We shall have our young men ready to deliver learned lectures on the procession of the equinoxes and calculate the exact time of the eclipses, and then come back to their homes to propitiate the demons who eat up the moon or the sun."

The gist of Mr. Paranjpai's remarks is that Hinduism is so full of superstition and false notions contrary to morals that the teaching of it will always do harm rather than good. Regarding social freedom he remarks: "We talk about equality, while our religion enjoins strict distinctions between the various castes. The advocates of religious education must, to be logical, revive all the old-world injustice. No, this is not progress, it is retrogression." About Hindu priests he says: "Our priests are not what people foolishly believe them to be. Their success is nothing else but the credulity of their dupes." It is only to be expected that this bold and outspoken article should have aroused considerable indignation among those modern "reformers" whose cry is "Back to Hinduism," regardless of what Hinduism is or whether it has any real teaching to offer.

Unpopular though such sentiments undoubtedly are in the India of to-day, there can be no doubt that the best friend of the people would be one who should ruthlessly declare the utter inadequacy of the Hindu religion for modern civilised men. The confession which ancient Greece and Rome, with all their splendid civilisation, had to make, can surely be no matter of shame for modern India to make in her turn. When we note the mental robustness of Japan, and the readiness of its people to adopt whatever is best from the common treasury of human knowledge and culture, we cannot help wishing that similar qualities would show themselves in the educated men of India. The desperate clinging to childish superstitions and a pessimistic pseudo-philosophy is unworthy of rational minds. That philosophy, such as it is, is destructive of any real religion and of any real morality. As an able observer says: "The Hindu, strange as it may seem to say so, has little or no appreciation of the spiritual world as that world appeals to us. To him even God in the last refuge is impersonal: personality is a disease, an episode of the present state. In practical life the bad spirit has nothing to fear, and the good nothing to hope for, in a world into which no vestige of memory or personal continuity is allowed to enter. And so it comes about that the most solemn warnings, and equally the most gracious promise, of the gospel fall on dead, or at the best wonder-stricken, ears, the dynamic lost."

It is this difference of mental attitude that makes the progress of Christianity so slow in India, and it is here that the necessity of Christian education comes in. Something more permanent and constant than occasional preaching is required to evangelise the Hindus. A ground has to be prepared, an atmosphere created, before the gospel can find its entrance into the heart, or the great promises and blessings of true religion be valued and desired. An integral part of the missionary enterprise in India must still be the influence of our schools and colleges, though, as time goes on, more and more attention must be devoted to the care of Christian youth and the training of Christian preachers and teachers. Such outlay should not be grudged; it is an absolute necessity of the situation, not a questionable "extra" or luxury.

Again, I say, the true friends of India are those who would change its root-ideas. There is a kind of vague tolerance and would-be broadmindedness among many, who as a rule have little real knowledge of the subject, and who will declare that the Hindu has a very fine religion, though they do not care much for the Hindu individually. Better, we think, though less easy and careless, is the attitude of those who regard the Hindu personally with friendly appreciation, but have a clear insight, based upon knowledge, into the practical worthlessness of his religion and theosophy.

Let us take, as a concrete illustration of the ineffectual character of the attempt to regenerate India through its old religion, the actual religious teaching now given in Government or Hindu schools and colleges, which profess to impart moral training in addition to secular knowledge. The effort is a praiseworthy one, with the spirit of which we have much sympathy; but what is its practical outcome? I am informed that the religious teaching given in Hindu institutions consists mainly of the Sanskrit Bhagavad-Gita. The leading (practical) doctrine of the Bhagavad-Gita, extolled so highly by Hindus generally, is that we must do the work of our calling diligently, regardless of consequences. Why? Because otherwise the *rules of caste* will be corrupted and break down! The book is a hotch-potch of all kinds of Hindu doctrines, with a little bit to please everyone in turn; but its real object is evidently to maintain *caste*, which at the date when it was written was threatened by the spread of philosophic speculation, as opposed to the orthodox worship of the deities and reverence for Brahmans. On the theoretical side, again, it teaches that we must perform the duties of our avocation, and as soldiers slay and kill even our countrymen and relatives if so required, because it really does not matter what we do. Arjuna felt a natural dislike to slay his kinsman in battle, because he had a kind, good heart. He consulted the divine Krishna on the point. What was Krishna's reply? Was it to the effect that he ought to follow the dictates of feeling and conscience? Not so; he exhorted him to go into the battle and fight his best, regardless of consequences, because, to quote the parodist of Byron, "Nought is everything, and everything is nought." Our actions and circumstances are illusory. I am the world, and the world is I. What basis of morals is to be found in such a notion? It is simply subversive of every ethical principle. It is the very acme of the mock-sublime—it is philosophy run to seed and become ridiculous. This *travesty* of principles which may in themselves contain some element of truth is to be seen in nearly all Hindu ideals. Speak of self-sacrifice, and the Hindu will relate with gusto a story of some holy man who allowed a tiger to eat him, out of mere good-nature, and wished him a good appetite as he was being crunched by the teeth of the savage beast. Speak of filial duty, and you are told of the five Pandavas, who, when they had won Draupadi as a bride for one of their number in the public contest, informed their mother that they had brought something of value, and she unwittingly told them to divide it

THE GORI-GANGA RIVER, WITH MISSION CAMP

among them, whereupon they took Draupadi as their common wife. Speak of charity, and you are told about the hospital for fleas which some pious soul endowed in Western India.

Deeply as we must appreciate the interest and historical value of Hindu religion, and much as we may admire what is admirable in it, no thoughtful Christian who has studied the subject can doubt that India's national and social as well as individual redemption depends, not on any reform or development of Hinduism, but on the adoption of Christianity.[1]

Some recent discussions have opened the question as to a possible amalgamation of Christianity with the doctrines of Hinduism, and one writer has even gone so far as to say that the character of the future Christianity of India will be largely Vedantist. With such a view I cannot agree. It is, of course, possible that a union of the kind may be attempted, but it would be, like Vedantism itself, a system of philosophical subtleties and verbiage, attractive to a few intellectual minds, but without life or moral power. There can be no development of pantheism and pessimist surrender of personality into the veritable Christian gospel. The Christianity that India needs is the Christianity of Christ, the gospel of the Incarnation, of the Cross, of a renewed humanity, and of eternal hope.

[1] Since writing the above I have read the late Dr. J. Murdoch's pamphlet, entitled *India's Greatest Educational Need: The Adequate Recognition of Ethics in her Present Transitional Stage*, and am glad to find my remarks in substantial agreement with those of the veteran Christian reformer. Dr. Murdoch mentions the desire on the part of many parents in India for direct moral teaching to be given to their sons, leading many of them to prefer mission schools and colleges.

The union of Christian thought with Greek philosophy may be pointed to as a parallel instance, but in reality the comparison will not hold. Greek speculation was a real search after truth, it was an attempt to use the reason impartially on subjects of highest import. It could therefore readily combine with a religion which recognises the spirit of man as the candle of the Lord. Hindu philosophy, on the other hand, is an assumed knowledge of matters, many of which are beyond human ken; and it does not proceed by the method of investigation and proof, but is a tissue of arbitrary statements. Hypotheses are laid down without proof, and a system is evolved to suit them. It claims to possess a superhuman theosophic knowledge of the universe, which aims at satisfying the curiosity of the human mind rather than its desire for truth; and its claim cannot be rationally upheld.

CHAPTER XIII

CONCLUSION

THE main line of interest followed in the preceding pages has been that of religion, and India's religion is certainly her most interesting possession and her chief significance for the world in general. Those who have studied Hinduism are aware that it contains a depth of religious and philosophic thought far beyond what a superficial view might seem to disclose. Pantheism is a system whose roots go very deep; it is not easily displaced. It appears to Hindus to include all other forms of religion, and to be infinitely superior. It can only be met and satisfied by a true, thorough, and consistent religious view of the world, such as we believe to be inherent in the Christian system. This means that the nature of Hindu thought must be studied by Christian advocates with a completeness and earnestness such as they have seldom devoted to it; and the special adaptation of the religion of Christ to the Hindu, and its special power and fitness to supplant the pantheistic creed of the people, have to be realised by strenuous observation and reflection. The battle has yet to be fought between the highest ultimate forces of the two opposed religions. So far as one is competent to judge, it t compromise and adaptation are out of the question. The root-ideas of Christianity and Hinduism are as far as the poles asunder, and can never be reconciled. They are as oil and water, and cannot be made to mingle by any process of amalgamation known to our spiritual chemistry. It is true that there are certain movements and tendencies of the human mind which are illustrated in both religions alike, but Pantheism is in the fullest sense the idea of Hinduism, and its denial of human personality is absolutely destructive of those ethical distinctions that are the life and soul of Christianity. The Hindu idea of salvation is deliverance from personal existence, while the Christian views it as deliverance from evil, and the attainment of a renewed and perfected self. God to the Hindu is the ocean, into which he falls as a drop to lose his individuality. To the Christian consciousness God is the Father of Spirits, with whom he is to live endlessly, in distinction yet in filial relation. Hinduism is pantheistic in the wrong sense: identifying the world with God, declaring that all that is, is God. Moral distinctions are thus annulled, and God is the author of evil. Good and evil are both alike to Him. As the Bhagavad-Gita says:

> To him who wisely sees,
> The Brahman with his scrolls and sanctities,
> The cow, the elephant, the unclean dog,
> The outcast gorging dog's meat, all are one.

What room can there be for progress or improvement in human life when "all are one," and the vile is equally divine with the pure and noble? Vedantism, which has taken such firm hold of the Indian mind as how we treat our fellow-men, either in thought, word, or deed. It is on the basis of personality, of true individual existence, that all the really beneficial moral systems have grown up. Greek philosophy, Roman law, Christian civilisation, and the modern ideal of liberty, all rest on this indispensable basis. The educated Hindu of to-day, agitating for political rights, must first lay the foundations of his religious and ethical system anew, before he can logically claim to be treated as a personal being. The spiritual is the true source and creator in human affairs. Material civilisation itself, with all that makes up the worth and beauty of life, depends on the ultimate spiritual ideas and motives at work in the heart of the nation. In the interesting development of national life that we have recently witnessed in Japan, it is clear that this great fact has been realised by the keen and thorough minds that have been moulding the destinies of that remarkable country. They have felt that the old religions of the land, Shinto and Buddhist, were incapable of supplying the needed basis of national life, and they have been led to consider the fitness of Christianity to be the foundation of their civilisation. Probably it is not by such *doctrinaire* considerations that a religion can become a powerful element in national development, yet the truth remains acknowledged that Christianity, and Christianity alone, has in it the force required for the growth of the highest moral, social, and political life.

But India is a great home of spiritual forces; its people, though at present lost in the mists of a pantheist theosophy, are endowed with a remarkable genius for religion. There, religions are constantly being born; movements of subtle thought, and sometimes of earnest spirituality, are in constant process of evolution. The rise of Buddhism witnessed a real moral reformation, and a turning of the people in their myriads from empty formalism to a higher ideal of mercy, truth, and love—the cultivation of the good deeds that flow from the good will. Divorced though it was from the true idea of God, it yet witnessed to the moral nature that is His most precious gift to men. It was an awakening of conscience, such as has preceded every great religious movement in the past. The conversion of India to Christ, we may well believe, will be the effect of a moral impulse, the desire for a higher spirit and standard of personal living. It will be the attraction of the good, the pure, the unselfish, and the beautiful in life and conduct, and its ideal will be found in Jesus Christ. It is the absence, so far, of this moral need and yearning dissatisfaction that keeps back the regeneration of India, and allows many, who ought to know better, to remain content with the partial and imperfect, or even with the low and unworthy, rather than turn to the light. But India will receive the gospel when the need of it is felt. Our hope and confidence is that forces are at work which in God's good providence will awaken the dormant conscience and arouse among the multitudes of the land an earnest longing after the excellency of the knowledge of Christ. None of the varied effort that has been so long and faithfully put forth will be labour in vain. We remember that with God a thousand years are as one day, or as a watch in the night; and from our disappointment and hope deferred we learn to wait upon the Lord, to wait patiently for Him, to have larger thoughts of the divine wisdom, and to rest in the greatness of the hope that is rising and growing broad in the world's heart. We think of the great tidal influences that are the life of God in the soul of humanity, of the Power that makes for righteousness bringing to birth the conscience of India, through law and order, through the influence and example of just and benevolent foreign dominion, through the written and spoken Word of God, through the purer and truer thoughts of a Western literature permeated by Christian influences; and we believe that when conscience is awakened there will be a great hunger after God, after the living God; and that in ways too subtle and marvellous for our understanding all the tangled threads, and all the hidden influences, and all the faithful toils of these years of working and waiting will be found united in perfect harmony in that "far-off divine event," the conversion of India. Yet why should we say "far-off"? A statesman and observer of established repute, and one certainly with no bias towards the cause of Christian missions (Sir Alfred Lyall), has expressed his belief that India "will be carried swiftly through phases that have occupied long ages in the lifetime of other nations." We would go forward in the spirit of Carey's noble watchword, "Expect great things from God; attempt great things for God," seeing that "the providential plan is often a long-coming preparation, and then a rapid development."

The analogy of the Buddhist movement in India to Christian propagandism has not remained unnoticed. I observe that the correspondent of an Indian newspaper who waited on Dr. Barrows when he visited

India as Haskell lecturer in 1896, put to him the following questions: "Do you not see any similarity between the spread of Christianity to-day and the spread of Buddhism in ancient times?" and again, "With the primitive means of communication, was not the spread of early Buddhism marvellous?" Dr. Barrows pointed out that there was a reason for the wide and rapid spread of Buddhism, carried through the land as it was by bands of earnest men, and felt by the people to be a welcome relief from the formalism and bondage of the Brahmanical priesthood; but that Christianity had had to meet, and had overcome, far more formidable antagonism in its early history. His concluding words, in answer to these questions, were: "A system like Christianity, demanding perfect loyalty to God and equal love to men, and permitting no compromise, like that of Buddhism when it consented to be one of the three religions of China, makes progress by overcoming the obstinate pride and all the entrenched wickedness of man, and therefore I regard its early advance as one of the chief wonders of history. Its real progress to-day among non-Christian peoples is owing to the special presence and power of the Holy Spirit, inspiring love, creating purity, renewing the soul."

It may be added that Buddhism was an indigenous faith in India, a popular movement chiefly, though not exclusively, among the non-Brahmanical classes; that it was championed by the powerful Kshatriya order against the claims of the Brahmans; whereas Christianity labours under the disadvantage of being generally regarded as the religion of the foreign conqueror; and patriotism is supposed to consist chiefly in resisting it, and clinging to the old faiths as an inheritance that the foreigner cannot take away, embodying a social system that is the chief entrenchment of Eastern reserve as opposed to foreign aggression. We may say with truth that the spread of Buddhism had everything in its favour, and that Christianity, from a worldly point of view, has everything against it. Buddhism, again, presented a very simple theory of life, attractive to the natural temper of the East—a quietist despair of earthly activity, to which the Indian is only too prone. To such a temper the easiest thing in the world was to turn Buddhist monk or nun; and religion in Buddhist countries practically amounts to that. Christianity, on the other hand, presents a complex ideal—active, non-ascetic, social, and demanding a reality of moral effort: not to retire from life, but to live it intensely and nobly—that is apt to stagger the Oriental, whose common answer to the preaching of Christianity is a *non possumus*, a murmured "who is sufficient for these things?"

Yet the rapid and wide extension of early Buddhism has surely some lessons for us to-day. India is a country where such things can be. The climate and conditions of life admit of almost literal obedience to the instructions of our Lord to His first disciples and preachers, given as they were for a special work of evangelisation and suited to Eastern lands. The European missionary, indeed, would not find it practicable to become a wandering faqir, in the narrower sense; nor would he by so doing exhibit the true spirit and ideal of the Christ who "came eating and drinking," and whose glory is that He has ennobled the common life of men. Any outward asceticism that he could practise would seem rank luxury compared with the half-clothed wretchedness of the Indian poor, reduced almost to the bare elements of animal existence. Yet he seeks to fulfil the essential requirements of his calling, in patient toil, and daily renewed hopefulness, and sincere good-will to the people among whom he dwells. He cannot denationalise himself, nor put away the tone and temper of civilised life that are part of his nature; nor would it be good for him to do so. He fulfils his duty far better by exhibiting an example of wholesome Christian living in personal and family relations, than he could ever do as a fanatical preacher of a retreat from the world as evil. India has had enough of that. Its religion for thousands of years has known no gospel but that of ascetic abandonment of life, and the result to-day is almost *nil.* It is an impossible and useless ideal, a system of selfish concern for one's own soul and an ignoring of the social duties that constitute man's true nature and end. *Christianity rests on a true theory of life, and Hinduism on a wrong one.* This fact can never be too much emphasised, and India's regeneration can only be in abandoning its false spiritual foundation.

The final success of the Christian movement in India, it is generally acknowledged, depends on the Christians of the land. We are, like the disciples in Galilee, "waiting for power from on high" to inspire men of apostolic type to go forth with gracious might and influence among their fellow-countrymen. It would be unjust to deny that there have been, and are, powerful and sainted characters among the Indian Christians—men of whom any country might well be proud; but circumstances have been against their acquiring a widespread influence. India as a nation is only just beginning to realise its unity. Up to the present it has been a congeries of local communities, and a man's influence has been necessarily confined to his immediate surroundings. These conditions are rapidly changing. We are waiting for the Man and the Hour, and we trust that ere long both will come—the men and the opportunities. While remembering that "not many wise, not many mighty are called," we are fully aware that men of might and wisdom are urgently needed, and in God's own good time will be raised up, as St. Paul himself was, men of spiritual force and daring, endowed with a great heart and a great mind. Perhaps the chief duty of the foreign missionary now is in giving the best of himself to the young men of the Christian community, that they may be fitted to take up and carry on the great work of evangelisation. The soil is being prepared in many ways: through Christian preaching and education; through the widespread reading of the Bible that is undoubtedly going on all over India; through the general effect of Western education; through the wearing down of the barriers of caste by modern conditions and industrial changes; through the widening of the horizon that is caused by the freedom and breadth of modern life, with its world-wide communication; and, not least, by the quiet influence of Christian women in the homes of those arbiters of their country's future, the mothers of India.

It has appeared to the writer that one of the most powerful influences for the spread of a strong and enduring type of Christianity exists in the contact of specially qualified workers with the educated youth, especially in the great centres of educational activity. One knows something of the Indian student, his character and possibilities; and whatever may have been said, often perhaps hastily and unsympathetically, we know him to be a hopeful factor in the national life—necessarily the hope of India. Young India resembles the youth of other lands in being capable of generous ideals and strong affections. He is especially drawn towards culture and refinement in those whom he meets. When he sees the Christian faith embodied in the best type of civilised man,—let us say, in the worthiest product of British and American university life,—his sympathies are keenly evoked; and when the character of Christ is presented in the way most fitted to appeal to him, he feels that "we needs must love the highest when we see it." There is a great and distinct work in India for our best minds and most cultivated brains. One has dreamed at times of a united Christian university or central seminary, where some of the best-trained men of the West might give themselves to the distinct teaching of Christianity in its highest and widest aspects, and whither distinguished visitors from Britain and America might bring the inspiring touch of their personality to bear on the young men of India, whether Christian or non-Christian. We see foreshadowings of such an ideal already in the educational work of several of the missionary societies, and in the Haskell lectureship; but what is needed is the strong impulse of united action.

Let us endeavour, in conclusion, to gather up in a few sentences the leading thoughts of the foregoing pages, and to reduce to something like clearness the view of

Indian religious and social life that has been to some extent illustrated.

The ground of Indian religion in all its manifestations is a pantheistic philosophy which tends to make the world unreal, and in its most important school of doctrine, the Vedantist, plainly declares life to be an illusion. The current religions are regarded by the higher thought of Brahmanism as accommodations to popular ignorance and weakness, Brahma alone having reality. Those faiths, while often pathetically witnessing to true religious affections and longings, do not rest on any worthy idea of the divine nature; and the mundane, and often comparatively modern, origin of the various cults can be clearly shown, as has been pointed out in some of the preceding chapters. They have certainly no more religious authority than the mythology of ancient Greece and Rome, and, as enlightenment spreads, they must inevitably share the same fate of neglect and oblivion. The social system of the Hindus, elaborated by Brahmans whose real convictions were based on the pantheistic view of the world, was necessarily an artificial system, designed (quite rightly of course) to maintain the social fabric in enduring solidity, but taking for its binding principle the institution of caste. Every man was to belong to some caste, to fulfil its duties, and to remain in it. The constitution of society was declared to be eternally fixed. The Brahman was to be the head of the body politic, the Kshatriya the arm, the Vaishya its body, and the Shudra its feet. The Bhagavad-Gita, seemingly the only ancient scripture which all Hindu sects to some extent really recognise, leans all its weight on the caste principle, which is indeed the be-all and end-all of

Hinduism. Hinduism is at bottom a social system, in which the individual may believe, and for that matter openly profess, any religious creed he likes, provided that he does not break with his caste. Men are tolerated who frankly declare themselves to be Christians at heart, so long as they keep to caste regulations. The intense excitement and bitter persecution attending the baptism of converts in the higher classes are the logical expression of the Hindu social system, and its instinctive movement of self-defence, for its very life depends on the maintenance of caste.

Caste itself seems to have an essential connection with pantheism, which carries with it a kind of fatalism. Only under a pantheistic despair of betterment, and confusion of moral issues, could such a system as Indian caste have grown up and prevailed for so many ages. Indian pantheism has no message for the modern world; it is divorced from the ideas of progress and liberty. A Christian civilisation, in short, such as the British Government of India essentially is, can alone provide the material, the basis, and the guiding power for the modern state; but until the nation itself is Christianised, such a civilisation must remain external, artificial, and *socially* powerless. The absence of a consistent ethical view of life, in the breakdown of the caste system, is the most lamentable feature of the present confusion, and that also can only be erected on a Christian basis. For caste is already doomed, by the new conditions and the new order of facts in India, and the time is fast approaching when society can no longer be regulated by the idea of caste. As time goes on, its inadequacy as a social rule will become more and more evident.

No one will suppose that the real motive of the Christian enterprise in India is here stated, or that these are the actual considerations that have driven Christians over the world to preach the Cross, but it is surely not wasted effort to show that from every point of view, whether that of the Christian, the statesman, or the thoughtful well-wisher of his species in general, the work of Christian missions in India is justifiable, is useful, and in fact is necessary.

As a modern historian has said, "The image of Christ remains the sole basis of all moral culture, and in the measure in which it succeeds in making its light penetrate is the moral culture of the nations increased or diminished."

INDEX

Adwaita system of Vedantism, 15.
Agni, 180, 182, 185.
Airi, a demon, 218, 224, 225.
Almora described, ch. II.; foundation of, 39, 40, 107; verses on, 53.
"Almoriana," 146.
Amazon kingdom in Tibet, 91–93.
Anariya, story of, 215–217.
Animal folk-lore, 267–269, 272.
Animism, 202–204.
April Fool's Day, 251.
Apsaras, 212.
Argha, 195.
Arpan, 195.
Arti, 195.
Arya Samaj, 165.
Aryan gods, 165, 166.
Aryans in India, 83, 86, 88.
Ascetics, 155–161.
Asiatic Researches, 16, 137, 142, 152, 235.
Askot, 101.
Asoka, 90, 148; his edicts, 88, 89, 168.
Atkinson, E. T., quoted, 16, 97, 101, 108, 137, 138, 153, 158, 185, 186, 198, 199, 225, 227, 232.
Ayahs, 44.

Bacon quoted, 276.
Badarinath peak, 36; shrine, 128, 129, 151–154, 270, 271.
Badi custom, 233–235.
Bageswar, 57, 66.
Bagwali stone-throwing, 61, 235, 236.
Balighat pool, 67, 117.
Bam Sah, 119, 120, 124.
Baniyas, 42, 167, 174, 239, 259, 260.
Barbers, Indian, 278.
Bareilly, 17.
Barrows, Dr., quoted, 303, 304.
Batchelor, Rev. J., quoted, 181.
Bathing, religious, 59, 149.
Batten, Commissioner, 125.
Baz Bahadur Chand, 31, 111–113.
Bears, 34, 71, 272.
Benares, 128, 132.
Benfey quoted, 82.
Besant, Mrs., 12, 290.
Bhabar, 21, 22, 29, 31, 114, 269.
Bhagavad-Gita, 293, 294, 298, 309.
Bhairava, a form of Siva, 158, 160, 171, 250.
Bhairava Jhamp, 150.
Bhim Tal, 30, 32.
Bhima, 73.
Bhishma Chand, 107.
Bholanath, a deity, 221.
Bhotiyas, 30, 57, 59, 77, 87, 112.
Bhotiya ponies, 24, 59, 60, 93.
Bhuts, or ghosts, 218 ff.
Bijai Chand, 109.
Binsar, 64, 115.
Bir Bal, 108.
Bir Chand, 105.

Bir Deo, 99, 100.
Birth ceremonies, 236.
Blinding as a punishment, 110, 111, 115, 116.
Boars, 34, 71.
Boer camp at Bhim Tal, 32.
Brahm and Dham, 226.
Brahma, 172, 177.
Brahmana scriptures, 132, 282.
Brahmans, origin of, 174 ; supremacy of, 176; missionary operations of, 174 ; in Kumaon, 41, 67, 262-264.
Brahmapura, 90, 91, 92, 132.
Brahmo Samaj, 165.
Bridges, 145.
Brighton corner at Almora, 38.
British administration, 135.
British Government, its responsibility, 287, 288.
British invasion of Kumaon, 125.
Budden, Rev. J. H., 52, 55.
Buddha, 88, 132, 148, 282, 283.
Buddhism, early spread of, 303-305.
Buddhism in the Himalaya, 89, 97, 186.
Buddhism, rise of, 168, 302.
Buddhism, suppression of, 148.
Buddhist scriptures and remains, 84, 88, 283.
Burial of ascetics, 160, 265.
Burnell, Dr., 93.

Calcutta Review, 16, 26.
Canning, Lady, 20.
Caste, 14, 167, 291, 293, 294, 310.
Ceremonies, domestic, 238.
Chakor, or partridge, 34.
Chamberlain's duties, 110.
Champawat, 39, 102, 106, 129, 226.
Chand dynasty in Kumaon, 40, 99, 102-117, 126, 273.
Chaprasi, 66, 271.
Charas, a hemp drug, 275, 276.
Chatterjea, Bankim Chunder, 164.
Chaumu, a deity, 223.
Cheena hill, 26.
Cholera in Kumaon, 51, 172.
Chorgaliya, 23.
Christianity, need of, in India, 12, 13, 287, 295, 301, 310.
Christians, Indian, 306, 307.
Climate, effect of, 285.
Climate of Kumaon and Garhwal, 87.
Colebrooke, 95, 142.
Cremation, 246, 247.
Crooke quoted, 158.
Curzon, Lord, 48.

Dak bungalows, 31, 66.
Dalip Chand, 109.
Dancing, religious, 207, 208.
"Dandi," 24, 70.
Dandi ascetics, 160.
Darma valley, 30, 77.
Dasehra festival, 253.
Dasyu, 83.
Davids, Prof. Rhys, 84, 89, 95, 132, 232.
Debi Chand, 113.
Debidhura, 82.
Demonism, 204 ff., 231.
Dhankuri, 68, 71.
Dip Chand, 117.
Diwali festival, 252.
Doms, 42, 82, 239, 260-262.
Doti, 25, 52, 101, 102, 223.
Draupadi, 129, 294.
Dubois, Abbé, 190, 242.
Dungaria, 206.
Dwarahat, 101.

Earthquakes, 152.
Educated, Christian work among, 307, 308.
Education, Christian, 292, 293.
Education in Kumaon, 45 ff.
Eggeling quoted, 182.
English education in India, 46-50.
Exorcism, story of, 213-215, 217.

Fairies, 212, 213.
Family life, Hindu, 242, 243.
Fatalism of Hindus, 14, 285.
Fish-feeding, 68.
Flora of Kumaon, 70, 72, 145.

Folk-lore of Kumaon, by G. D. Uprety, 16, ch. XI.
Forced labour in Kumaon, 25, 67.
Fossils, 81.
Fraser quoted, 120–122.
Free-thinkers in Kumaon, 266, 267.
Funeral rites, 246, 249.

Gagar range, 26, 32, 33.
Gambling, 61, 252, 253.
Gananath, 64.
Gandharvas, 213.
Ganesa, a god, 171, 194, 237.
Ganganath, a god, 222.
Ganges, 133 ; its source, 141.
Gangoli, 112, 259, 271.
Gantua, 205 ff.
Gardner, Colonel W. L., 124, 127.
Garhwal, 19, 20, 109, 112, 119, 258, 277.
Gaumukhi, or prayer-bag, 198.
Gayatri, 171, 197.
Geography of the Hindus, 136, 137.
Ghantakarna, a deity, 221.
Ghat, petitions for redress, 209.
Ghi, or clarified butter, 249.
Ghosts, worship of, 212 ; belief in, 218, 219.
Gogra river, 69.
Gohna landslip and lake, 28, 154.
Gola river, 29.
Gold in Kumaon, 60.
Goriganga river, 76, 77, 230.
Goril, a deity, 222.
Gosains, ascetics, 157.
Goudge, J. E., quoted, 253.
Govisana, kingdom of, 22.
Grain, proverbs relating to, 257.
Granite hill, 34.
Greek thought, 296.
Gumti river, 57, 98.
Gurkhas, 23, 37, 41, 117, 118–125, 254.
Gurkhas, regiment of, 39, 40, 50.
Gurral, or Indian chamois, 34, 68.
Guru, 197.
Gyan Chand, 105.

Hafiz Khan, 17, 19.
Handsborough, Dr., 19.
Harak Deb Joshi, 63, 67, 118, 119.
Hardwar, 52, 144.
Haru, 226 ; class of deities, 210.
Hastidal, 64, 145.
Hawalbagh, 64, 145.
Heber, Bishop, 37.
Himalaya, sacredness of, 131, 133.
Hinduism, essence of, 286 ; fatalism of, 14, 285 ; revival of, 12, 290.
Hiradungri hill, 63.
Hodgson, Brian, 199.
Hoffmeister's *Travels*, 146 ff.
Holi festival, 250.
Honiberger quoted, 276.
Human sacrifice, 159, 173, 208.
Humour, Indian, 265, 279, 280.
Hundes and Huniyas, 30, 112.
Hunter, Sir W. W., quoted, 133, 217.
Hunter, story of a, 143, 144.
Huxley quoted, 86.
Hwen Thsang, 22, 90 ff., 132.

Ice-tables, 75.
Indra Chand, 104.
Inscriptions, Sanskrit, 58, 98.
"Ishta Devata," 170, 194.

Jageswar temple, 116, 117.
Jainda Kiral, story of, 106.
Jains, 167.
Janeo, or sacred thread, 191.
Jangama ascetics, 161.
Japan, 292, 301.
Jhusi, 40, 102.
Jibbu, an animal, 78.
Johar valley, 30, 77, 119.
Joshi Brahmans, 104.
Joshimath, 97.

Kabir, 154, 170, 171, 187.
Kailas mountain, 112, 129, 137, 138.
Kakar, or barking deer, 34, 68, 269.

Kali river, 105.
Kali, wife of Siva, 100, 159, 235.
Kali Yuga, 14.
Kalimatiya hill, 63.
Kalinga, siege of, 122.
Kalki incarnation of Vishnu, 170, 188.
Kalsi, inscription at, 88, 89.
Kalua or Kalbisht, a deity, 226.
Kalyan Singh or Chand, 39, 40, 107.
Kanphata sect, 158–161.
Kapalika ascetics, 160.
Kapila, 168, 282.
Kapilavastu, 283.
Kapkot village, 68, 76.
Karboja, or sheep-pack, 30, 79.
Karma, 281 ff.
Kashmir Hindus, 132.
Katyur kings, 58, 97–101 ; gods, 205, 210, 226.
Keats quoted, 252.
Kedar, a name of Siva, 180.
Kedarnath, 128, 142–151, 270.
Khabish, a demon, 214.
Khagmara Fort, 39, 40, 106, 107.
Khan Bahadur Khan, 19.
Khassiyas, 40, 42, 84, 85, 86, 87, 101, 104, 259, 260.
Khati tribe, 273.
Kosala, kingdom of, 88, 132.
Kosi river, 37, 38, 64, 130, 145, 146.
Krishna, 12, 129, 170, 189, 190, 201 (note), 250, 251, 294.
Kshetrpal, a deity, 227.
Kucherry at Almora, 41.
Kukri knives, 60.
Kumari, wife of Siva, 178, 184.
Kumbh year, 152.
Kurmachal, 129.
Kusa grass, 248.
Kutila writing, 98.

Lachua Kothari, story of, 279, 280.
Lakes in Kumaon, 27.
Lakshmi Chand, 58, 60, 109.
Lal Guru, 44.
Langur monkey, 33.
Lassen quoted, 169, 282.
Lawrence, Lord, quoted, 288.
Left-hand sects, 156.
Leopards, 58.
Leper asylum at Almora, 35, 52, 53, 55.
London Missionary Society, 35, 54, 55, 63, 81.
Lucretius quoted, 286.
Lyall, Sir Alfred, 174, 303.

M'Crindle's *Ancient India*, 89, 92.
Mackenzie, 18.
Madua, or millet, 51, 257.
Magadha, kingdom of, 88, 132.
Mahabharata, 83, 129, 169, 185, 189.
Mahamari, or plague, 23, 51.
Mahseer fish, 31, 68.
Makara, 159.
Malwa Tal or lake, 32.
Mana pass, 141, 275.
Mandakini river, 141, 142, 146, 149.
Mangal, the planet Mars, 196.
Mansarovar lake, 112, 137.
Mansiari, 77, 78.
Mantras, 196, 197.
Manual of the Ten Rites, 236.
Mara faction in Kumaon, 104, 110, 236 (note).
Marks, sectarial, 192.
Marriage rites, 241–245.
Marriage, Hindu idea of, 243.
Masan, a demon, 214, 218, 220.
Max Müller, 174.
Mayo, Earl of, 50.
Meals, daily, 249.
Meat-eating, 193, 249.
Megasthenes, 88, 92.
Melas, or fairs, 56 ff.
Meru, Mount, 134, 135, 136.
Mlechchha, 83.
Mogul emperors, 105, 107, 112, 114, 117.
Moira, a fort, 50.
Monal pheasant, 34, 68.

Monkeys, 33, 65.
Mora fly, 76.
Moral training, need of, 288 ff.
Mountains, worship of, 177.
Murdoch, Dr. J., 295 (note).
Musk deer, 108.
Mutiny, the, 17 ff., 288 (note).

Nagas, 84, 232.
Naini Tal, 18, 24, 26, 38; landslip at, 27, 28.
Name-giving ceremony, 238.
Names, caste, and titles, 240.
Names, personal, 239–241.
Nanda Devi, a goddess, 113, 172; her festival, 251.
Nanda Devi peak, 36, 69, 79.
Nandakot peak, 73.
Narayan Sah, 41.
Naukachiya lake, 32.
Nepal, 19, 20, 50, 95 ff., 118, 235.
Neutrality, religious, 288, 289.
Nilakantha, epithet of Siva, 138.
Nirankara, a god, 223.
Nirvana, 284.

Oak forests, 32, 64, 275.
Oldenberg, H., 166 (note).
Oracles, 215.
Ordeals, 253, 254.

Panch Chule peaks, 36.
Pandavas, 129, 294.
Panth Brahmans, 264.
Pantheism, 297, 298, 309.
Paranjpai, Mr., quoted, 290, 291.
Parvati, wife of Siva, 129, 143, 178.
Pasupati cult, 86, 171, 183.
Pathans, 23.
Penth markets, 56.
Personation, 210.
Phallic emblems, 177.
Phartiyal faction, 104, 110.
Philosophy, effect of Indian, 281, 287.
Philosophy, Indian, characterised, 283 ff., 296.
Phurkia, 72, 76.
Pilgrim roads, 144, 145.
Pinda offerings, 195, 246.
Pindar river, 70, 71, 72.
Pindari glacier, 62 ff., 134.
Pine or chir trees, 32.
Places, folk-lore connected with, 270–272.
Popular religion in the Himalaya, 162 ff.
Possession, 204 ff.
Priests of temples, 194.
Proverbs, 255 ff.
Punoo, a Bhotiya, 74.
Puranas, 12, 175, 176; Bhagavat Puranas, 13.
Puranic religion, 201.
Purohita, or family priest, 193.

"Rags of superstition," 33.
Rainy season, 38.
Raja, title of, 103.
Rama, 130, 169, 170, 189, 201 (note), 247.
Ramananda, 170, 187.
Ramanuja, 187.
Ramayana, 169.
Ramayana of Tulsi Das, 11.
Ramsay, Sir H., 19, 22, 28, 52, 55, 80, 125.
Ramsay College, 41, 55.
Ranikhet, 29.
Rao, Sir T. M., 13.
Rawal, or high priest, 147, 153.
Rhododendron forests, 32, 33.
Rice crops, 51.
Rice-throwing, 245.
Risley, Mr., quoted, 203, 231.
Rohillas, 17, 23, 114, 123; invade Kumaon, 116.
Romany, 43.
Rosaries, 194, 195.
"Royal" gods, 205 ff.
Rudra Chand, 107, 109.
Rudraksha rosary, 195.
Runiya, a demon, 225.

Sadhu, or ascetic, 265.
Saka, or Scythians, 84, 88.

Sakti, or female energy of the deity, 158, 171, 186, 198, 199.
Sanchi topes, 89.
Sankara Acharya, 94, 95, 97, 147, 148, 152, 178, 183, 184.
Sankara Vijaya, a book, 160, 170.
Sankhya school, 168, 282.
Sanskrit language in the Himalaya, 132.
Sanyasis, 157.
Sarda river, 69.
Sarju river, 57, 66, 67, 68, 98, 105, 117.
Satyanath, a deity, 221.
Sects, reforming, 170.
Seshnag, 40.
Shib Deo Joshi, 117.
Shor, 105.
Sibbald, 18.
Silk in Kumaon, 105.
Singhavahini, a goddess, 194.
Sita, 130, 170.
Siva, 31, 42, 58, 96, 129, 130, 134, 138, 177–186.
Smith, Robertson, 177.
Snake-worship, 84, 232.
Snowy range, 34, 36.
Som Chand, 102.
Sraddhas, 248, 263.
Sri Ballabh Upadhya, 63.
Sri Chand Tiwari, 106.
Srinagar in Garhwal, 28, 112, 113, 144, 154.
Strachey, Sir J., quoted, 26, 64.
Sun-god, 171; worship of, 238, 239.
Suvarnagotra, 92.
Sweepers, 43–45.
Systems, Six, of Indian philosophy, 168, 283, 284.

Tantras and Tantric system, 64, 69, 94, 158, 169, 186, 196, 199.
Tapoban, forest retreat, 156.
Tarai, 20, 87, 104, 117; sport in the Tarai, 23.
Tea cultivation, 99.
Tea-drinking, 249.
Tejam camp, 76.
Temple worship, 179.
Temples, 57; of Siva and Vishnu, 199, 200.
Tennyson quoted, 273, 278.
Terraced fields, 50.
Thakuri rajas, 101, 258.
Thal mela, 61.
Theosophical movement, 13.
Tibet, 30, 77, 81, 136.
Tigers, hill, 58, 271, 272, 273, 274, 280.
Tihri state, 125, 141.
Tirmal Chand, 110.
Tonga, a kind of carriage, 23.
Traill, Commissioner, 75, 113, 125, 217, 218, 253.
Transmigration, 281 ff.
Trinity, Hindu, 172, 182.
Trisul peak, 36.
Troup, Colin, 18.
Turanian races, 184, 199, 285.

Udyan Chand, 105.
Untadhura pass, 76, 77.
Upanishads, 282.
Uprety, G. D., 16, 60, 202, 206, 211, 218, 232, 243, 256.
Uttara Kurus, country of, 137.

Vairagis or Bairagis, 156, 157.
Vaitarani river, 247.
Vallabha, 187.
Vallabhacharis, 190.
Veda, 83, 164.
Vedantism, 14, 15, 165, 284, 295, 299.
Vedic religion, 166, 179.
Vishnu, 128, 129, 151, 187, 190; avatars of, 188, 189, 247.
Vishnu temples, 190, 191.
Vivekananda, Swami, 14, 165.

Waddell, Colonel L. A., quoted 22, 81, 126.
Waterfalls, 72.
Weber quoted, 82, 95.
Wellington, Duke of, quoted, 300.
Wheeler, Talboys, quoted, 174.

Widows and widow-remarriage, 244, 245.
Wilford, 137.
Williams, Sir Monier M., 231.
Wilson, H. H., quoted, 159, 160, 170, 179, 187, 251.
Wool trade, 78.
Worship, daily, or Sandhya, 197, 241.

Yama, the Indian Pluto, 247.
Yantra, 196.
Yoga system, 156, 284.
Yogis, 155, 246, 264-266.